A Dictionary of
FOOD HYGIENE

R C BOWMAN

BA, BSc(Hons), MSc, MEd, Cert Ed, MCIEH, MIOSH

and

E D EMMETT

BSc, Cert Ed, CBiol, MIBiol

Published by Chadwick House Group Ltd.

Cover photographs reproduced by the kind permission of
E.T.I., Dominion Way, Worthing, West Sussex BN14 8NW and
Fosters Refrigeration, Kings Lynn, Norfolk PE30 4JU.

PUBLISHED BY CHADWICK HOUSE GROUP LTD.

Chadwick House Group Ltd is the trading subsidiary of the Chartered Institute of Environmental Health (CIEH), the professional and educational body for those who work in environmental health in England, Wales and Northern Ireland. Founded in 1883, the Chartered Institute has charitable status and its primary function is the promotion of knowledge and understanding of environmental health issues.
A Royal Charter was granted in 1984. The majority of CIEH members work as Environmental Health Officers in local authorities; some work in central government, academia, as independent consultants and in positions overseas.

The Chartered Institute is also the leading awarding body for vocational food safety and health & safety qualifications in the United Kingdom. Chadwick House Group Ltd manages the development and promotion of these qualifications. The company is a major publisher of environmental health publications, including the weekly Environmental Health News, the monthly journal, Environmental Health and the food safety quarterly bulletin, Food Forum. The company also publishes a variety of books, videos and reports on food safety, health & safety, housing and environmental protection.

Further information about Chadwick House Group publications can be obtained from CHGL Publications Division on 0171 827 5872 / 0171 827 5882. Fax 0171 827 9930, General Switchboard 0171 928 6006.

More information about the CIEH can be accessed through the CIEH Website at www.cieh.org.uk

ISBN- 0 900103 12 4

Text © R C Bowman, E D Emmett 1998

The right of R C Bowman and E D Emmett to be identified as authors of this work has been asserted by them in accordance with Copyright, Designs and Patents Act 1988.

The authors wish to thank members of staff at Cannock Chase Council for information supplied.

All rights reserved. No part of this publication may be reproduced or transmitted in any form or by any means, electronic or mechanical, including photocopy, recording or any other information storage and retrieval system, without permission in writing from the publisher or under licence from the Copyright Licensing Agency Limited.
Further details for such licences (for reprographic reproduction) may be obtained from the Copyright Licensing Agency, of 90 Tottenham Court Road, London W1P 9HE.

This is a Second edition
First published in 1992

The authors and publisher cannot be held responsible for any consequences arising from the use of the information in this book, although it has been checked thoroughly and to the best of our knowledge.

We would be grateful for any suggestions which would improve the next edition.

Contents

Entries, A-Z   1- 228

Appendix 1 : Food Law   229

Appendix 2 : Scientific names   241

Appendix 3 : Abbreviations   244

Appendix 4 : Major causes of food poisoning   247
            and food-borne disease

Abattoir Large, often factory-type slaughterhouse, which may include a processing plant. The term is also commonly used to mean any slaughterhouse.
See: Cross-contamination, Pennington report.

Aberdeen typhoid outbreak In 1964 an outbreak of typhoid fever occurred which involved many people in Aberdeen, Scotland. It was caused by canned corned beef produced in Argentina. The cans were cooled after processing with unchlorinated water from a river and it is suspected that the typhoid organisms entered the seams while they were expanded after heating. *See*: Canning, Infections (waterborne), *Salmonella typhi*.

Abrasion An area of grazed skin which is a potential site for bacterial growth leading to an infection. The covering of such areas with a suitable waterproof dressing is advisable for food handlers. *See:* Appendix: Food Law, Personal Hygiene, Pus.

Abrasives Various gritty substances used in the formulation of cleaning agents. An abrasive cleaner used incorrectly or on the wrong surface can cause scratches and surface damage which, although almost invisible to the naked eye, may harbour micro-organisms. This has been noted even with surfaces as durable as stainless steel.

Abscess A localised region of pus surrounded by inflamed tissue in an infected part of the body. It may be the cause of bacterial food poisoning if the pus is not contained.
See: Personal Hygiene, *Staphylococcus aureus*.

Accelerated Freeze Drying (AFD) A method of food dehydration in which:
- small pieces of quick-frozen food are placed under vacuum and then gently heated
- ice crystals in the food turn directly into water vapour without first melting; this effect is called sublimation
- the food remains more or less the same size and after processing has a brittle and sponge-like character
- during rehydration water enters faster and more completely than with conventionally dried products
- the final quality is quite close to that of the fresh item.

Typical products include coffee, whole prawns, peas and other similar sized items. The main problems with the process are its expense and that the dried product is brittle and may powder if roughly handled. Shelf-life is long (months or more) as long as the packaging remains intact. The rehydrated food should be stored and treated as though it were fresh. *See:* Dehydration.

Acetic (ethanoic) acid A preservative used in the food industry. It inhibits organisms responsible for both food poisoning and food spoilage. It is more effective against yeasts and bacteria than moulds, and it is a component in mayonnaise, pickles and many sauces. *See:* Acid, Food Preservation, pH.

Acetobacter A group of Gram-negative bacteria used in the manufacture of vinegar. They oxidise alcohol (ethanol) from, for example wine or apple juice, producing acetic (ethanoic) acid. They can be responsible for spoiling beers and wines, producing a vinegary taste.

Acetylandromedol Now known as Grayanotoxin.

Achromobacter A group of Gram-negative bacteria found in the intestinal tract of man and animals. They can cause food spoilage of beer, dairy products, eggs, and other foods. (Many of the species of *Achromobacter* have been renamed as species of *Alcaligenes*.)

Acid A chemical substance which, when dissolved in water, releases hydrogen ions (H^+). Most bacteria cannot tolerate strong acid conditions; they grow best at around pH 6.5, but can grow at pH values between 4 and 9. This sensitivity to strong acid conditions is used in the method of food preservation by pickling, where vinegar (a weak solution of acetic/ethanoic acid) is used to stop the growth of micro-organisms. In general, yeasts and moulds are more tolerant of acid conditions than bacteria, so foods with a low pH (below pH 4.5) are not usually spoiled by bacteria. They are more susceptible to spoilage by yeasts and moulds.

Acid foods (classification) In canning the heat treatment required depends upon several factors including the pH of the food to be processed. In general, pathogens do not grow below pH 4.5 but foods are commonly divided into several categories. These are:

- high acid (below pH 3.7, e.g. pickles and some fruits)
- acid (pH 3.7 to 4.5, e.g. tomatoes and some fruits)
- medium acid (pH 4.5 to 5.0, e.g. most vegetables and mixtures such as soups)
- low acid (above pH 5.0, e.g. meats, fish, milks and some vegetables).

The more acid the food the less heat is required during canning. *See:* Botulinum cook, Canning.

pH scale

- 14 — Highly alkaline
- 12
- 10 — Caustic soda solutions (10+)
- 8
- 7 — Neutral point (pure water)
- 6 — Most foods(meat,fish, many vegetables)(4.5-7)
- 4 — Most bacteria will not grow (4.5)
- Acid foods (tomato, many fruits, vinegar)(3-4.5)
- 2 — Strong acids
- 0

Acidophile An organism that grows best in acid conditions, where the pH is in the range 2 to 5. (-phile = 'lover') *See: Lactobacillus.*

Acidophilus milk A sour-tasting milk product in which lactose has been consumed by lactobacilli (bacteria). It is intended for people who have a lactose allergy.

Acinetobacter Food spoilage organisms (bacteria) affecting the colour and odour of meat, fish and poultry.

Acrolein An acrid-smelling breakdown product of glycerol produced when oils and fats are heated past their smoke point. Foods cooked in such fats or oils have an unacceptable flavour.

Act of Parliament Statute Law made by Parliament setting out the broad principles of law and often empowering the appropriate Minister to make regulations dealing with matters in more detail. *See*: Food Hygiene Regulations (various), Food Safety Act 1990.

Activity relation chart An aid in designing workplaces such as kitchens and food production areas in which the flows of staff, equipment, raw materials and products are marked on a plan. Information either from direct observation or from flow process charts is used, and the plan may show up deficiencies in layout from many points of view

including those of food hygiene, work study and safety.
See: Design of food premises, HACCP.

Acute
1. A disease of sudden onset, usually severe, lasting only for a relatively short time (hours or days). An example of such a disease is food poisoning. The symptoms last only as long as the pathogens (or their products) are in the body.
2. Rapidly acting (for example in the case of poison).
See: Bait shyness.

Additives Various substances are added to foodstuffs in order to affect amongst other things colour, flavour, texture, taste and nutritional value. A wide number of additives with an influence on food hygiene exist including:

- preservatives, such as sulphur dioxide, sodium nitrite, acetic/ethanoic acid, and benzoates inhibit the growth of micro-organisms and are added to a wide variety of foods
- antioxidants such as ascorbic acid and tocopherols prevent fat rancidity.

Emulsifiers, stabilisers, colourings and others are process or aesthetic additives although colourings may be used to disguise the true appearance of foodstuffs.

In Europe approved additives are given an 'E' number although there is some controversy concerning the safety of some of these. International agreement on additive safety is only partial and many countries have different approved lists and standards for safety testing. *See*: 'E' numbers.

Advisory Committee on the Microbiological Safety of Food (ACMSF)
A UK Government body reporting on food safety issues.

Aerobic plate count (APC) A laboratory measure of organisms, expressed as 'CFU/gram'. A CFU is a 'colony-forming unit'. Acceptable levels vary depending on the particular food but levels over 10^4/g are considered unsatisfactory as this indicates a high level of contamination, old stock or poor refrigeration.

Aerobe (Aerobic) An organism that will grow on the surface of a solid medium exposed to air, using the free oxygen present.

Aeromonas hydrophila A free-living Gram-negative bacterium found in aquatic environments, including both uncontaminated and contaminated fresh water and in sewage. It causes spoilage of milk and butter producing a 'fishy' flavour and it is also associated with spoilage of eggs. An outbreak of gastroenteritis, involving raw oysters which had been stored at minus 72°C for 18 months, illustrates the survival potential of this organism.

Aerosols Particles or droplets of moisture suspended in the air may carry micro-organisms. They may contaminate unprotected foods, resulting in food poisoning. Droplets are produced by sneezing, coughing, talking, whistling, etc.
See: Contamination of Food, Droplet infection, Personal Hygiene.

Aflatoxicosis Poisoning that results from ingestion of aflatoxins in contaminated food or feed. All animal species seem to be susceptible, the liver being the main site of damage suffering necrosis, cirrhosis, and carcinoma. For most species the LD_{50} values range from 0.5 to 10 mg/kg body weight.

Aflatoxin An endotoxin produced by some fungi, and hence is called a mycotoxin. It was first recognised in Britain and the US during the 1960s. Several mushrooms and toadstools produce mycotoxins, as do some moulds, such as members of the genus *Aspergillus* (e.g. *Aspergillus flavus*). Some species of *Penicillium*, while growing on moist stored foods such as peanuts, oats, wheat, soya beans and rice produce aflatoxin. The toxin is very resistant to heat. If animals are fed with feed contaminated with aflatoxin they can suffer the effects of poisoning. Aflatoxins have been found in milk from cows that were fed aflatoxin-contaminated grain. There is some evidence to suggest that low levels of aflatoxin are carcinogenic to animals, especially affecting the liver.

Agar-Agar (agar) A gelling (solidifying) agent originally used in cooking, which is extracted from a seaweed. It is now used world-wide to solidify bacteriological media, the solid 'agar gel' being used to culture bacteria in laboratories. It is well suited as a solidifying agent because after it has been melted in boiling water, it can be cooled to around 40 to 42°C before it hardens, and it will not melt again until the temperature is raised to about 80 to 90°C. Most micro-organisms cannot degrade it. Various agar formulations are used in the identification of bacteria taken from, for example a suspected contaminated food or from a food handler following an outbreak of food poisoning.

Aggressiveness A term used to describe the ability of bacteria to enter, spread and multiply inside the body of a host and so reach a susceptible tissue. It is one of the two properties (the other being toxin formation) which make some micro-organisms pathogenic. (Aggressiveness is also known as 'invasiveness').

Air conditioning A system of cleaning and adjusting the temperature and regulating the humidity of air used in public and commercial buildings and food stores.

Air drying
1. A method of preservation in which fruits, vegetables and sometimes cereals are dehydrated.
2. A method of allowing washed crockery, utensils etc to dry naturally without the use of a cloth. This removes the possibility of recontamination of the washed items by a soiled cloth.

Albumen (egg white) Egg white (a protein) is generally not a good medium for microbial growth due to the following reasons:
1. the low content of non-protein nitrogen
2. the unavailability of certain vitamins through combination with proteins
3. the lack of 'free' iron, which is needed by micro-organisms for enzyme activity
4. its (high) pH of 9.6.
Dried egg (both whole and white) has been involved in a number of outbreaks of salmonellosis world-wide. In order to prevent the growth of pathogens, dehydrated albumen is first pasteurised. *See*: Dehydration.

Alcaligenes A group of Gram-negative bacteria which produce an alkaline medium during growth. A number of species are known to cause spoilage of foods, such as 'ropiness' in milk and a slimy growth on cottage cheese. The organisms are widely distributed in nature, being found in faeces, soil, water and dust.

Alkali-therm A high pH and high temperature method of scalding and defeathering poultry carcasses.

Alcohol Term normally used for ethanol (ethyl alcohol), a constituent of fermented and distilled drinks. Most living organisms are not capable of tolerating high concentrations of alcohol. It has effects on the nervous system, is also an antiseptic and is sometimes used in wipes to reduce the numbers of organisms on probe thermometers. Alcohol gel disinfectant is used as a bactericidal hand cleaner and requires no water or drying.

Aleukia (Alimentary Toxic Aleukia) A serious, often fatal disease affecting red and white blood cell functions. It is caused by a mycotoxin produced by various species of mould when millet is allowed to remain in fields over winter and harvested late. Victims suffer from severe anaemia, haemorrhaging and massive uncontrolled infections. It is not a problem if grain is harvested and stored properly. *See*: Aflatoxin.

Algae
- A large group of plants, including single-celled forms that float on water, and the seaweeds. They can cause problems by fouling drinking water and producing poisonous substances.
- They grow in fresh water, some grow in moist soil, on the bark of trees and on damp walls and floors and in sea water.
- One group found in the oceans may, particularly in the summer months, grow extensively forming 'blooms' called red tides. They produce a powerful toxin which kills fish and may even kill humans. Shellfish, such as oysters or clams growing in such water concentrate the toxin in their bodies which can then cause illness in people eating them.
- Annually off the north-east coast of Britain, from around May to June, shellfish become toxic by filtering the alga *Alexandrium tamarense* from the water. Such blooms are confined to relatively small areas, but the number of them reported in recent years has shown an increase in both frequency and extent. (These blooms occur more frequently in the summer months and may be one reason for the saying "only eat oysters when there's an 'r' in the month"; none of the summer months May to August contain this letter.)

See: ASP, Blue-green algae, DSP, PSP.

Alimentary tract Alternative term for the digestive system.

Alimentary toxic aleukia (ATA) *See*: Aleukia.

Alkali A substance having a pH of over 7.0. Alkaline substances are rare in food, two examples being egg albumen (pH 7.5, increasing with age) and sodium bicarbonate/hydrogen carbonate (a component of baking powders). Caustic soda solutions used in cleaning may have pH values of above 10. *See*: pH.

Alkali production Some bacteria (e.g. *Pseudomonas fluorescens*) spoil foods by producing alkalis. They can cause a bitter flavour in milk.

Alkaloids Organic chemical substances which will react with acids to form salts. Examples include nicotine (often used as an insecticide in horticulture), solanin (a toxin developing in the skin of potatoes stored in the light), caffeine (a stimulant occurring in coffee, tea and chocolate) and capsicin (an irritant substance found in pepper). *See:* Honey.

8 Allergy

Allergy Consumption of certain foods by susceptible individuals may result in an allergic reaction characterised by a specific immunological response. Initial exposure produces no effect but sensitises the areas which become affected on future exposures. Many foods have been reported to produce allergic reactions of varying severity, including related fatalities; peanuts, strawberries, chocolate, milk and some food colouring materials have all been found to be responsible. Allergic reactions are also possible following exposure to animals, pollen, fungal spores and many other items.

Alpha amylase An enzyme present in egg yolk and used as an index of processing for pasteurised whole egg. The enzyme is denatured by heating to 65°C for two and a half minutes.

Alpha chloralose A rodenticide which lowers body temperature causing death by hypothermia. It is toxic to other animals and is ineffective at high ambient temperatures.

Aluminium A metal commonly used for making cooking vessels such as saucepans and also cooking foil.

Advantages
- Low cost
- Lightness
- Good thermal conductivity.

Disadvantages
- Acid foods dissolve aluminium; the metal has been linked with Alzheimer's disease because of the high level of aluminium found in the brains of sufferers of this disease.
- White sauces cooked in aluminium pans may discolour due to the presence of aluminium oxide.

Aluminium sulphate is a sedimentation agent used in water treatment and was involved in an incident in Cornwall, England in 1989 causing varied symptoms in a number of people who consumed accidentally contaminated water.

Alzheimer's disease Premature senility in which a region of the brain (the cerebral cortex) degenerates causing memory loss, paralysis and speech impairment. It has been linked with aluminium as a possible cause.

Ambient temperature The temperature of the surroundings, or room temperature. This may vary widely in a kitchen environment, but is often around 20°C, well inside the zone for bacterial growth. Any bacteria present in foods will grow and multiply rapidly. The need for correct storage of raw and cooked foods prior to and after cooking is essential. Leaving foods for prolonged periods at room temperature is a common cause of bacterial food poisoning. *See:* Temperature control.

American cockroach (*Periplaneta americana*) A large (up to 40 mm in length) reddish-brown insect occurring mainly on ships and in port areas in Britain. The somewhat pejorative name 'Roach City' has been applied to New York due to the large numbers of these insects found there. *See*: Cockroaches.

Amino acids A group of over 20 nitrogen-containing organic substances from which proteins are made. Amino acids are involved in the Maillard reaction and contain the amino group ($-NH_2$). *See:* Browning.

Ammonia A strong smelling gas which may taint goods such as meat through accidental exposure to it. The gas is often used as a refrigerant on board ships. It is produced in cheeses such as Brie and Camembert and it is also a sign of advanced putrefaction in fish.

Amnesic shellfish poisoning (ASP) Caused by the neurotoxic substance domoic acid produced from a marine diatom (*Nitzschia pungens*) and affecting shellfish such as mussels. The disease produces rapid symptoms (within 24 hours) of food poisoning but also short-term or permanent memory loss (within 48 hours) similar to Alzheimer's disease in elderly sufferers. The latter may also die from ASP as evidenced in an outbreak in Canada during 1987 due to eating blue mussels.

Amoebic dysentery (amoebiasis) A serious illness caused by the protozoan parasite *Entamoeba histolytica*. The illness occurs following the consumption of sewage-contaminated water or food contaminated with such water. The incubation period varies from a few days to four weeks and the symptoms include diarrhoea of varying severity (usually containing blood and mucus) and death is not uncommon.
Infection is rarely transmitted from acute cases; most cases arise through faecal-oral spread from excreters of cysts. The disease may be prevented by using only treated water supplies, together with effective sewage treatment, consequently outbreaks in developed countries are rare. Cysts resist standard chlorination.

Ampholytic Bactericidal detergent molecules derived from amino acids and used in liquid soaps.

Amphoteric A property of surface-active agents used in cleaning chemical formulations. In alkaline conditions they are anionic (negatively charged) and possess detergent properties while in acid conditions they are cationic (positively charged) bactericides. The range of bacteria affected is restricted. Amphoteric substances may be deactivated by a number of organic substances, including food residues.

Anaerobe (Anaerobic) An organism that is able to grow in the absence of oxygen. This is important with regard to food since it means that the simple exclusion of air (as in vacuum-packing) will not prevent all bacterial growth. A common food poisoning organism of this type is *Clostridium perfringens*.
See: Canning, *Clostridium botulinum*, Sous vide.

Andromedotoxin Now known as Grayanotoxin.

Animals Most wild, domestic and food animals are known intestinal and surface carriers of pathogens, parasitic worms and zoonotic diseases. For this reason live animals should not to be permitted in food rooms. The full extent of diseases carried by animals is very large and includes

    anthrax, brucellosis, glanders, malta fever, salmonellosis,
    swine erysipelas, taeniasis, trichinosis, toxocariasis,
    tuberculosis, undulant fever, vaccinia and Weil's disease.

Anionic Detergent molecules having a negatively charged hydrophilic head including soaps (stearates and laurates) and soapless detergents (alkyl benzene sulphonates). Most common detergents are anionic and tend to produce large amounts of foam.
See: Sanitiser.

Anisakis simplex A white-coloured roundworm (nematode) approx. 2 cm long which is a parasite of cod, salmon, herring and other fish. It causes an often painful illness, anisakiasis, in humans by the burrowing of the larva into the throat, stomach and intestines. Japan has the highest number of cases due to the consumption of raw fish (sushi). Freezing to less than minus 22°C for a week kills the nematode in fish. Other worms, such as *Pseudoterranova, Phocanema, Contracaecum* and *Hysterothylacium* have similar risks.

Anthrax A disease mainly of bovine animals and sheep, also affecting humans and caused by the Gram-positive bacterium *Bacillus anthracis*, spores of which develop when the organism is exposed to oxygen. They are frequently found on pasture land. Rapid death occurs in animals with bloodstained fluid exuding from body openings and the carcass quickly decomposes. The disease is highly contagious and must be notified. Affected carcasses should not be dissected but are incinerated or buried 2 metres deep in quicklime. People are infected by contact with animals, their hides or hair (weavers have contracted the disease in this way) or by eating affected meat. Human fatality is very likely if infection occurs; veterinary surgeons are in a high-risk group. *See*: Notifiable disease.

Antibiotics Chemicals (produced originally by some micro-organisms) which are able to kill or inhibit the growth of other micro-organisms. They were developed for the treatment of bacterial diseases, which is still their main use today. They have also been used in animal feeds (at low levels) to protect them from disease.

Traces of antibiotics have been found in milk produced by cattle being treated for a bacterial disease. If these antibiotic-resistant organisms are also present in the milk, cheese production may be affected, due to the antibiotic suppressing the starter culture. This results in the production of second grade cheese, useful only for processing.

Antibiotics have been used as food preservatives, their use in this area being strictly controlled.

Anticoagulants Substances such as bromadiolone, coumarin and warfarin which stop the normal clotting of blood. They are widely used in rodenticides since their slow or chronic action does not arouse suspicion in the animal. Death results from multiple internal haemorrhages. *See*: Bait shyness.

Antimicrobial agent Any agent that is effective in killing micro-organisms or inhibiting their growth. The term is usually used to describe chemical agents, but physical agents, such as ultra violet (UV) light or very high temperatures also have antimicrobial effects. *See*: Antibiotics, Antiseptics, Disinfectant, Sanitiser.

Antimony A component of some enamels used to coat metal items. Antimony is dissolved by acid foods and has been known to cause chemical food poisoning. Chipped or non-food grade enamelware should not be used with foodstuffs.

Antioxidant A substance preventing oxidation reactions such as the development of rancidity in fats and oils or the browning of cut surfaces of fruits. Examples include vitamin C (ascorbic acid) and its salts, vitamin E (tocopherol), propyl gallate, BHA and BHT. *See:* Additives.

Antiseptics Chemicals that oppose infection (sepsis), usually by inhibiting the growth of micro-organisms. They may be used on the skin and other tissues, and they may be dilute disinfectants.

Antitoxin A substance produced by the body or administered into it to combat bacterial toxins such as those produced by *Clostridium botulinum* or *Staphylococcus* species.

Ants
- The garden ant (*Lasius niger*) occasionally invades food premises but it is more of a nuisance than a carrier of disease.
- Pharaoh's ant (*Monomorium pharaonis*) however is a carrier of pathogens and nests in heated buildings such as hospitals and bakeries. It has been known to cause wound infections in hospitals.

Control measures
- All ants will eat widely, but seem to prefer sweet or protein foods. Storage of foods in closed containers is essential.
- Eradication in infected premises may be extremely difficult since a heavy infestation reaches all parts of the fabric of buildings and success relies on destroying the nests.
- Syrup-soaked baits may be effective as a control measure if their locations are suitable and feeding ants periodically destroyed.
- Other treatments include the use of poison baits which are carried back to the nest or spraying with a residual insecticidal lacquer.
- Juvenile hormone has been used to control Pharaoh's ants.

Appeals (UK Law) It is possible for a person convicted of an offence, for example under Food Hygiene Regulations, to appeal if they do not agree with the decision of the court. A similar procedure applies with alleged contraventions of other laws and also if there is disagreement regarding the contents of improvement, emergency prohibition or other notices. *See*: Appendix: Food Law.

Appert, Nicholas *See*: Canning.

Apples Not known to cause food poisoning directly but some varieties contain sufficient malic acid to dissolve metals such as copper. The outer skin may carry transient organisms and various chemicals, and so should be washed effectively before eating. An outbreak of *E. coli* 0157:H7 was reported in the USA and Canada in 1996 from the consumption of unpasteurised apple juice; 12 of the 45 persons affected developed haemolytic uraemic syndrome (HUS). *See*: Browning, Enzymes.

Apricot kernels Contain cyanide substances and are occasionally involved in food poisoning. Various spirits distilled from apricots have also been found to contain high levels of cyanide.

Aprons Part of the protective clothing of some food industry workers particularly those involved in wet or dirty processes. The material used should be capable of being cleaned and is often of impermeable plastic which may be hosed down.

Arbroath smokies Fish, commonly whiting or haddock, preserved by hot smoking. *See*: Food Preservation.

Argentine ant (*Iridomyrmex humilis*) A tropical species of ant found in warm buildings in temperate climates. It is an occasional invader of warm buildings including food premises. The species is aggressive towards other ants and tends to build nests in inaccessible parts of buildings making treatment difficult.

Arthropoda (Arthropods) A large group of animals including insects, ticks, lice, mites. spiders and crustacea. Some of these, such as flies and cockroaches are vectors of disease. (The name arthropod means 'jointed leg'.)

Ascarides *See: Ascaris lumbricoides*, Roundworms.

Ascaris lumbricoides
1. A large roundworm of pigs found in the intestines. The worm lays eggs which are excreted and hatch in the intestines of another pig. The larvae produced penetrate the walls of the intestine and are carried by the bloodstream to the heart and lungs and then to the trachea where they are swallowed, the cycle now being complete. Livers are often badly affected with white areas called 'milk spot' and are aesthetically unfit.
2. One of the most common intestinal parasites of humans. Worms are passed out of the body in the faeces or nose and throat and mature into infective larvae outside the body in soil or water. Infestation follows the ingestion of sewage-contaminated water or food, with a similar life-cycle as in the pig. Water treatment and good personal hygiene will help to prevent human infestation. The roundworm *Trichuris trichuria* causes a similar problem.
See: Roundworms.

Ascorbic acid
- Chemical name for vitamin C, a water-soluble vitamin, forming part of the intercellular cement which attaches body cells to each other.
- The deficiency disease is scurvy and is characterised by tissue breakdown

- including bleeding from gums and hair follicles, teeth loosening and eventually falling out, and the reopening of old wounds and bone fractures.
- The vitamin is destroyed by heat and by contact with oxygen and bicarbonates (such as sodium hydrogen carbonate). It is lost to a large extent in many food preservation processes such as canning and dehydration as well as during cooking.
- Ascorbic acid is a food additive used as an antioxidant, preventing browning in cut fruits and vegetables and as an improver in bread doughs.

Ascospore A sexual fungal spore, produced as a means of reproduction, in a sac-like structure called an ascus. There are usually 2 to 8 ascospores in an ascus. Such spores are produced by the members of the phylum Ascomycota, members of which include the unicellular yeasts and the septate moulds, e.g. *Penicillium* and *Aspergillus*.

Aseptic packaging Literally the term 'aseptic' means the absence of contamination by unwanted micro-organisms. In some canning and related processes (including filling of cartons with milk, fruit juices etc.) the closure of the pack is performed under aseptic conditions to limit the bacterial load on the product. In practice this is difficult since it means filling a sterile product into sterile containers and closing under sterile conditions. UHT dairy product packages are normally sterilised with hydrogen peroxide, although ethyl alcohol, ethylene oxide gas and UV methods are available.

Aspergillus A group of moulds (members of the Fungi) which are commonly found in soil and decaying vegetation, such as in compost heaps. Many species are involved in the spoilage of foods, and some are useful in the food industry (e.g. making soy sauce from soya beans, and rice wine from the fermentation of rice). They grow well in concentrations of sugar and salt and are therefore found in many foods which have a low water content. Many members of this group produce a deadly aflatoxin.

Aspergillus flavus A mould which commonly grows on seed crops, including peanuts, oats, buckwheat, rice and soya beans. It grows best if the crop has been damaged during harvesting or if there has been insect damage in storage. The aflatoxin produced can pass up the food chain and has been found in milk (from cows and humans) and eggs.

Aspergillus niger A mould which causes spoilage of refrigerated foods, such as sausages, and is responsible for much 'mouldy' bread. It has a number of uses in the food manufacturing industry, including the manufacture of citric acid (for the soft drink industry) and it is also used to manufacture a variety of enzymes.

Aspergillus oryzae A mould used to produce sweet syrups from corn and other starches and also in Japan to produce fermentable sugars for sake (rice wine) making.

Assembly systems
1. In large scale catering operations, such as hospitals and cook-chill, a conveyor belt system of plated meal assembly is often used with a central conveyor passing between work stations where hot and cold foods are plated by operators. Temperature control using insulation or heating/chilling may be required.
2. The *mise-en-place* system is widely used in which partly finished stocks are kept so that orders may be rapidly satisfied. Examples include components of sandwiches in sandwich bars, pre-prepared pizza bases and toppings and preparation of sauces before a service period. Maintenance of temperature control is important.

Assured Safe Catering (ASC) One of a number of HACCP-based systems designed for the catering industry. It follows catering steps (Purchase, Delivery, Storage, Preparation, Cooking and Service) rather than specific ingredients and applies controls, monitoring and corrective measures to these steps. Critical points are commonly temperature control, cleaning and staff training. Hazards are identified in the same way as HACCP as biological, physical and chemical. The system is meant to be simple and manageable with new users being advised to start with purchasing and delivery at first, make sure that the new regime works and then to extend the system to the rest of the operation stage by stage. There is a Department of Health manual on this system.

Astrovirus A cause of sporadic gastroenteritis in children under four years of age. Outbreaks occur mainly in child care settings, such as nurseries, hospitals etc. By the age of ten years most British and American children have antibodies against this virus. *See*: Viruses.

Asymptotic The absence of symptoms. *See:* Symptomless excreter.

ATP (adenosine triphosphate) A substance used in energy transfer in cells and so is omnipresent in biological material. A rapid test for cleanliness of surfaces is based on ATP measurement, ATP being found in micro-organisms and food. Freshness in wet and frozen fish may be determined by the level of ATP, which is broken down, on death, into hypoxatine. The test is colorimetric. *See*: TMA.

Australian cockroach (*Periplaneta australasiae*) Similar in appearance and habits to the American cockroach but having triangular yellow markings on the front wings.

Australian spider beetle (*Ptinus tectus*) A cosmopolitan and widespread beetle in food stores and warehouses feeding on all types of food, often cereals and spices. The larvae cause damage by boring into packaging materials. The adult beetle is 5-6 mm long and covered with dense golden brown hairs. They resemble spiders because of their long legs and narrow 'waist' between thorax and abdomen. *See*: Beetles.

Authorised officer An employee of an enforcement authority in the UK empowered to perform functions under various laws. As an example, an EHO employed by a local authority is authorised by the authority to enforce Food Hygiene law and will have identification to prove this.

Autoclave An instrument used in microbiology laboratories to sterilise materials such as glass, bacteriological media, water and chemicals by exposing them to moist heat under pressure. Materials are made sterile in a matter of minutes, e.g. 15 to 20 minutes at 101 to 135 kPa (15 to 20 psi). This produces a temperature inside the autoclave of 121°C. The higher the pressure used, the higher is the temperature obtained and the shorter the time required for complete sterilisation.

Autumn fly (*Musca autumnalis*) A swarming fly which enters buildings in the autumn and leaves in the spring. It lays eggs on animal dung and pupates in the soil before hatching in the summer to become a pest of horses and cattle. *See*: Flies.

Available water (a_w) A measure of the availability of water on a scale of 0.00 to 1.00 expressed as the relative humidity of the product compared with the relative humidity of the atmosphere in equilibrium. Most pathogenic bacteria grow well in a medium with an aw of at least 0.95 although many yeasts and moulds tolerate an a_w of 0.75. Freezing at below minus 15°C reduces the a_w of ice to around 0.85 and causes some bacteria to be killed. (Note: a_w is also known as Water Activity.)
See: Growth requirements (bacterial).

Avirulent Harmless, lacking in virulence. Such organisms do not cause disease.

Avocado A fruit unusual in its high fat content, often over 10%. It does not ripen until picked and is very susceptible to chilling injury during storage and enzymic browning when cut.

a_w *See*: Available water.
Bach process A heat-sealing process in which thermoformed plastic lids are applied to containers of food such as yoghurt.

Bacillary (bacterial) dysentery A diarrhoeal disease more common in tropical countries than in Britain, particularly affecting infants and young children.

Bacillus cereus 17

- Incubation period is from two to four days.
- Symptoms include diarrhoea, abdominal cramps, pain, fever, vomiting and, if severe, blood and mucus or pus in the faeces.
- Caused by members of a group of Gram-negative bacteria called the *Shigella*, and is therefore also known as shigellosis.
- Commonly spread by poor personal hygiene (i.e. faeces-contaminated hands), inanimate objects (such as toilet seats), food, water and flies.
- Treatment requires antibiotics and the essential replacement of body fluids, lost as a result of diarrhoea and vomiting.

Sanitary procedures, including effective sewage treatment, water purification, control of flies, together with sanitary preparation and serving of food all reduce transmission of the disease. The *Shigella* are the second most frequent cause of 'traveller's di

diarrhoeal type:
a variety, including meats, milk, vegetables and fish.
- Cooked rice should be refrigerated or kept hot until used.

It is a Gram-positive normally aerobic spore-forming bacterium, causing food poisoning due to the release of an exotoxin. *See*: Endospore, Enterotoxin.

Bacillus licheniformis* and *Bacillus pumilis Food spoilage organisms which may cause food poisoning at very high levels ($>10^6$/g)

Bacillus subtilis A Gram-positive aerobic to facultative spore-forming bacterium. It is naturally found in soil and vegetation. It can cause food poisoning, with an onset period from 10 minutes to fourteen hours, but commonly around 2 to 3 hours. Symptoms include headache, nausea, vomiting, occasionally diarrhoea and abdominal pain. It usually results from a chance contamination and is not associated with any particular food, but meat, pastry and rice dishes are commonly implicated. It is also responsible for spoilage of foods, such as canned cured meats and causes 'ropiness' in bread. The organism is used in some biotechnology processes, to produce enzymes in 'biological' washing powders, as well as in the production of antibiotics.

Bacillus stearothermophilus A heat-resistant organism (thermophile) causing the development of acids (but not gas) in canned foods resulting in a spoilage condition known as 'flat-sour'. It is an anaerobic spore-former found in low-acid foods such as vegetables and milk.

Bacon A pork product produced by curing which kills most bacteria and parasites such as tapeworms and roundworms. Certain *Staphylococcus* species survive the high salt concentration (they are called halophilic) and may cause food poisoning if temperature control is not adequate. Bacon should be cooked thoroughly before consumption. *See*: Pork.

Bacon beetle *(Dermestes lardarius)* A pest of skin, hide, biscuits and protein foods. Remains of dermestid beetles have been noted in mummies and the beetle is known to feed on dead rodents and bonemeal.

Bacteria (singular Bacterium)
- There are over 1 700 known species of bacteria, only some of which are pathogenic.
- The vast majority are free-living and play useful roles in nature, including:

a) the recycling of materials via the processes of decomposition of organic matter, as in soil
b) the treatment of sewage
c) soil improvement, by the production of nitrites and nitrates.

People have also been using bacteria for hundreds of years in the production of food, such as cheese and yoghurt. A few forms are photosynthetic. In recent years bacteria have been increasingly used in industrial processes (biotechnology), for example in the production of drugs.

Bacterial cell (structure) The bacterial cell has a much simpler structure when compared to the typical animal or plant cell; the bacterial cell is described as prokaryotic, and the typical animal or plant cell is described as eukaryotic. Not all bacteria possess a capsule (also known as a slime layer). Similarly only some forms possess flagella, which are used for locomotion, and some possess fimbriae.

Bacterial cell

Bacterial Classification.

- Bacteria are generally unicellular (single cells), often existing in groups or aggregates of cells.
- Individual cells are extremely small, and most are no larger than 1 to 2 micrometres in diameter, and 1 to 10 micrometres in length. (1 micrometre

= 1 millionth of a metre.) One simple means of classifying bacteria is based on the shape of the cell. The main groups are:

1. the coccus group (pl. cocci), which are spherical
2. the bacillus group (pl. bacilli), which are rod-shaped
3. the vibrio, which are comma-shaped
4. the spirillum group, which are spiral or corkscrew shaped.

Of the four groups, the coccus group may be further subdivided into colonial forms, the cells existing in groups or clusters. The shape of the cell is used to help in identifying bacteria. Another aid to identification is a special staining procedure, called the Gram stain. *See*: Diplococcus, Staphylococcus, Streptococcus.

Bacterial growth. Bacteria are living organisms and so have the usual requirements for growth.

- Food
- Warmth
- Moisture
- A certain gaseous environment such as oxygen
- A certain pH
- Time

During periods of growth and reproduction, usually by binary fission, the cell is described as vegetative. A doubling of numbers of bacteria may occur in 10-20 minutes under ideal conditions.

Endospores (spores)
- When conditions become unfavourable for growth, some forms of bacteria are able to enter a resistant phase known as an endospore or spore.
- This enables them to survive under adverse conditions, such as the very high temperatures obtained during cooking.
- If and when conditions again become favourable, they return to the vegetative phase and continue to grow and reproduce as before.

Toxins
- Bacteria produce and release chemical poisons called toxins and it this these that are responsible for some symptoms of many diseases, including food poisoning.

Note: Bacterial endospores are NOT produced as a means of reproduction, which is the case with fungi. *See*: Binary fission, Endotoxins, Enterotoxins, Exotoxins, Growth requirements (bacterial), Spores.

Bacterial growth curve When bacteria are grown in a closed system (one which contains all the necessary growth requirements; nothing being added or removed) in liquid growth medium, and the population is counted at intervals, it is possible to plot a growth curve. Such a curve shows four typical phases of growth over a period of time:
I. The Lag Phase: During this phase the bacteria are adapting to the new environment. It can last from a very short time to several days. There is some reproduction, but the number does not increase since the reproduction rate is equal to the death rate. The end of the lag phase and the beginning of the next phase occurs when the bacteria have made the necessary adaptations.
II. The Log Phase: Reproduction is occurring at the maximum rate. The bacterial cells are reproducing exponentially and there is minimum cell death. As nutrients become scarce and the wastes accumulate, there is a decrease in the growth rate and the curve turns into the next phase.

Bacterial growth curve

III. The Stationary Phase: Growth and reproduction slow considerably to a point where the reproduction rate equals the death rate. This is often due to the loss of a growth factor, such as a vitamin or amino acid, or a sudden change in pH. This eventually leads to the final phase.

IV. The Death or Decline Phase: This is the reverse of the log phase, where death of cells occurs at an exponential rate. Death rate greatly exceeds reproduction rate. Accumulation of wastes is a common cause. Eventually the whole population of cells will die out.

Bacterial Growth Curve (Implications) Knowing how a population of cells increases through time has practical implications in the food industry.

1. An awareness of the bacterial growth curve may be used to explain the spoilage of certain foods, such as milk. Pasteurised milk may be kept in a refrigerator for a few days only before it spoils, even if unopened. The spoilage agents are those organisms in the milk which are unaffected by the pasteurisation process. During unopened storage or after opening, the spoilage organisms present enter the lag phase. Each time the milk is taken from the refrigerator the temperature increases sufficiently to allow the micro-organisms to adapt to their environment. The longer it is left outside the refrigerator, the quicker the lag phase will proceed. Once the lag phase is completed the milk may spoil in three to four hours. Continued refrigeration will extend the lag phase, but it will finish eventually and the milk will be spoiled.

2. If bacteria are given ideal conditions, such as in a warm kitchen or food production environment, there may be a rapid increase in bacterial cell numbers, as the bacteria enter the log phase, and this may result in an outbreak of food poisoning. The easiest way to stop this is to use proper temperature storage of foods.
See: Temperature control of foods.

Bactericidal soaps (and lotions) Preparations containing bactericidal substances, designed to reduce the numbers of bacteria (particularly staphylococci) on the hands. In order to be effective they require persistent and consistent use.

Bactericide An agent designed to kill bacteria, such as a disinfectant. ('-cide' means 'killer' or 'killing'.)

Bacteriology A branch of biology that is concerned with the study of bacteria.

Bacteriological standard The quality, acceptability or potential safe shelf-life of foods may be measured in part by the numbers of micro-organisms present. There are several available laboratory methods including
- **Total viable count (all living bacteria)** Numbers greater than 10^4

organisms/gram indicate an unacceptable level of contamination.
- **Faecal organisms** An indication that contamination from intestines of humans or animals is present.
- **Specific pathogens** *Staphylococcus* species, *Bacillus cereus, Clostridium perfringens* and *Salmonella* species among others may be tested for specifically to highlight any problems such as poor personal hygiene or cross-contamination.

As an indication of levels, *Salmonella* species should be absent, *C. perfringens* is relatively safe at 10^3/gram and *S. aureus* at 10^2/gram. These figures are intended as a guide only. *See: E. coli*.

Foods may be tested as part of a quality control system such as HACCP or after samples are taken by an EHO. In Britain there are no legal standards at present although there is power in the Food Safety Act 1990 to make regulations concerning the levels of bacterial contamination in foods. *See*: Individual organisms.

Bacteriophage (phage) A type of virus that infects bacterial cells.

Bacteriophage (phage) typing A method of identifying bacteria using specific strains of bacteriophage. An example is *Salmonella enteritidis* phage type 4, the organism associated with causing food poisoning following consumption of raw or lightly cooked eggs. They are highly specialised in that they attack only members of a particular species or even strains within a species.

Bacteriostatic Halting the continued growth of bacteria but not necessarily reducing their numbers. Substances such as antiseptics used on the skin possess this property.

Bain Marie
1. Equipment for keeping food hot, consisting of metal containers, with or without lids, suspended over hot water in a cabinet. There is also a dry, mobile version heated by gas or electricity. Construction is usually of stainless steel. Food should be capable of being held above 63°C, out of the danger zone.
2. A heated water bath used to keep containers of sauces, for example, hot but not boiling or to cook these gently.

Baits Substances placed in traps to attract food pests. They may be poisonous to kill pests or non-poisonous to estimate the scale of an infestation. A rodenticide bait may contain a mixture of poison and cereals, meat, fish or other food. Baits are not effective if there are other food supplies available. Bait boxes must be numbered, marked as being poisonous and placed at known locations marked on a plan of the premises.

Bait shyness Refusal of rodents to eat further bait if earlier consumption of the bait has caused illness but not death. Another bait may be substituted.

Bakeries Produce a wide range of products such as breads, cakes and pies some of which are high-risk foods containing meat, eggs and cream. Warm conditions around ovens have provided ideal conditions for cockroaches and stored cereals are sometimes infested by various beetles.

Balai products Products such as intestinal casings, gelatin and lard for human consumption.

Bamboo shoots Natural, non-cultivated varieties of bamboo may contain cyanogens which release hydrogen cyanide by enzyme action when the plant cells are damaged. *See*: Cyanide.

Banana May contain small amounts of lectin, a substance interfering with the normal action of the digestive system.

Bandages These are required in first aid kits, the numbers and types depending on the number of people employed and the risks of the work. A bandage is not a waterproof dressing, cannot be cleaned and should not be worn where it could come into contact with food. A finger bandage could be satisfactory if protected by a waterproof finger stall which would prevent any bacteria infecting an injury from getting onto food.

Barbecues
- The main risk is that foods may be cooked on the outside but fail to reach an adequate internal or centre temperature. Chicken for example may be pre-cooked in an oven and then finished on the barbeque.
- This is a particular problem with 'made up' food such as beef burgers since any bacteria present will be spread all through; undercooked chicken may also be a problem if *Salmonella* organisms survive.
- Other risks are from cross-contamination, poor defrosting, and insufficient cooking.

Barrier cream Protects the skin of the hands from drying and cracking after repeated hand washing. The cream may be bactericidal. Food-use cream is unperfumed and will not taint food.

Basidiospore A sexual fungal spore, produced as a means of reproduction, formed externally (on a basidium); usually four spores per basidium. Such spores are produced by the mushrooms and puffballs.

Basins
- Separate wash-hand basins should be provided for food handlers to wash their hands before, during and after food preparation.
- Soap, nail brush, suitable drying facilities and hot water may be required.
- A notice requesting users of toilets to wash their hands is useful.

Beans Many beans (such as red kidney beans) and pulses are known to contain toxic chemicals such as haemmaglutinin. They must be thoroughly cooked before consumption. *See*: Red kidney beans.

Beef
- Meats may be contaminated with bacteria by cross-contamination at the time of slaughter or during delivery, storage and preparation.
- The spores of bacteria such as *Clostridium perfringens* may be present on the surface of beef having come from the soil via the animals' feet and hide.
- The insides of joints or pieces of meat normally contain few bacteria and rare beef, unless minced, poses only a slight health risk with tapeworm.
- Cooked beef is a high-risk food and must be refrigerated to below 8°C or kept hot above 63°C.
- Regulations in the UK restrict the sale of beef on the bone as a control measure for BSE/CJD.

See: Appendix : Food Law, BSE, *E. coli*.

Beef burgers Since any bacteria on the surface of the beef are mixed throughout a beef burger, they must be cooked thoroughly so that any organisms in the centre are destroyed. An outbreak of food poisoning in Britain in 1991 involving *E. coli* was attributed to undercooked beef burgers.

Beef tapeworm (*Taenia saginata*)
- The cysts (larvae) of this inhabit beef muscle, particularly those with a high blood supply such as the heart, diaphragm and cheek.
- These are difficult to detect since they are small (pea sized at most) pearly-white objects embedded in muscle.
- Humans are infected by eating undercooked meat.

- The tapeworm, up to 15 metres long, develops from the cysts in human intestines and attaches with hooks/suckers to the walls of the intestine which may tear and bleed.
- Segments containing eggs are periodically released and pass out with the faeces. They may contaminate grazing land starting the life cycle again.
- Cysts are destroyed by thorough cooking or freezing at minus 10°C for at least 14 days.
- The cysts are called cysticercus bovis, cattle being the intermediate host.
- Around 60 million cases per year world-wide are estimated. Treatment for humans is safe and effective.

Beetles (Coleoptera) Many varieties affect food causing spoilage but not food poisoning. Affected food is unfit for human consumption. Infestations are often difficult to deal with and fumigation with methyl bromide or other substances may be the only solution if an entire building has become infested. There are very many beetles, almost one for every different food, including Australian spider, Bacon, Biscuit, Broad-horned flour, Cadelle, Cigarette, Coffee bean, Confused flour, Copra, Dried fruit, Flour, Golden spider, Khapra, Long-headed flour, Maize, Meal worm, Merchant, Pulse, Rice, Rust-red flour, Saw-toothed grain and Spider beetles.

Benzene hexachloride (BHC) A persistent insecticide also known as HCH (hexachlor hexane). The gamma isomer is effective against a wide range of insect pests and is used in powder, spray, dust and ointment forms. It acts against the central nervous system of insects and may affect mammals.

Benzoic acid A preservative used to prevent mould and yeast growth in fruit juices, pickles, soft drinks, coffee essence, salad cream, beers and other foods. Sodium benzoate, calcium benzoate, potassium benzoate and ethyl 4-hydroxybenzoate have similar uses. These substances may cause adverse reactions in asthma sufferers and persons having skin allergies.

3,4 benzpyrene A carcinogenic substance occasionally found in smoked products. The EU safe level is 3ug/kg but levels up to 10ug/g were detected in a French survey in 1995.

Besatz Impurities such as weed seeds, fungi, rodent hairs, dust, stones and other physical contaminants in wheat grain. It is called dockage in the USA.

Best-before date A dating system used to indicate the shelf life of a product during which it is at its best quality. Typical foods have long shelf lives of months or more and are low risk.

- Examples include cakes, crisps, biscuits, canned food and drinks.
- There is little risk of food poisoning.
- It is a quality statement, the eating quality of the food deteriorates slowly after the date.

High-risk foods should have a 'use-by' date since they are perishable and may cause food poisoning.

BHA and BHT Synthetic antioxidants, butylated hydroxy anisole and toluene, used to prevent oxidative rancidity in foodstuffs. The safety of both substances has been in question and there are restrictions on use in infant foods although BHT has been sold as an antiviral agent, and BHA is reputed to protect against some carcinogens.

Biguanide A detergent/bactericide (sanitiser) used for glass-washing.

Binary fission
- A process of cell division in a number of single-celled organisms, including bacteria, in which one cell divides into two daughter cells.
- Each daughter cell produced is similarly able to divide resulting in 4 cells, then 8, 16, 32, 64 etc.
- Bacteria are able to reproduce in this way in as little as ten to twenty minutes, and will continue doing so as long as their surroundings remain favourable.

Binary fission results in large numbers of cells being produced in a fairly short period of time. *See*: Bacterial growth curve.

Biodegradability The ability of a substance to be broken down into non-toxic or non-polluting end-products after its use. Many plastics are non-biodegradable as is the chemical disinfectant hypochlorite. Hydrogen peroxide, a bactericidal chemical, is biodegradable as it breaks down into water and oxygen.

Biologically active principles (BAPs) Naturally occurring toxins such as pulegone and menthol in peppermint and corn mint oils, safrole in cinnamon and coumarin in cassia. These and others are used in herbal teas, mint sauce and chocolate mints.

Biotechnology The application of micro-organisms, their processes or products in industry. Historically, micro-organisms such as yeasts and bacteria have been used in fermentation and cheese making for example. Modern uses include sewage treatment and pharmaceutical manufacture. DNA 'cut and paste' techniques are used to change flavour, texture and other parameters such as resistance to disease. DNA may also be moved across species, for example form fish to tomato. DNA testing of foodstuffs for

Biphenyl An anti fungal preservative used on the outsides of fresh fruit, especially citrus fruits. Washing with detergent helps remove it.

Birds Pests of food rooms, particularly sparrows and pigeons.

Problems
- They carry food poisoning bacteria such as salmonellas and also carry insect pests.
- Droppings and feathers may cause physical contamination of food.
- Birds deface buildings and nests may create a fire risk.
- The diseases psittacosis and ornothosis, caused by *Bedsonia* organisms, are carried by many species including parrots and budgerigars, causing fever and pneumonia in humans.

Control
- Buildings may be proofed against entry by screens or netting over doors and windows.
- Narcotising with alpha chloralose is a possible control measure.
- External window ledges may be sloped or treated with soft materials to discourage perching or nesting.

See: Zoonoses.

Birdseye, Clarence An American pioneer of freezing who developed the commercial operation of this preservation method during the 1920s. *See*: Freezing.

Biscuit beetle (*Stegobium paniceum*) A pest of stored cereal products. It is small, reddish-brown in colour and covered with yellow hairs. It is the most common insect pest of domestic food stores. In the USA it is known as the Drug store beetle.

Biscuits Many are both low in water and high in sugar and are thus not capable of supporting the growth of bacteria. They are however attractive to rodents and insect pests and should be stored in containers with tightly-fitting lids at a low humidity (RH 60%) at between 10-15°C. *See*: Dry goods store.

Black Ant (*Lasius niger*) Also called the Garden ant and sometimes invades food rooms. Unlike Pharaoh's ant it is not known to carry disease and is more of a nuisance although infested food should be regarded as unfit. Infestations may be persistent and it is important to practise good housekeeping so that food is not available. Destruction of ants is by insecticidal dusts and sprays which must be used carefully in food areas.

Black bat, Black beetle, Black clock Alternative common names for the Oriental cockroach, *Blatta orientalis*.

Black death Another name for the Great Plague (bubonic plague) that swept across Europe in the fourteenth century. It is spread from rat to human by the rat flea (*Xenopsylla cheopis*) and resulted in around 25 million deaths (one third of the population). The causal organism is *Yersinia pestis*, outbreaks still occur but are rare.

Black fungus beetle (*Alphitobius laevigatus*) A black oval beetle about 5 mm in length infesting damp stored cereal grain.

Black pudding A cooked meat product made from blood, oats, cubes of fat and seasonings encased in a skin of animal intestine. It should be refrigerated during storage as it is a high-risk food.

Black rat (*Rattus rattus*) The least common of the two main species found in the UK. It is also called the ship's rat and is rarely found away from sea ports. It is smaller and more slender than the brown rat and climbs easily throughout buildings. Distinguishing features include a dark brown/black body, large ears, pointed snout and a tail longer than its body. *See*: Rats.

Black spot Surface spoilage of meats caused by localised spots of mould, usually *Cladosporium herbarum*.

Bladder worm The larvae (also known as cysts or cysticerci) of a tapeworm which are localised in the skeletal muscles, for example, of cattle or pigs. If the meat of an infected animal is undercooked and eaten the surviving larvae will attach to the lining of the intestine and develop into a mature tapeworm. *See*: Tapeworms.

Blanching Treatment of vegetables by boiling water or steam for a short time, often less than a minute, prior to freezing. The heat of the process destroys spoilage enzymes which would otherwise cause browning, loss of flavour and development of off-odours during frozen storage. Enzymes which destroy Vitamins A and C may also be destroyed. Other effects of blanching include driving out trapped air and destruction of surface bacteria. Over-blanching may result in the cooked product losing firmness of texture.

Blast Chilling

Blast Chilling
- A fan-assisted refrigeration cabinet designed to lower the temperature of hot cooked food rapidly to around 5°C prior to refrigerated storage.
- The maximum time for this should be 90 minutes so that pathogens do not multiply to dangerous levels.
- The size and thickness of food has a great effect on chilling time. Joints of meat to be chilled should be a regular shape and no heavier than 2.5 kg.

See: Cook-chill.

Blast freezing Similar to blast chilling but hot cooked food is reduced to minus 18-22°C prior to freezer storage. Quick freezing is essential to preserve food quality. *See*: Cook-freeze, Freezing.

Bloaters Whole ungutted herring preserved by dry salting and cold smoking. *See*: Curing.

Bloom
1. The desirable appearance in fresh meat due to the reaction of the protein myoglobin with oxygen. Further oxidation produces metmyoglobin, a brownish-grey substance indicative of increased age of meat.
2. The result of extensive growth of algae in summer months.

Blowflies (*Calliphora, Lucillia, Phormia* and *Sarcophaga*)
- Large flies about 10 mm in length, breeding in raw and decaying meat and other foods.
- Some breed on live animals and in faeces.
- They are most active in warm weather.
- Eggs are laid, hatching within 24 hours into larvae or maggots. These burrow into the affected food while feeding on it.
- After some days the maggots migrate, often at night, into the soil and with in a week of hatching from the pupae the flies are able to lay eggs.

Blowflies are known carriers of *Salmonella* and *Clostridium* species. Affected food is termed 'flyblown'. Alternative names are bluebottle, greenbottle and grey flesh fly. *See*: Flies.

Blown cans Cans in which gas has been produced develop protruding ends, are termed 'blown' and the contents are unfit to eat. Some *Clostridium* and *Bacillus* bacteria are heat resistant (thermoduric) and may survive if the can is under-processed releasing hydrogen and carbon dioxide gases during storage. There are various stages:

- flipper - the can end may be forced back with light thumb pressure but flips out if the can body is struck
- 'springer' - pressure on a protruding end causes the other end to spring out
- 'hard swell' or 'blown' - both ends protrude.

Blown cans are most common if cans are stored at temperatures above 15°C, or if under-processing occurs.

Bluebottle Alternative name for blowfly. *See*: Flies.

Blue-green algae (Cyanobacteria) A group of photosynthetic micro-organisms which grow as a slimy or jelly-like growth on soil or on the surface of water. Under certain conditions they may grow extensively in water forming scums or blooms. This usually occurs in late summer or early autumn and the algae eventually die and are decayed by other aquatic micro-organisms. They may release toxins which poison fish and other animals. Sheep and goats have died through drinking contaminated water. The toxin most often implicated is microcystin produced by the alga *Microcystis*. The toxin causes liver damage and people drinking contaminated water, (even accidentally during swimming) are also at risk. Direct contact with the alga may cause eye and skin irritations and the toxin causes liver damage.

Body blank A piece of tin-plated steel from which the body of a can is formed.

Body fluids All body secretions, human and animal, may contain bacteria, including many types which are pathogenic. These fluids, which include saliva, blood, pus, urine and faeces, may contaminate food. Strict personal hygiene is needed to prevent contact between body fluids and food.

Boils Infections of hair follicles by bacteria such as staphylococci resulting in a painful red swelling with a yellowish top or head.

- The head contains pus, a liquid mixture of bacteria, toxins (also white blood cells) which is highly infective. Pus must not be allowed to come into contact with food.
- In severe cases, food handlers are excluded from work until the condition has cleared.

See: Septic lesions.

Bone taint Off-odours caused by putrefying bacteria in deep-seated parts of muscle near to the bone. The bacteria gain access from lymph nodes in the surrounding tissue and multiply rapidly if conditions are favourable.

Booklice (Psocids) Small or minute wingless insects, varying in colour from grey/brown to yellowish, infesting a wide range of stored products, mainly packaged cereals. Other foods and packaging materials may also be affected. They thrive in warm and damp conditions, feeding on mildew and mould and may carry pathogens. Dry conditions are the best defence against booklice. Affected food is unfit.

Boric acid A long-lasting, slow acting insecticide used to kill ants and cockroaches. It is often applied at high concentrations and may cause damage to humans and animals.

Botrytis A mould affecting stored food products. *Botrytis cinerea* is also called 'noble rot' and is a desirable condition affecting grapes used to produce various sweet wines in Sauternes and Rheingau. *See*: Moulds, Mycotoxins.

Bottling A preservation process similar to canning in which food is heated in sealed glass containers to destroy pathogens. Home bottling of vegetables has sometimes resulted in cases of botulism since the temperature reached by domestic methods is not high enough to destroy spores of the bacterium *Clostridium botulinum*.
See: Botulism, Botulinum cook, Canning.

Botulinum cook In the canning and related industries, the bacterium *Clostridium botulinum*, being very heat-resistant, is used as a process indicator for foods which have a pH over 4.5. If it is destroyed, then other pathogens are also killed and 'commercial sterility' is achieved. *See*: Canning, Fo value.

Botulism A disease caused by the toxin of the Gram-positive anaerobic bacterium *Clostridium botulinum,* several types of which affect the central nervous system.

- First symptoms normally occur within 18-36 hours and include lassitude (tiredness), headache and diarrhoea.
- Difficulty in speech, loss of balance, constipation and double vision follow within a few days.
- The disease is often fatal since the brain centre controlling breathing is often affected.
- Diagnosis may not occur since the disease is uncommon and symptoms may be unclear.
- Recovery is slow and may be incomplete.

The organism is found widely in the environment; the disease has been caused by home bottled vegetables (asparagus, green beans and others), canned fish (tuna and salmon), duck pate and hazelnut yoghurt but is relatively rare. Because of the severity of symptoms, cases often attract great publicity. Less than 100 cases per year are reported annually in the USA and far less elsewhere.

Bowel The gut or small and large intestines.

Brachonids Small or minute black insects (wasps) which breed inside other insects, their presence indicating a large population of them. *See*: Ichneumon flies.

Brawn A meat product made from pig's head meat, ox cheeks and beef and pork trimmings. Diced meat is cooked and moulded with gelatin or gelatinous stock. It is normally served cold and since it is a high-risk food, should be refrigerated during storage. *See*: Meat products.

Bread Not a well-known cause of food poisoning, its water content being too low for bacterial growth, although mould growth is often a problem. Oven temperatures will kill any bacteria present in flour although survival of spores of *Bacillus subtilis* and others may result in 'rope', causing an unpleasant odour and sticky yellow-brown spots in affected bread. Sandwiches and similar bread-based products may contain high-risk foods as fillings. *See*: Appendix: Food Law, Moulds, Mycotoxins.

Brining The immersing of prepared sides, pieces or slices of pork in brine (a solution of approximately 25% salt, 3% potassium or sodium nitrate and sometimes other substances such as 1% sugar in water) during the production of bacon by curing. Brining of vegetables prior to pickling to reduce their water content which would otherwise dilute the vinegar is also practised. *See*: Sauerkraut.

British Food Manufacturing Industries Research Association (BFMIRA)
A research laboratory providing various services such as food analysis to the food industry.

British Pest Control Association (BPCA) The professional body of pest control operators which lays down industry standards. Members must conform to a code of practice.

Broad-horned flour beetle (*Gnathocerus cornutus*) A brown-black beetle about 4 mm long having very large lower jaws (mandibles). It infests food stores.

Broad Street pump In 1854 the public water pump in Broad St (now Broadwick St) in Soho, London, was the centre of a major outbreak of cholera. The epidemiologist John Snow (later knighted) linked the sewage-contaminated water supply with the outbreak.

Brodifacoum An anticoagulant rodenticide causing death by prevention of blood clotting. Although classed as a chronic poison it may be effective after a single feed. *See*: Warfarin.

Bromadiolone An anticoagulant chronic rodenticide often formulated as a paste and extruded from a pressure gun. *See*: Warfarin.

Brown FK 154 A mixture of azo dyes used to colour kippers. Some research suggests that the dye causes genetic mutation in bacteria.

Brown house moth (*Hoffmannophila pseudospretella*) A pest of stored cereal grains, particularly if these are damaged. *See*: Moths.

Browning Food spoilage may occur due to a reaction in cut surfaces of fruit and vegetables. The reaction is promoted by oxidase enzymes released when cells are damaged and the resultant brown colour is caused by oxidation of phenols in the cell. Several methods including blanching, immersion in salted water, treating surfaces with lemon juice or other weak acids and the use of preservatives such as sodium metabisulphite are used to prevent browning. The enzymes are inhibited by heat, low pH, ascorbic acid (vitamin C), sulphite and chloride ions while immersion in water limits the availability of oxygen. *See*: Blanching.

Brown rat (*Rattus norvegicus*) The commoner of the two main species found throughout the UK. It is larger than the black rat, has a blunt snout, small ears and a tail shorter than its body. The body colour is brown/grey with a pale belly. It is capable climbing but is not as agile as the black rat.

Brucella abortus
A Gram negative bacterium causing brucellosis in cattle and undulant fever in humans.
- It causes a severe and sometimes fatal fever which may recur periodically for years in humans after infection from infected milk or milk products or contact with affected animals.
- It occurs mainly in dairy farmers, the veterinary profession, and slaughterhouse workers with the first symptoms not appearing for several months after infection.

- The disease is difficult to cure with sufferers having pains, bronchitis, high temperature and sweats.
- The word 'undulant' means 'wavelike' and illustrates the periodic nature of symptoms.
- It is also called Malta fever, Cyprus fever and Gibraltar fever. David Bruce, an army surgeon, investigated the disease in the early 1900s. *Brucella melitensis* was identified.
- Brucellosis has increased generally in the Mediterranean region during the 1980s.

Brucella melitensis A Gram-negative bacterium causing a condition in goats similar to that caused by *Brucella abortus* in cattle. A large outbreak affecting 135 persons in Malta during 1995 was linked to consumption of Gbejniet, a cheese pastry made with unpasteurised goat's milk.

Brucellosis *See*: *Brucella abortus*.

Bruising A cause of enzymic browning in fruits and vegetables when cell enzymes are released. Severe bruising causes decay to speed up and food to become rapidly unfit to eat. *See*: Browning, Enzymes.

Brush strips Fixed to the bottom edges of doors in proofing of buildings against entry of pests.

BSE Bovine spongiform encephalopathy or 'Mad Cow Disease' is caused by a prion (a protein-like infectious particle) and affects the nervous system of cattle. Cooking of food has little effect on the prion.
- Loss of balance and difficulty in muscle co-ordination are known symptoms.
- A similar disease, scrapie, exists in sheep.
- There is concern that infected feed containing animal protein has spread the disease among food animals.
- It is also thought that the consumption of infected meat may lead to Creutzfeldt-Jacob disease (CJD) in humans.
- Movement and export/import bans have been used as a control measure.
- Improved slaughterhouse hygiene in which care is taken not to allow particles of the brain or spinal cord of affected animals to cross-contaminate other carcasses has also been practised.
- Spinal cord and thymus are removed from slaughtered animals over 6 months old and destroyed. The head meat from cattle, goats and sheep may also be removed from the human food chain.

- Detection of the illness requires a sample of brain tissue, hence confirmation of the disease is not possible until after death of the animal.
- In the UK, a programme of slaughter of very large numbers of cattle has been instituted and cattle over 30 months old are not allowed to enter the food chain.
- There is some evidence of maternal transmission of BSE to calves.

Buckie (*Buccinium undatum*) A mollusc about 10 cm in diameter having a pale coloured thick spiral shell containing dark coloured flesh. Also called the whelk.
See: Shellfish.

Buckling (*Buccinium undatum*) Salted hot smoked herring fillets.
See: Curing, Smoking.

Buffers Chemical additives which resist changes in pH of foodstuffs. Many salts of citric, tartaric, malic and phosphoric acids are used.

Buffets Food presented on open display, often self-service.

- Cases of food poisoning have resulted.
- Contamination during service is very likely.
- High-risk foods may be left at room (ambient) temperature for buffet service for up to four hours, but must be of good quality beforehand.
- Refrigerated displays for cold buffets are preferred.
- Topping up with fresh food is undesirable since the previous food may be contaminated.

See: Appendix: Food Law.

Building Regulations Comprehensive regulations covering every aspect of the construction of all types of premises including food premises.

Building, proofing In order to prevent rodents, birds and insects gaining access to buildings many measures are possible including

- fitting wire cages to the tops of vent pipes
- ensuring close fit of doors and windows
- mesh screens over opening windows.

Gaps around pipes passing through walls, broken drains, defective water seals in gullies, sinks and WCs and air bricks will also allow entrance to pests as will more obvious holes in walls and ceilings.

Bulgarian bacillus Original name given by Metchnikoff in 1910 for the Gram-positive bacterium *Lactobacillus bulgaricus*. He proposed that yoghurt consumption would prolong life and attributed this property to the organism.

Burnett, Sir Macfarlane A Nobel prize winning Australian microbiologist who showed the value of hand washing after the compulsory hand washing of schoolchildren's hands led to reduction in cases of poliomyelitis.

Butcher's shops
- Risk of cross-contamination from raw to cooked meats is very high and foods and equipment must be kept separate.
- Food intended for sale as pet food must not be kept with human food.
- Adequate refrigeration must be provided.
- Disposal of waste can cause problems with pests and other animals such as dogs and cats.

See: Pennington report.

Butter Due to its high milk fat content (over 80%) butter is not known to have caused food poisoning. It is a perishable food and should be kept between 1-4°C although it may be safely frozen for several months. Butter deteriorates due to the action of micro-organisms which cause rancidity resulting in the production of glycerol and free fatty acids; oxidation reactions form organic peroxides. The taste and smell of rancid butter is due to butyric acid.

Bye laws Laws which apply locally in the UK. One example is the banning of dogs entering food shops.

***Byssochlamys* moulds** These can affect some canned products. They are heat resistant, a comparatively rare property of moulds.

Cadelle beetle (***Tenebroides mauritanicus***) A distinctively shaped flat black insect about 15 mm long, the adult having a marked 'waist'. It feeds mainly on cereals and is often persistent in flour mills. The habit of larvae burrowing into wood provides harbourage for this and other pests.

Cadmium A metal used to electroplate steel and other metals such as those used in the manufacture of utensils and other equipment. Acids such as fruit acid may dissolve it causing chemical food poisoning. Cadmium-containing glazes used for pottery and some enamelware also suffer from this problem and are not food-grade.

38 Calcium propionate

Calcium propionate A preservative used in dairy and bakery products, particularly against moulds and 'rope' organisms.

Calcivirus A cause of viral gastroenteritis in children between 6 and 24 months of age. Outbreaks occur mainly in child care settings, such as nurseries, hospitals etc. More than 90 per cent of all children have developed an immunity to this illness by the age of 6 years. *See*: Viruses.

Campden tablets A disinfectant containing sodium or potassium metabisulphite often used in brewing for 'sterilising' (disinfecting) equipment and finishing, or stopping, fermentations. The active agent is sulphur dioxide, which is a strong bactericide.

Campylobacter A group of Gram-negative bacteria causing the food-borne disease campylobacteriosis/campylobacter enteritis or simply gastroenteritis. Outbreaks caused by this group have shown a dramatic increase in numbers over recent years. In Britain in the early 1990s around 30 000 cases per year have been reported; in the US it causes more disease than *Salmonella* and *Shigella* species combined.
- The bacterium (a spirally-curved bacillus) is a non-sporeformer, with an optimum temperature of 43°C.
- It is microaerophilic to anaerobic, and is sensitive to low pH.
- The onset period for the disease varies from two to seven days.
  The infective dose is relatively low.
- Symptoms, probably caused by the release of an enterotoxin, start by resembling influenza, are sometimes termed 'flu-like' and include diarrhoea, which usually contains blood.
- The illness generally lasts from 7-10 days to several weeks with few fatalities.
- Complications, such as meningitis and endocarditis (inflammation of the lining of the heart) are possible.
- Foods commonly involved are mainly raw or undercooked meat (especially poultry), and offal; raw and inadequately heat-treated milk and contaminated water have been found to be responsible for large outbreaks.
- Contamination is usually from the excreta of humans and animals, birds (particularly poultry), cattle and domestic pets. Person-to-person spread in young children is also possible.
- Wild birds pecking milk bottle tops are reported to have infected this foodstuff.
- Properly cooking chicken, pasteurising milk, and chlorinating drinking water will all kill the bacteria.

In common with other food-borne diseases, small numbers of organisms are able to cause an infection. The usual species are *Campylobacter jejuni* and *coli*.

Candling A non-destructive method of visibly examining the insides of eggs by exposing them to a bright light. Various defects such as imminent hatching, large air spaces and blood spots may be seen.

Canning A method of food preservation developed in the early 1800s in France by Nicholas Appert who won a prize from the Emperor Napoleon for his efforts. It was originally called 'Appertisation'.

1. The process relies on heat to destroy micro-organisms (pathogenic and spoilage), the aim being to achieve commercial sterility.
2. The pH of food is important in determining the amount of heat required since pathogens (in particular *Clostridium botulinum*) generally do not grow below pH 4.5.
3. Other factors affecting length of heat treatment include the size of the can and whether or not the contents are liquid or solid; solid contents require a longer process.
4. Cans are made from tin-plated steel and may be lined with protective coatings or lacquers.
5. The end seam joining lid to body is of some importance and must have the correct dimensions (overlap) to ensure proper closure.
6. The head space is normally a vacuum, this being measurable and is an index of effective processing or shelf-life.
7. Canned foods have shelf-lives varying from a few months (tomatoes) to many years (corned beef).
8. Cans should be stored at 10-15°C in dry conditions; food should not be stored in opened cans otherwise corrosion will occur.
9. Canned meats may be stored in a refrigerator for a few hours before use to make slicing easier.
10. Long term storage of cans in refrigerators may lead to corrosion (rust) and then contamination.
11. Canned foods are generally very safe but any high-risk canned food must be treated as though it were fresh once the can has been opened. For example opened canned ham must be refrigerated (in a suitable container, not in the can) and used within a few days.
See: Aberdeen typhoid outbreak, Acid foods, *Bacillus stearothermophilus*, Blown cans, Botulinum cook, Fo, Sterilisation, Sulphiding.

Capon Male chicken killed at 12 weeks. It is sometimes treated with a hormone implant to increase speed of body weight production.

Capsule The bacterial capsule (also known as a slime layer) is a complex structure and

forms the outermost layer of some types of bacteria. It has two main functions:
1. to confer virulence on pathogenic bacteria, and
2. to cement together those forms that exist in groups or aggregates of cells, e.g. the staphylococci.
The specific composition of the capsule is the basis of serotyping of bacteria, which otherwise are identical. *See*: Serological typing.

Carbon dioxide A gas used to control growth of spoilage organisms such as the aerobes *Pseudomonas* and *Achromobacter*. Examples include storage of chilled meats and fruits and vegetables at an atmosphere of up to 10% carbon dioxide. The gas may be added in large storage rooms or be the result of wrapping food in selectively-permeable films.

Carcinogenic The ability of an agent to cause cancer; such substances include many chemicals and various forms of radiation.

Carpet beetle (*Anthrenus* species) A wide variety of small beetles (up to 4 mm long) whose body scales give them a variegated appearance (patches of different colours). They occasionally infest food but are more commonly found in woollen materials and fabrics.

Carrier An individual who harbours disease-causing organisms inside the body and excretes them, without suffering from or showing any symptoms of the particular disease.

1 Incubation carriers: most people excrete organisms during the incubation period of a disease without showing symptoms.
2. Convalescent carriers: people who excrete organisms while recovering from a disease, with symptoms having ceased.
3. Healthy carriers: this is the most potentially dangerous group to public health. These food handlers show no signs of illness at any time, but they excrete pathogenic organisms. They are unlikely to pay the necessary extra attention to their personal hygiene, unlike incubation and convalescent carriers.

Carriers may also be described as:

    a. chronic carriers, who excrete the pathogenic organisms throughout their lives

    b. casual carriers, who excrete the pathogenic organisms for a short period only, e.g. for weeks or months.

All carriers are likely to spread disease. They are difficult to identify and therefore treat,

Ceilings 41

both of which are required in order to stop them from excreting the organisms. (Carriers may also be described by the medical term 'symptomless excreters'.)

Carveries These have a particular food hygiene hazard in that cooked meats are offered for sale for lengthy periods. They may also suffer from lack of temperature control and problems of contamination. Overhead infrared heaters are sometimes used to maintain temperatures. The maximum time cooked meat should be kept (displayed) at below 63°C is two hours, and no more should be displayed than is reasonably necessary.

Cash (handling of) There is evidence that money, both coins and notes, can provide a temporary residence for micro-organisms which could then be passed on to food. Control measures could include hand-washing or the use of separate staff.

Casual staff Persons who occasionally help out may not be aware of the problems of hygienic food handling and care should be taken that their knowledge of this is sufficient. Training of such staff should be such that food is safely produced and their work practises should be of the same standard as other food handlers. Increased supervision may also be used to control this situation. *See*: Due diligence, Training of food handlers.

Cationic detergent A surface-active molecule with a positively-charged active group (ion). Often slightly acidic (pH 6-7), they have limited powers of detergency but are bacteriostatic and find uses as disinfectants in sanitisers. An example is the variety of quaternary ammonium compounds.

Cats Live animals carry many diseases which may be transmitted to humans by way of food and so cats should not be allowed in food rooms or to use utensils etc used by people. Hairs and other items may also contaminate food. *See*: Animals.

Caustic potash An alkaline cleaning agent possessing corrosive powers similar to caustic soda.

CDR (Communicable Disease Report) A weekly bulletin, produced by Central Public Health Laboratory (CPHL), circulated to EHOs and the medical profession, giving details of food poisoning and other communicable diseases in England and Wales.

CDSC (Communicable Disease Surveillance Centre, London) Part of the Central Public Health Laboratory (CPHL) dealing with food poisoning and other diseases. It receives around 250 000 reports annually from 250 local and NHS laboratories and collates them into a database. There are also facilities for identifying and typing salmonellas and VTEC.

Ceilings All parts of food rooms including ceilings should be constructed so that they can be maintained in a clean condition, even though they are not surfaces which normally come into direct contact with food. A gloss painted surface would be adequate, as long as flaking did not occur. The time between cleaning and redecoration is judged according to needs. *See*: Design of food premises.

Cell membrane A structural component of all cells. In animal cells it encloses the contents of the cell, but in bacteria (and plants) the cell membrane is surrounded externally by a tough cell wall. The cell membrane is selectively permeable, controlling the movement of substances into and out of the cell; in addition, in bacteria it is concerned with cell respiration and, in some pathogenic forms, the production of toxins. The outer membrane contains molecules which are toxic to humans. *See*: Endotoxins.

Cell wall (bacterial) Encloses the bacterial cell. It is a fairly rigid structure and gives shape to the bacterial cell. There is a procedure, known as the Gram stain, which assigns all bacteria to one or other of only two groups, depending on the result of the stain. It is a useful aid to identification. The different reactions to the Gram stain are thought to be due to differences in the composition of the cell wall.

Cellulose A complex carbohydrate, the main component of the cell wall in plants and most algae.

Central Public Health Laboratory (CPHL) Located at Colindale (London, England), a major research institute concerned with food microbiology. *See*: PHLS.

Centre temperature (Core temperature) The centre of food is the last part to reach the desired temperature during cooking or cooling and is often measured using a probe thermometer. Key temperatures are:

a. minimum 75°C should be reached during cooking and reheating
b. 63°C is the legal minimum for hot food in the UK (82°C in Scotland)
c. minus 18°C for frozen foods
d. 1-4°C as good practice for food in refrigerators. (8°C maximum by UK law).

    Important Points
1. Air temperature in equipment (e.g. in an oven or refrigerator) may be different from the temperature of the food.
2. The outer temperature of food will be different from the internal temperature.
3. Probes must be positioned accurately by trained persons.
4. Probes must be disinfected after use.
5. Temperatures at several spots should be taken.
See: Appendix: Food Law.

Cereals Not often associated with food poisoning except for outbreaks involving the

bacterium *Bacillus cereus.* Storage of cereals and related products must be such that pest infestations, including beetles, other insects and rodents are prevented. In damp conditions, mould growth is a problem.
See: *Aspergillus*, Dry goods storage, Rice.

Cestoda (Cestodes) *See*: Tapeworm species.

Changing facilities A separate room in which staff may change from outer clothing into work wear and in which outer clothing and footwear may be stored is desirable. It is undesirable to keep outer clothing in food rooms unless it is in a cupboard or locker. This is to prevent contamination of food by dust, clothing fibres, etc.

Chadwick, Edwin One of the founding figures of public health in England during the middle of the nineteenth century and the first president of the Sanitary Inspectors' Association (1883). The current headquarters of the Chartered Institute of Environmental Health is in Chadwick House, London.

Cheese Milk products made in a variety of ways from animal milks by the action of bacteria such as *Streptococcus lactis.* Hard cheeses of the cheddar type are not high-risk foods. Cheeses ripened with moulds or micro-organisms and those made from raw milk are safest when refrigerated. Outbreaks of food poisoning from cheeses have been due to *E. coli, Listeria monocytogenes, Salmonella* species, *Staphylococcus aureus* and others. Cheeses made from raw milk are liable to contain many species of micro-organisms including pathogenic moulds. *See*: Dairy products, High-risk food, Milk.

Chemical bonds Atoms are strongly linked to form compounds by various bonds such as covalent and ionic, an example being the chemical bonding of sodium and chlorine to form common salt. Hydrogen bonds weakly attach adjacent molecules of water and other substances.

Chemical food poisoning Many 'one-off' cases of food poisoning and other diseases have been noted due to accidental contamination of foods with chemicals ranging from pesticides to cleaning chemicals. Two infamous events include

1. mercury contamination of fish in Minamata Bay, Japan, which caused congenital deformities and brain damage in humans
2. a major incident in Spain in which hundreds of people died as a result of consuming contaminated cooking oil.

Chemical disinfectants/sterilants *See*: Hypochlorite.

Chickens

1. On a live chicken, and other birds, there may be large numbers of bacteria on the skin, plus others from the feathers, skin and faeces.
2. Contamination may come from feedstuffs, such as fish meal and animal protein; pasteurisation of such feedstuffs is recommended.
3. Contamination of the skin and the lining of the body cavity occurs at various stages in and following slaughter such as washing, plucking and evisceration (removal of innards).
4. There is contamination of eggs with salmonellas.
5. The giblets (gizzards, hearts and livers) are also frequently contaminated.
6. In the 1970s and 1980s, 60 to 80% of chicken carcasses were found to be contaminated with species of *Salmonella*, but during the early 1990s less than 50% contamination was reported in Britain.
The following bacteria have been isolated from poultry and poultry products: *Alcaligenes, Bacillus, Corynebacterium, Enterobacter, Escherichia, Flavobacter, Proteus, Pseudomonas, Sarcina (Micrococcus), Salmonella* and *Staphylococcus*. In addition a number of yeasts have also been isolated.

Consequently, careful thawing, storage, and thorough cooking of all chickens (indeed all poultry) are essential. It is also important that any blood from poultry is not allowed to contaminate other food. *See*: Cross-contamination, Eggs (various entries), *Salmonella* (various entries), Thawing of food.

Cheese mite (*Tyrophagus casei*) A pest of cheese and other foods and also responsible for the characteristic flavour and surface appearance of Altenburg cheese. When ripe, the cheese is covered with a grey-white powder consisting of live and dead mites.

Chilled foods Foods kept under refrigeration, normally between 1-4°C, to extend their shelf-life by a few days. Such foods are perishable and often high-risk, temperature control being required by law in the UK. *See*: Appendix: Food law, Cook-chill, Danger zone, Refrigerators.

Chlorine

1. The hypochlorites (chemical disinfectants) release chlorine, which is toxic to many organisms due to its powerful oxidation of structural protein, causing death of cells.
2. Action takes a few minutes and sufficient time (contact time) should be allowed for when an item is to be disinfected.
3. Chlorine compounds are hindered by heavy soiling of surfaces by food

residues and may also corrode metals.
4. They also have a strong taste and odour and must be rinsed from food contact items.
5. The non-biodegradability of hypochlorites is also an issue, but these substances are both cheap and effective.
See: Disinfectants, Hydrogen peroxide, Hypochlorite.

Chocolate Confectionery products high in both fat and sugar, rarely involved in food poisoning. In 1982/3 an outbreak of food poisoning due to the bacterium *Salmonella napoli* occurred under very uncommon circumstances including a very low infective dose (less than 100 organisms). A more frequent cause of complaint with chocolate is the presence of a white surface deposit due to migration of some ingredients over a long storage period. Generally chocolate is a low risk food which may be safely stored at room temperature.

Cholera
- A disease of the gastrointestinal tract caused by the bacterium *Vibrio cholerae*.
- It is transmitted via the faeces through water, contaminated foods (particularly shellfish harvested from polluted water) and rarely from cholera carriers.
Person to person spread by the faecal-oral route contributes to epidemic spread in underdeveloped countries where sanitary facilities and personal hygiene are poor.
- The incubation period is usually around two to three days, but can be as little as 4 hours.
- The effects on the sufferer are due to an enterotoxin which causes diarrhoea, as much as 20 litres (35 pints) per day; there is also violent vomiting.
- The severe fluid loss, without treatment, results in death.
- The mortality rate without treatment is over 50%; treatment requires replacement of lost body fluids, together with antibiotics.
- Vaccines are available.
- It is a rare disease in developed countries, due to efficient sewage disposal and water purification.

Chopping boards
a)   Wooden boards
1. Traditionally used, but wood may be an unsuitable material since it is difficult to clean, it is easily cut and it absorbs moisture.
2. Wooden chopping boards must be in excellent condition if they are to be used for food preparation.

3. The practice of salting boards after use does not have any great effect on *Staphylococcus* organisms.
4. Wooden boards may harbour bacteria from some foods prepared on them and so contaminate other foods later prepared on the same board.
5. Survival of some bacteria on wood is inhibited by naturally occurring toxins present in the wood itself.
6. American research on oak boards has showed 99.9% disappearance of salmonellas when cleaned, disinfected, and dried overnight.

b)   Polypropylene and synthetic boards
1. Modern materials, such as polypropylene, are now available and are claimed to be tougher and non-absorbent.
2. They may be colour coded, for example red for raw meat, green for vegetables, blue for fish.
3. These boards, in common with wood, may be deeply scored and become difficult to clean.
4. Some users report a safety problem in that plastic boards are slippery.

Ideally separate blocks and boards should be used for different foods, particularly for raw and cooked foods. This helps to control cross-contamination.

Chromobacterium lividum   A Gram-negative spoilage bacterium causing greenish-blue to brownish-black spots on stored beef.

Chronic disease   A disease that develops slowly over a long period of time. Often irreversible.

Cider   Both cryptosporidiosis and *E coli* outbreaks have been found in this product as well chemical food poisoning from zinc derived from a galvanised fermentation vessel.

Cigarette beetle (*Lasioderma serricorne*)   A pest of tropical products including cocoa, mainly infesting tobacco during storage and manufacture. The adult resembles the biscuit beetle but is smaller.

Ciguatera   A type of neurotoxin food poisoning similar to paralytic shellfish poisoning, caused by a number of tropical species of fish (groupers, barracudas, snappers, mackerel, and other species of warm-water fish). Not all fish of a particular species or from a certain locality are affected. It causes at least 50 000 cases per year world-wide but is very uncommon in the UK, the extent in the USA being unclear. The causative agents are marine algae (dinoflagellates) including *Gambierdiscus toxicus*, *Prorocentrum concavum* and *P. mexicana*. The disease may be fatal (up to 20% mortality). Initial signs of poisoning occur within six hours and include numbness and tingling which may spread to the fingers and toes, nausea, vomiting, and diarrhoea. The disease is normally self-limiting within several days from onset but, in severe cases, the neurological symptoms may persist for months or longer.

CIP (Cleaning-in-place) systems A method used to clean equipment, often involving pipe work, without first dismantling it. Cleaning chemicals and rinses may be pumped through equipment to remove contamination, food residues and deposits. Simple systems are found in the licensed trade and are used to clean beer pipes, while more complex operations exist in food factories, including milk processing plant.

Cladosporium A group of green moulds which are responsible for spoilage of a wide range of foods, including fresh meat, fruits, vegetables and cheese. It can grow at temperatures down to minus 4°C. The most frequent spoilage agent is *Cladosporium herbarum*, the growth of which appears dark green to black. The spores of this organism are very commonly found in the atmosphere. Other species cause green, brown or black discoloration.

Examples of spoilage include:

1. black spot on meat, especially freshly butchered and stored at 0 to 4°C, particularly if there is drying out of the surface of the meat
2. green mould rot of stone fruits, e.g. peaches, apricots, plums and cherries
3. cheese, where the mycelium and spores are dark or smoky in colour, producing dark colours to the cheese
4. another member of this group is *Cladosporium cladosporioides* which causes softening of cucumbers.

Clean-as-you-go A motto in food hygiene indicating that it is the food handlers' personal duty to clean up food waste caused by themselves thus avoiding any build-up. Fresh deposits are easier to remove than older ones.

Cleaning Cleaning has been described as being the largest day-to-day maintenance operation in any food business.

Problems
1. Cleaning is often regarded as a low status job and is frequently neglected.
2. Cleaning staff are often untrained.
3. Inadequate cleaning and the subsequent build up of deposits is high on the list of reasons for closure of food premises and prosecutions.
4. A food business may be judged on its cleanliness by both customers and enforcement officers.
5. Pests are attracted to dirty food premises.

Solutions
In the ideal situation, cleaning should be performed by a specialist team who arrive fresh on the job with the means to operate effectively. In practice, cleaning is frequently performed in a haphazard way by tired staff who have just finished a long shift of food production.

Cleaning schedules The key to managing cleaning operations is to systemise the approach by preparing a schedule stating

> **WHAT?** (items to be cleaned)
> **WHO?** (persons responsible)
> **HOW?** (method of cleaning)
> **WHEN?** (frequency)

The schedule, or plan, should include details of all equipment needed and state any safety precautions necessary. It must be capable of being checked or monitored to ensure that the system is working. Checking may be visual or microbiological (by taking swabs). Complete cleaning schedules may be purchased 'off the shelf' from cleaning chemical suppliers.

Cleaning-in-place systems *See*: CIP.

Cling film A thin plastic self-sticking film used to cover foods both during storage and in certain cooking methods including microwaving. It is important to use the correct grade of film.

The plasticiser chemical used in some film has been reported to be both fat-soluble and carcinogenic and its use in contact with fatty foods is not advised. The space between food and cling film may have a very high humidity and provide favourable conditions for mould growth if storage is long-term.

Cloakrooms Food handlers should have somewhere away from the food rooms to place their non-work clothes. This may take the form of a changing room or similar. If clothes are taken into food rooms then lockers or cupboards, must be supplied.

Clostridium botulinum
- An important and deadly food poisoning bacterium.
- A Gram-positive anaerobic bacillus, and a spore-former, so the organism will survive high temperatures.
- The most heat resistant of all food poisoning organisms.

Clostridium difficile

- Causes a disease known as botulism, the food poisoning being due to the release of a neurotoxin (an exotoxin). Seven types of botulism are recognised (A to G) based on the toxin produced by each strain. Types A, B, E and F cause human botulism.
- Toxin production is least likely when the environment is aerobic, below 5°C, below pH 4.5, and in the presence of nitrites, as in smoked meats and fish.
- The onset period for the disease is usually 18 to 36 hours (exceptionally 12 to 96 hours).
- Duration of the illness varies from death in 24 hours to eight days, or slow con valescence over six to eight months.
- First symptoms include slurring of speech, double vision and loss of balance since the toxin affects the nervous system (it is a neurotoxin).
- Death may result due to disturbances of various brain centres such as that involved in the control of breathing.
- The illness is rare in the UK and the US (less than 30 cases per year), but is a severe disease with a very high mortality rate.

Foods commonly involved are any food which is not acid (above pH 4.5) particularly in any improperly processed or contaminated canned or bottled foods, which provides anaerobic conditions. Contamination of soil, meat and fish is likely since spores of the organism are widely distributed in nature.

Clostridium botulinum Type A was found in Mascarpone cheese (a rich triple cream product) in Italy, some as part of home-made tiramisu in a 1996 outbreak.

Infant botulism (thought to be caused by the ingestion of *Clostridium botulinum* spores) was first identified in the USA in 1976 with over 900 reports since then. Contaminated honey has been linked to some cases. A single case in Scotland in 1993 was associated with lumpfish caviar.

(There is another type of botulism, known as wound botulism, which results from the infection of a wound by *Clostridium botulinum* alone, or with other micro-organisms. Toxins produced reach other parts of the body via the blood stream. This type of botulism does not involve food.)

Clostridium butyricum   Occasionally implicated in milk-borne food poisoning in infants.

Clostridium difficile   A Gram-positive bacterium which has been found to be responsible for a number of outbreaks of diarrhoea in London and Staffordshire (England) in the early 1990s. Affected individuals were hospital inpatients on geriatric wards. It is thought that the organisms were allowed to grow in the bowel due to the effects of

50 Clostridium nigrificans

antibiotic therapy, which had been prescribed for other medical conditions. Some strains of the organism produce a weak toxin and have an optimum temperature for growth of 30 to 37°C. *Clostridium difficile* is carried by 1-3% of healthy adults and 10-20% of hospital patients treated with antibiotics.

Clostridium nigrificans See: Desulphotomaculum nigrificans.

Clostridium perfringens A Gram-positive anaerobic bacterium, a spore-former and so often survives normal cooking.

- Grows between 15 to 50°C.
- The illness is often due to the organisms multiplying (>10^6 cfu/g may cause illness) during long, slow cooking and storage.
- Causes food poisoning symptoms as a result of an enterotoxin (endotoxin) released during sporulation (spore formation) in the digestive system, not in foods.
- It usually requires extremely large numbers of organisms to be present in the food for the illness, which is relatively mild, to occur.
- The onset period for the disease is 8 to 22 hours and the duration of illness is 12 to 48 hours.
- Symptoms are mild, with abdominal pain, flatulence and diarrhoea, rarely accompanied by vomiting, but often with nausea.

Foods commonly involved are meat dishes, such as stews or rolled joints, particularly when they are not cooled rapidly and refrigerated after cooking, or if they are not re-heated thoroughly, i.e. those subjected to poor temperature control. Contamination is usually from excreta, raw meat, poultry or soil. Institutional cooking (e.g. schools, hospitals, prisons, factory canteens) where large quantities of food are prepared several hours before serving is typical of the location of this type of food poisoning.

An outbreak of illness thought to be caused by eating chicken in a floating Cantonese restaurant in Amsterdam affected a party of tourists. The chicken had been stewed a long time in advance of service and was poorly stored.

Processed meats with sodium pyrophosphate (a bacteriostatic substance), an acid pH and high salt when kept under refrigeration have less growth of *Cl. perfringens*.

Note: This organism was formerly known as *Clostridium welchii*.

Clostridium sporogenes A Gram-positive spoilage bacterium of canned foods. It is a proteolytic organism (i.e. it breaks down proteins), producing foul-smelling (putrid) compounds. The food may be partly digested. Affected cans swell and may even burst. It affects particularly canned meats and fish. Spoilage is ordinarily prevented by adequate refrigeration, and the cause is due to under-processing.

Clostridium thermosaccharolyticum A Gram-positive spoilage bacterium of canned food. It is a saccharolytic organism (i.e. sugar-splitting), and causes gaseous spoilage of canned vegetables, producing a sour/fermented/cheesy odour. It typically forms acid and gas in low and medium acid foods, and affected cans swell and may burst.

Clostridium welchii The former name for the bacterium *Clostridium perfringens*.

Closure orders *See*: Emergency prohibition notice and order, Improvement notice.

Clothes moth (*Tineola bisselliella*) Occasional pests of stored products. *See*: Moths.

Clothing
- Protective clothing is worn to protect food from risk of contamination and not to keep other clothes clean.
- Persons handling open food should wear clean and washable overclothing at all times.
- Light coloured uniforms are preferred (soiling is obvious).
- The design of such clothing should minimise physical contamination of food by having no pockets or buttons. Sleeves may be present or absent depending on the work in hand.
- Comfort of the wearer should not be neglected; some fabrics are better than others in this respect.
- Colour-coded uniforms may be appropriate in operations where the prevention of cross-contamination is vital.

Other items of clothing may include head and beard coverings, gloves, aprons, footwear and wellington boots. All of these must be capable of being cleaned and kept in that condition. *See*: Protective clothing.

Cloths These are often implicated as the vehicle on which food poisoning bacteria are spread from place to place. Cloths must be used with great care, the disposable type being preferred in many situations. Cloths for re-use should be disinfected with hot water or chemicals.

Cobalt 60 A radioactive isotope finding industrial and medical use as a source of X-rays. *See*: Irradiation.

Coccus A term which describes the shape of certain bacterial cells; such cells are spherical. *See*: Bacterial Classification.

Coccidiosis A protozoan infection in rabbits caused by *C. serialis* and *C. pisiformis* resulting in small white cysts in the abdomen and yellowish areas in the lungs and liver. Affected animals are condemned.

Cockroaches Insects causing widespread infestation of food stores and related areas, particularly those which are heated.
1. Cause physical contamination.
2. Rarely exist in small groups and are generally nocturnal.
3. Infestations may be very difficult to deal with since eggs are capable of surviving in poor conditions for long periods even though the adults may be destroyed by a programme of treatment.
4. As with other pests, treatment is a professional task involving insecticides and poison baits. Juvenile hormone may also be used.

Several species are known, including the American cockroach (*Periplaneta americana*), reddish-brown in colour, up to 40 mm long, German cockroach (*Blattella germanica*), pale brown in colour, up to 15 mm long and the Oriental cockroach *(Blatta orientalis),* dark coloured, up to 25 mm long. All are known potential carriers of food poisoning organisms such as salmonellas.

Cocoa moth *(Ephestia elutella*) Also known as the warehouse or mill moth, it affects chocolate and tobacco as well as general foods.

Coconut *See*: Desiccated coconut.

Codes (date) Date-coding of goods gives information to suppliers and consumers regarding shelf-life of products and is also useful to investigators if problems arise. Many systems are in operation from 'secret' coding to open dating. *See*: Best-before date, Stock rotation, Use-by date.

Codes of Practice Advisory or guidance documents produced by various bodies including government and professional organisations. As such, these have no legal weight but if a Code of Practice is ignored and a statute or other law is broken, then this would be evidence that insufficient care had been taken. There are also statutory Codes of Practice which give guidance to EHOs amongst others on how to enforce certain legal provisions in a uniform way. *See*: Inspections.

Codex Alimentarius A subsidiary of the Food and Agriculture Organisation (FAO) and the World Health Organisation (WHO) which develops food safety standards and codes for adoption by governments. Examples include HACCP systems, laboratory procedures, commodity standards for many foods, food preservation techniques and permitted levels of pesticide residues.

Codworm (*Phocanema*) A pale coloured roundworm parasite, about 20 mm long, which encysts in both organs and flesh making badly affected fish unfit.

Cold chain A term used to describe the unbroken storage requirement of chilled high-risk foods from production to consumption. Such a chain includes all storage and transport used by all persons whether manufacturer, wholesaler, retailer or consumer. *See*: Temperature control.

Cold (effect on bacteria) *See*: Growth requirements (bacterial).

Cold room A large walk-in refrigerator.

Cold spots (in microwave cooking) Microwaves may be deflected (refracted) by ice crystals in frozen food so that some areas receive little heating and consequently remain frozen. Rotating or moving the food during heating helps to overcome the problem. *See*: Microwave ovens, Runaway heating.

Cold storage *See*: Chilled foods, Freezers, Refrigerators.

Cold store taint The absorption of odours by foods during cold storage. The use of containers with lids and proper wrapping reduces this risk.

Coliforms A group of bacteria which are commonly found in the large intestine (or colon, hence the name). They make up a large part of the intestinal flora of man and other vertebrate animals where they are normally kept under control. Examples of such organisms include *Enterobacter aerogenes, Escherichia coli, Shigella dysenteriae,* and *Vibrio cholerae* .
Note: These organisms are strictly referred to as FAECAL coliforms, since other coliforms are more commonly found in plant and soil samples. Their presence is generally undesirable in foods, since if they are detected in some foods, e.g. oysters, it is considered to be an indication of sewage contamination and so there is the possibility of intestinal pathogens being present. Also their growth in foods results in spoilage, causing the production of 'off' flavours.

Colon The large intestine.

Colony (bacterial) A population of micro-organisms which have grown on the surface of a solid medium (commonly agar) as the result of the reproduction of one or a few cells. Colonies have characteristics, such as texture, size, shape and colour, and these are fairly constant for a given species. Such characteristics are useful in distinguishing one micro-organism from another with the naked eye.

Colony count Microbiological technique involving counting the number of colonies of organisms after a specified time period. Uses of such figures include quality control of raw materials and products, and assessment of cleaning processes.

Colour coding A system of controlling cross-contamination by using different coloured equipment for individual foodstuffs or in separate areas. A common scheme is raw meat-red, cooked meat-yellow, poultry meat-white, vegetables-brown, raw fish-blue and salads/fresh fruit-green. Typical items coded would include chopping boards, uniforms and knife handles. *See*: Clothing.

Commensalism A form of symbiosis in which one individual benefits but the other is not harmed. Such relationships exist in many forms of life, including man and a variety of micro-organisms, including certain bacteria and yeasts. Examples include *Streptococcus viridans* (a bacterium) found in the mouth, and *Candida albicans* (a yeast) found on the surface of the skin. Note: Such a relationship may change under certain conditions and the organisms may become pathogenic.

Commercial sterility The near-total destruction of all micro-organisms and spores such as is achieved in canning. Some non-pathogens will survive but the product is judged to be safe. *See*: Sterilisation.

Committee on Medical Aspects of Food and Nutrition Policy (COMA)
UK Department of Health Committee reporting on medically related agriculture and food issues such as the links between ill health and nutrition.

Communicable disease A disease capable of being transmitted from one person to another, e.g. food poisoning. *See*: Notifiable disease.

Communicable Disease Surveillance Centre (CDSC) Run by the PHLS at Colindale, London. It receives around 250 000 reports annually from 250 local and NHS laboratories and collates these in the LabBase database. There are also facilities for identification and typing of salmonellas and VTEC.

Compaction Large volumes of waste packaging materials such as cardboard boxes may be reduced in size by pressing them into bales in a compactor. Such bales have an additional advantage in that harbourage for pests is reduced.

Compensation In the event of an enforcement officer such as an EHO making a professional mistake which is proved to be harmful to a business or person, compensation may be claimed.

Condensed milk

1. The sweetened type is a high sugar product, not considered to be high-risk. Preservation is by a combination of osmosis and heat.
2. The unsweetened type undergoes a severe heat treatment and is as safe as other

canned foods. If water is added after the can is opened then this product must be treated in the same way as fresh milk.

Conduction A method of heat transfer in solid materials in which molecular vibration transfers heat to adjacent molecules. Cooking methods using conduction including griddling and the heat from microwaves travels in solid foods by this method.

Conidiophore A fruiting aerial hypha, produced by some mature fungi, bearing conidiospores.

Conidiospore A type of reproductive asexual spore produced by some types of fungi. It may be unicellular or multicellular, and is not enclosed in a sac. Such spores are produced in chains at the end of a conidiophore. *Penicillium* (a common spoilage mould) reproduces by means of conidiospores.

Confectionery Products with a large sugar content, not normally considered to be high-risk foods.

Confused flour beetle (*Tribolium confusum*) A dark coloured insect, around 6 mm long, being a pest of stored cereal products. *See*: Beetles.

Consultant in Communicable Disease Control (CCDC)
The so-called 'proper officer' of the local authority to whom infectious diseases are notified by GPs and who passes on statistical information to the Office for National Statistics in the UK.

Consumer protection A large amount of legislation intended to protect consumers is enforced by various agencies including Trading Standards Officers. Some food issues are included such as the weight of pre-packed goods and labelling.

Contact dust Rodenticidal or insecticidal powder not for food room use. Poison may be eaten by the animal during grooming or may be taken back to nests.

Contact time The length of time taken for a disinfectant chemical to achieve the desired effect. It is normally in excess of 3 minutes for hypochlorite on food-contact surfaces.

Contamination of foods Most natural foodstuffs are either of plant or animal origin, and both have their particular surface populations of micro-organisms. Animals also have an intestinal population and they also liberate micro-organisms in their excretions and secretions. Both groups may, from time to time, suffer from parasitic disease, and so they will also carry those particular pathogens. Contamination may also occur from an outside source; the main sources being:

1. plants, fruits and vegetables (bacteria, yeasts and moulds)

2. animals, including meat, hides, hooves, hair, faeces, and for poultry, feet, feathers and eggs (mostly bacteria)
3. sewage (bacteria and viruses)
4. soil (bacteria, yeasts and moulds)
5. water (bacteria and viruses)
6. air (bacteria, fungal spores and viruses)
7. food handlers (bacteria and viruses)
8. kitchen surfaces and equipment (bacteria, yeasts and moulds).

Controlled atmosphere In the storage of meats, fruits and vegetables the addition of carbon dioxide is used to slow microbial growth and delay ripening. In some fruits such a pears and melons the addition of the gas ethylene hastens ripening at the end of the desired storage time.

Convalescent carrier *See*: Carrier.

Convection A method of heat transfer occurring in gases and liquids by convection currents. Since heat rises, these currents move away from the heat source and circulate throughout the substance being heated. In the reheating of large volumes of food such as soups and stews it is important that convection does not leave cool spots.

Cook-Chill A method of interrupted catering in which food is

1) prepared

2) cooked to a core temperature of 70°C

3) rapidly chilled to 3°C

4) stored at 3°C (this may include transport)

4) regenerated (reheated) to 70°C

5) eaten immediately.

The whole process must not take more than five days. In practice this means a day for production, three days storage and a day for reheating and consumption, but many operators reduce this. There is a set of guidelines (UK), produced in 1989, available from the Department of Health regarding cook-chill.

Temperature control at all stages of the process is vital and probe thermometers are frequently used. If food during storage reaches 5°C it must be eaten within 12 hours. If 10°C is exceeded the food must not be eaten. The system, which operates on a factory basis, must be carefully controlled at all times since there is a danger from *Listeria monocytogenes*. Typical cook-chill users include hospitals and supermarkets with the end-users (consumers) often some distance away from the place of production.

Advantages of cook-chill

a. Wide menu choice and increased palatability leading to less wastage.
b. 24 hour production.
c. Economies in purchasing raw materials in bulk.
d. Centralised standards.
e. Better portion control.

Cook-Freeze A system similar to cook-chill but with an extended shelf-life due to storage at minus 18°C.

Cooking of food (effect on bacteria)

1. Fresh food, cooked thoroughly and served immediately, should never cause food poisoning due to micro-organisms.
2. If food is cooked thoroughly it should ensure that all bacteria in and on the food will be killed (except for spore formers).
3. The safest method of cooking is to use a short, high temperature method; this means that the food is quickly taken through the 'danger zone' of bacterial growth, to reach a temperature at which the death of bacterial cells starts to occur.
4 To ensure that bacteria are destroyed, cooking times and temperatures must be carefully calculated.
5. It is important to realise that cooked food may cause problems if it is allowed to cool too slowly, or if it is allowed to be re-contaminated.
See: Cooling of Food, Cross-contamination.

Cooking oils In use, these reach temperatures in excess of 160°C. Care is needed, particularly with the cooking of frozen foods, since it may result in the surface of a product being cooked but the centre temperature (core temperature) being inadequate for thorough cooking.

Cooling water In the canning industry, contaminated water has been a cause of food poisoning. *See*: Aberdeen typhoid outbreak.

Cooling of food Cooked food required for cold service after cooking should be cooled to a temperature of between 10-15°C within 90 minutes before refrigeration to avoid the multiplication of bacteria which have survived the cooking process, or the germination of spores which have not been destroyed. Large single items of food such as meat may need to be cooked in pieces no heavier than 2.5 kg (5 to 6 lb) while large volumes of liquid (more than 25 litres, or 44 pints) may be split into smaller shallow

58 Copper

portions to help rapid cooling. Hot food must not be placed directly in a refrigerator. Cooling may be done in a cool room (10-15°C) or in a blast chiller.

Copper One of a number of metals which may cause food poisoning. It can enter food from water pipes or from the action of acid foods on copper pans.
See: Metals.

Corynebacterium A group of Gram-positive bacteria, some members of which are pathogenic to humans and animals. Some cause disease and spoilage in plants, such as tuber rot of potatoes and fruit spot of tomatoes.

Corned beef Canned meat product ('corn' originally meaning salted) which although generally safe has been involved in food poisoning. *See*: Aberdeen typhoid outbreak, Canning.

Cornflour A potential source of *Bacillus cereus* organisms.

COSHH (Control of Substances Hazardous to Health) Regs 1994 (and as amended) Legislation requiring employers to assess the risks in use of all chemicals which may be a danger to health. These are defined under separate regulations and include toxic, harmful and corrosive substances. Employees must receive training and information regarding uses and risks. The use of very dangerous chemicals may require regular health checks. In the food industry the major COSHH problems are found in cleaning chemicals such as bleaches and caustic soda. *See*: Cleaning (various entries).

Coughing (and open food) Coughing results in a violent release of micro-organisms from the mouth and throat into the air. Many of these micro-organisms are in small clusters, surrounded by mucus. This helps to prevent them from drying and so they remain infective for longer. Any such clusters of bacteria landing on unprotected high-risk food may well be the starting point of an outbreak of food poisoning.
See: *Staphylococcus aureus*.

Courts Most food hygiene offences in England and Wales will be heard at a local Magistrates Court (Summary offences) and there is provision for appeals from these to go to a Crown Court. At higher levels are the Court of Appeal, House of Lords and European Courts. Other countries have different systems.

Covering of food In order to prevent airborne contamination, open food (for example that on display in shops) must be covered. *See*: Aerosols, Dust.

Coxiella burnettii An organism (a rickettsia) which causes Q fever in humans. After inhalation of the organisms, mild respiratory symptoms may follow. The acute illness itself is characterised by the sudden onset of a severe headache, muscle pain and fever which may remain very high for more than a month if not treated. It is rarely fatal, but endocarditis (inflammation of the lining of the heart) occurs in about 10% of cases. Incubation period may be from 5 to 10 years. Around 100 cases per year are reported annually in England and Wales, mainly from contact with animals by veterinary surgeons, abattoir workers, farmers and others. It may occasionally be transmitted by contaminated milk.

Cream A high-risk milk product, often pasteurised or sterilised, which should be refrigerated unless packed in a can or similar container. Various legal standards define the composition of creams (double cream is 48% fat). Hygiene precautions for cream also extend to imitation cream. *See*: Danger zone, High-risk food.

Creutzfeldt-Jakob Disease (CJD) A fatal disease, a transmissible spongiform encephalopathy (TSE), in humans. It has a long incubation period (up to 15 years or more), and is described as the "human equivalent of BSE", with which it is thought to be linked. It affects the brain, causing memory loss, dementia, disorientation and death usually within 6 months of diagnosis. Although mainly affecting people over 65 years of age, a new variant has appeared with a much shorter incubation period which affects younger people. In the UK 12 confirmed cases were diagnosed by June 1996.

Crockery Chipped or cracked crockery should be discarded since the damaged areas are porous and may harbour bacteria.

Cross-contamination

```
┌─────────────────────────────────────────────┐
│          Source of Contamination            │
│ Raw food, Refuse, People, Animals, Insects, │
│              Soil, Dust, Rodents            │
└──────────────────────┬──────────────────────┘
                       │
                       ▼
┌─────────────────────────────────────────────┐
│                  Vehicles                   │
│ Hands, Hand-contact surfaces, Food,         │
│              Equipment, Clothing            │
└──────────────────────┬──────────────────────┘
                       │
                       ▼
┌─────────────────────────────────────────────┐
│              HIGH-RISK FOOD                 │
└─────────────────────────────────────────────┘
```

Cross-contamination The transfer of bacteria from one food, often raw to another food, often cooked. Cross-contamination requires a 'vehicle'.

Examples are:

1. using the same knife to cut raw and cooked meats, or handling them without washing the hands in between
2. wiping up meat juices from a raw chicken with a cloth, and using the same cloth to dry a plate used for sandwiches
3. failure to wash the hands properly after using the lavatory and then preparing sandwiches or a trifle
4. preparing salad vegetables on a chopping board, the soil from which may contaminate e.g. hard-boiled egg later sliced
5. washing the hands thoroughly but then drying them on a soiled cloth prior to preparing food.

Crown Immunity (UK) Premises occupied by Crown agencies may be excluded from the provisions of various laws. As an example, prior to Feb 1 1987, Food Hygiene Law did not apply to hospital kitchens. Some Crown premises remain exempt from both Food Hygiene and Health and Safety legislation.

Crustacea A term used to describe a class of arthropods (literally 'jointed limbs') including crab, crayfish, lobster, prawn, scampi, shrimp and wood lice.
See: Shellfish.

Cryogenic freezing A type of quick freezing in which food is immersed in liquid nitrogen. The process is extremely rapid but expensive and tends to be used for high value products such as strawberries and prawns.

Cryovac (Tm - W R Grace Ltd) The vacuum packing of fresh meat in a special plastic laminate which prevents the entry of oxygen and moisture and also physically protects the product. Shelf-life is said to be doubled at chill temperatures.
See: Anaerobic, *Clostridium botulinum,* Sous vide, Vacuum packing.

Cryptolestes Small beetles (2-3 mm in length) sometimes infesting damp stored foodstuffs. The red-rust flour beetle is one example.

Cryptosporidium A unicellular parasite belonging to a group of micro-organisms known as coccidial protozoa. It was considered to be a commensal up to the mid 1950s when it was found to be a cause of fatal enteritis in turkeys. It was later found to cause diarrhoea in a wide range of animals, and in 1976, was shown to be able to cause illness in humans.

An increase in 1995 in England and Wales has been noted and in Maine, USA in 1994 an outbreak from cider made from apples thought to be contaminated with calf faeces from trees growing on animal pasture was recorded. Several hundred cases associated with eating fruit including raspberries were reported in the USA in early 1996 possibly via contaminated water.

- The most common species responsible for infections in humans and live stock is *Cryptosporidium parvum.*
- The organism can grow only in living hosts.
- Infection occurs when cysts (known as oocysts) are swallowed and fol lowing a complex life cycle, faeces containing more infectious cysts are released from the body.
- The cysts are highly resistant to disinfectants, including bleach. They are killed by freezing (minus 20°C for 30 minutes), by heat (55°C for 5 to 10 minutes, or a few seconds in boiling water), and by some chemicals.
- The disease, known as cryptosporidiosis, most commonly affects children aged one to five years. Cases have been noted in children after educational vis its from contact with animals such as lambs.
- The incubation period is about seven days.
- Symptoms include watery diarrhoea, abdominal pain, vomiting and fever, and last from one to three weeks. There is no current effective treatment.
- Source of infection may be animal or human and person to person spread is not uncommon. Water, raw milk and offal have all been identified as vehicles of transmission with cases noted in England in 1993 linked to unfiltered water from a borehole. Infection in sheep and cattle is common and may be passed to water supplies via contaminated slurry and manure.

A survey in 1996 showed that 300 000 homes in Hertfordshire (England) were affected with *Cryptosporidium,* a suggested reason was increased muckspreading combined with leaking supply pipes.

Culture media There are many media available for supporting the growth of micro-organisms in the laboratory. Essentially there are two types of media: liquid media (for bacteriological work) known as broths, and solid media, commonly nutrient agar gel. It is possible to select for the growth of particular micro-organisms, by including in the broth or agar gel something to actively encourage the growth of a particular organism. Conversely, the incorporation of substances to discourage or inhibit the growth of all micro-organisms except for the one desired are available. There are special solid media for culturing fungi, again based on agar, such as potato dextrose agar (PDA) and malt agar, containing crushed boiled potato and malt extract respectively. Both bacteria and fungi will show appreciable growth in or on such culture media within 24 hours or so in the laboratory. Such laboratory isolation and growth is a vital first step in identifying a suspected causal agent of disease or spoilage.

Note: Viruses cannot be cultured by these methods, as they can only grow and multiply inside a living host cell.

Curing

1. A method of food preservation, with ancient origins, in which meat or fish is immersed in a solution of salt and potassium or sodium nitrate.
2. Increased osmotic pressure creates conditions unfavourable to microbial growth by reducing the available water. Staphylococci however tolerate salty conditions.
3. During the process, nitrate is converted to nitrite which reacts with haemoglobin forming a pink-coloured substance (the characteristic colour of bacon and similar products).
4. The traditional (Wiltshire cure) process takes some weeks and modern developments include 'in-slice' curing and tumbling, both of which achieve curing in a day.
5. Some products may be smoked or have additions of sugar.
See: Corned beef, Halophile, Nitrate, Nitrite.

Custard A milk product and thus a high-risk food. It must either be kept hot (above 63°C) or cold (below 8°C). A danger is that custard may be prepared in advance, become contaminated and then not reheated to a sufficiently high temperature. Similarly, baked egg custard is high risk.

Cutlery *See*: Cleaning schedules, Washing up.

Cutting board *See*: Chopping boards.

Cyanobacteria (Blue-green algae) A group of micro-organisms which are subject to rapid multiplication in fresh water and are a known health risk to humans, fish, domestic and wild animals. Symptoms may prove fatal and include dizziness, headaches, muscle cramp, gastroenteritis and vomiting. Persons most at risk are those in direct contact with infected water. *See*: Algae.

Cyanogens Cyanide-containing substances found mainly in the seeds of foods including apples, pears, apricots and plums and also in various nuts and beans such as almond and kidney beans. Fatal poisoning has been noted following consumption of roasted apple pips. The tropical root vegetable manioc and the lima bean require thorough cooking to drive off the cyanide as hydrogen cyanide gas.

Cyclohexane Used in solvent extraction of natural flavourings. A small residue of

1mg/kg is thought to be acceptable.

Cyclospora cayetanensis
- A single-celled parasite (a protozoan), infections of which were first diagnosed in the late 1970s.
- Transmitted through infected faeces by the faecal-oral route, swallowing cysts found in contaminated food or water.
- *Cyclospora* is not infectious at the time it is excreted in the faeces. It becomes infectious (sporulates) days or weeks after excretion, especially in warm temperatures and high humidity.
- Direct person to person transmission is unlikely.
- Incubation period is up to 7 days; illness lasts for several days to a month or longer.
- Symptoms include watery diarrhoea (which can persist for a month or more), loss of appetite, bloating, flatulence, nausea, vomiting, stomach cramps, lassitude and fever.
- Drug treatment is available and effective.
- There were several hundred confirmed cases in the US over a two month period (May/June) in 1996, with many cases associated with the consumption of fruit (in particular raspberries, and mixtures of berries and other fruits). In the UK there are around 50 confirmed cases annually.
- Infections are known to occur in many countries, with contaminated water thought to be responsible.

Cysticercus bovis, cellulosae and tenuicollis The cystic stages of the beef tapeworm (*Taenia saginata*), the pork tapeworm (*Taenia solium*) and the dog tapeworm (*Taenia hydaginata*) respectively.

Cytoplasm That portion of a cell between the outer cell membrane and the cell nucleus or nuclear region. It consists of fluid in which are the cell's organelles, which are the components of the cell having specific functions within the cell.

Dairy products
1. The protein content of many dairy products makes them attractive to bacteria and they are classed as being high-risk foods.
2. Milk is subject to a great deal of food law such as the requirements for heat treatments of pasteurisation and sterilisation. It has been involved in outbreaks of both food poisoning and food-borne disease.
3. Soft cheeses ripened with moulds or other micro-organisms may be prone to growth of *Listeria* species, especially if raw milk has been used in their preparation.
4. Hard cheeses are regarded as less of a risk.

5. Cream has also been implicated food poisoning outbreaks when cross-contamination has occurred.
See: Butter, Cheese, Cream, Milk, Yoghurt.

Damaged goods Damage to packaging, containers and cans may allow food to become contaminated with micro-organisms or physical contaminants. Such foods should be regarded with suspicion and discarded if there is any doubt about their fitness. Food escaping after container damage may attract pests and also spoil other foods.

Danger zone This is the range of temperatures, around 5 to 63°C, in which food poisoning bacteria may multiply. Within the danger zone are

- room (ambient) temperatures (often around 20°C and above)
- human body temperature, 37°C.

This latter is the optimum or best temperature for the growth of many pathogens and high-risk foods should not be kept within the danger zone of temperatures for long time periods. This is the principle of temperature control and includes the use of refrigeration, cooking and hot storage. If a hot, cooked item requires refrigeration it must not remain in the danger zone for more than 90 minutes.
See: Appendix: Food Law, Cooling of food, Mesophile, Temperature control.

Dark mealworm (*Tenebrio obscurus*) A dull/matt black or brown insect, about 10mm in length; it is a pest of stored cereal products including flour. It thrives in damp and dark conditions producing large (over 20mm long) yellowish-brown larvae.

Dark-cutting meat A self-explanatory term used to describe meat of poor keeping quality, the colour being due to the muscle protein myoglobin. The most common cause is the slaughter of fatigued or stressed animals whose muscle glycogen reserves are low. This results in a high ultimate pH (over 6), glycogen being converted into lactic acid after death. 'Glazy' bacon has a similar cause.

Date codes Foods are marked with dates indicating either when they were produced or their last date for consumption.

'USE-BY' DATE

High-risk perishable foods which could cause food poisoning have a 'use-by' date indicating the last day upon which the food is safe to eat; examples include meat and dairy products and cook-chill items.

'BEST-BEFORE' DATE

Foods which deteriorate in quality but which are unlikely to cause food poisoning may have a 'best-before' date indicating that taste, appearance and other quality or organoleptic factors are likely to change after this date. Examples include potato crisps, biscuits, confectionery and canned drinks.

Other foods such as canned and dehydrated foods, bread, fresh fruit and vegetables do not have date codes. It is desirable to mark delivery dates on them where possible so that proper stock rotation can be carried out. Out of date stock should not be used or sold. Manufacturers' codes are often present, with some systems being difficult to decipher. *See*: Appendix: Food Law.

DDT (Dichlorodiphenyl trichlorethane) An insecticide developed in the late 1930s and widely used because of its toxicity to a large number of species. It was originally thought to be non-toxic to mammals but this has not proved to be the case. Higher life forms concentrate DDT in their tissues eventually building up lethal or damaging doses. Its use has been severely curtailed because of these environmental effects.

Deadly nightshade A plant which occasionally causes acute poisoning if eaten.

Death Cap mushroom (*Amanita phalloides*) A highly poisonous mushroom. The appearance of it is unspectacular, being small and pale-coloured, and it is suspected that mistaken identity is the cause of at least some cases of poisoning. Symptoms appear up to 12 hours after ingestion. The grey squirrel is able to eat this variety without harm. *See*: Mushrooms.

Death phase Alternative term for decline phase. *See*: Bacterial growth curve.

Decomposition/decomposers An indication of food spoilage in which the structure of cells is broken down by both micro-organisms (decomposers) and enzymes to produce undesirable changes such as liquefaction and off-odours.

Deep freeze

Advantages
- At commercial deep freeze temperature of minus 18°C and below, the activities of many micro-organisms are very much reduced with multiplication being virtually non-existent. Enzyme action is also slowed considerably.

- Shelf-life is greatly increased.

Disadvantages
- Deep freezing does not kill the majority of pathogens at temperatures commonly used. On thawing, bacteria will start to multiply as soon as the danger zone is reached.
- Spoilage enzymes are also inhibited at deep freeze temperatures but will continue to work slowly and eventually cause loss of quality.

See: Freezers (various entries), Spoilage of food, Star symbols.

Defaecate
The act of expelling faeces from the human or other body. *See*: Intestinal flora.

Defrosting
1. In refrigeration equipment, ice tends to build up as a coating on internal surfaces. This reduces the efficiency of refrigerators, freezers and chillers and should be periodically removed. Removal may be manual with a scraper or automatic using a built-in system. Automatic systems are designed so that the product does not reach an unacceptably high temperature.
2. An alternative term for thawing.

Dehydration
1. Loss of water by the human body sometimes as a result of continued vomiting and diarrhoea during an attack of food poisoning. It may be so severe as to cause death, as has been noted in cases of salmonellosis.
2. A method of food preservation which uses various techniques to remove water from foodstuffs and so make them unsuitable for the growth of micro-organisms.
- Dried foods have a very long history, early products (c.3 000 BC in Mediterranean regions) being produced by sun-drying; plums and grapes producing prunes and raisins, apricots and other fruits were also sun-dried. The method is still in use.
- More modern methods include the spray-drying of milk and other liquids.
- Dehydrated foods may be kept in closed containers at room temperature for long periods but as soon as water is added (reconstitution or rehydration) they must be treated as if they were fresh foods; this is particularly important for high-risk foods such as milk, gravy and soups.

See: Accelerated Freeze Drying, Available water, High-risk foods.

Delivery of foodstuffs. A vital part of the food chain and one in which cross-contamination and loss of proper temperature control is possible.

- Goods entering food areas must be carefully checked to ensure that they are received in a satisfactory condition before storage or use.
- Attention should be paid to date codes.
- Packaging and containers must be intact.
- Temperatures of chilled frozen foods should be checked.
- Avoid any contamination by keeping foods separate and not exposing them during delivery.
- All goods should be carefully checked against invoices and weighed if necessary.
- Vehicles and delivery persons must be hygienic.
- It is becoming increasingly common for detailed specifications of foods (including delivery conditions such as temperatures) to be demanded from suppliers.
- Samples may be taken for analysis.

Delivery vehicles
- These and containers used in them must come up to the same standards of construction and hygiene as food rooms.
- The internal surfaces of delivery vehicles should be capable of being easily cleaned and food should not subjected to any possibility of contamination.
- Segregation of foods should occur if deliveries are of mixed foods.
- Certain temperatures may be required for the transport of chilled or frozen food and deliveries of such food may be rejected if temperatures are incorrect, for example chilled foods above 5 or 8°C or frozen foods above minus 18°C.
- Refrigeration and insulation of vehicles is normally required for high-risk foods.

See: Appendix: Food Law.

Department of Health (DoH) UK Government department which has major interests in food hygiene and food law. There are links between the Department of Health and MAFF (Ministry of Agriculture, Fisheries and Food), particularly if food safety is an emergency of national concern.

Dermatitis An often painful inflammation of the dermis of the skin which may be caused by contact with a sensitising substance. The skin cracks and infection may result. Many chemicals, including those used in cleaning and washing up have caused it, particularly through repeated use although cases have arisen from a single contact. Affected areas of skin must be protected both to avoid food contamination and making the condition worse. In severe cases, sufferers may not work in food areas.

Dermestid Common name for the Dermestes beetles. *See*: Bacon beetle, Hide beetle.

68 Desiccated coconut

Desiccated coconut Dried coconut flesh is not normally associated with food poisoning. It is of historical interest because of outbreaks of typhoid and paratyphoid fever and salmonella food poisoning during the 1950s in many parts of the world, caused by contaminated coconut and its use in cakes and confectionery. Improved hygiene practices in the countries of origin of the product have proved effective.

Design of equipment in food premises Equipment must be such that it is
- capable of being easily cleaned
- non-toxic and impervious
- corrosion-resistant
- smooth, non-cracking and hard-wearing.

Stainless steel and certain plastic materials are often quoted as being ideal. Items of equipment should not cause physical contamination of food, for example from loose bolts.
See: Appendix: Food Law, Chopping boards, Colour-coding, Copper, Metals, Polypropylene, Stainless steel, Wood, Zinc.

Design of food premises
- Mains services (such as gas and water) must be available.
- Regard must be given to location, bearing in mind planning restrictions and registration requirements.
- Buildings should be proofed against pests and comply with current legislation.
- The principle of linear work flow helps to minimise risk of cross-contamination.
- Similar requirements to materials used in food equipment apply to food premises.
- All surfaces such as floors, walls and work surfaces must be capable of efficient cleaning.
- Facilities for staff changing and personal hygiene must be incorporated.
- Adequate storage facilities including refrigeration are essential.
- Adequate lighting and ventilation are required.

Desserts Those which contain milk/milk products and are above pH 4.5 should be kept refrigerated. Some yoghurts may be included.
See: Appendix: Food law, Milk products.

Destroying Angel mushroom (*Amanita verna/virosa*)
A highly toxic mushroom closely related to the Death Cap mushroom.

Desulphotomaculum nigrificans A Gram-positive spoilage bacterium which causes sulphide or 'sulphur-stinker' spoilage in low acid heat-processed canned foods, such as peas and corn. It produces hydrogen sulphide (rotten eggs smell), without any discoloration in peas, but in corn there is some blackening of the product. The organism is fairly easily killed by heat, and its presence in the food is evidence of under-processing. There is no external evidence of spoilage as there is no swelling of the can. Note: The organism was formerly known as *Clostridium nigrificans*.

Detergents
- Cleaning agents used to remove grease and other substances from surfaces, utensils and equipment.
- They reduce surface tension and are described as surface active agents (surfactants).
- Grease is dispersed in water, suspended and prevented from resettling; this is known as emulsification.
- Detergents should not form scum, be non-toxic and be easily rinsed off.
- Common soapless detergents are anionic and have negatively-charged, water-liking (hydrophilic) heads.
- Cationic detergents (positively-charged heads) are often bactericidal and used in sanitisers.

See: Amphoteric, Quaternary Ammonium Compounds, Soap, Soapless detergent.

Dettol One of a number of trade names for the antiseptic/disinfectant substance chlorxylenol. It has a strong taste and odour and has no use for food-contact items but may be used in other areas such as toilets and drains.

Diarrhetic shellfish poisoning (DSP) Caused by toxins released by the marine algae *Dinophysis* and *Prorocentrum* particularly in Japan, although the problem has spread world-wide; the first reported cases in England were in 1994, associated with imported mussels. Gastroenteritis is the main symptom and since the toxins are heat-stable the best preventative measure is to monitor contamination of shellfish beds. A dose of 40ug may produce diarrhoea which normally subsides within a few days. Other symptoms, rapidly occurring, including chills, nausea, abdominal pain and vomiting. Other shellfish such as oysters and scallops may be infected.

Diarrhoea A common symptom of food poisoning in which loose or liquid faeces are expelled with some frequency and violence. The cause is due to the presence of pathogens, toxins or other substances in the intestines. *See*: Food Poisoning.

Diazinon An organo-phosphorus residual insecticide used in lacquers to control cockroaches and also in fly strips. It is toxic to mammals.

Dichlorvos A chlorinated organic insecticide used as a fumigant and in fly strips.

Diguanides Cationic detergents used in glass washing.

Dinoflagellates Unicellular, free-floating algae. Certain marine forms produce neurotoxins that cause paralytic shellfish poisoning. The disease spreads to humans when large numbers of dinoflagellates are eaten by molluscs (e.g. mussels), which in turn are eaten by humans.

Dioxins A group of organochlorine chemicals widely found as environmental contaminants. They have uses as herbicides and in PVC used in food packaging. Dioxins are known to cause skin disfigurement and are potential carcinogens, but the likelihood of causing illness from food packaging (migrating from packaging to the food) is considered to be remote.

Diphtheria An infectious disease caused by three types of the Gram-positive *Corynebacterium diphtheriae*, affecting the throat of humans. The bacterium produces a powerful toxin which affects the heart and nervous system and may be fatal. The disease is contracted by the respiratory routes or through wounds and skin infections and has been spread via milk contaminated by dairy workers.

Diphyllobothrium latum Fish tapeworm causing various abdominal disturbances including flatulence, pain and diarrhoea occur over a week after eating undercooked fish. It is reported as once being common around the Great Lakes of the USA with more recent outbreaks in Los Angeles (1980) from sushi, a Japanese raw fish dish. *See: Anisakis simplex.*

Diplococcus Cocci that divide once and remain attached in pairs. ('diplo'= two). *See:* Bacterial Classification.

Diptera Literally 'two winged', the rear pair having degenerated to rod-like structures. This order contains a large number of species of flies including the housefly and bluebottle, both of which are significant carriers of bacteria capable of causing food poisoning.

Diseases (in food handlers) As a general rule, all food handlers must report diseases or infections, which could be transmitted to other people, to their supervisor who should inform the authority for controlling diseases (in the UK this is normally done by an

Disinfectant/Disinfection

Environmental Health Officer). *See*: Exclusion of food handlers.

Dish-washing An important part of cleaning, the effectiveness of which is paramount to ensure that no food on which micro-organisms may grow is left on plates. The image of a food business is frequently judged by the cleanliness of its crockery and utensils.

Two-sink system
1. Pre-clean or scrape to remove large food items.
2. Wash or main clean at around 55°C with a detergent to remove grease; this low temperature prevents foods such as eggs being cooked onto the plates.
3. Disinfecting rinse in a second sink containing water at about 85°C, or cooler water with a suitable chemical sanitiser; this removes detergent, reduces the bacterial load and heats up plates so that they may air dry without the use of cloths.
4. Air drying.
5. Finished items should be stored where they will not become contaminated.
6. Lightly soiled articles such as glasses are washed first so that the detergent does not become contaminated straight away.
7. Wash and rinse chemicals must be freshly made according to manufacturers' instructions and changed when necessary.

The single sink system is similar but requires filling and emptying. Mechanical dish washer cycles resemble the two-sink system. *See*: Cleaning.

Disinfectant/Disinfection
- Disinfection is the reduction of the numbers of micro-organisms to a safe or acceptable level.
- It does not imply total destruction nor a significant reduction in the numbers of spores.
- Common disinfectants include: heat (water at 82°C applied for one minute is a common use), various chemicals such as hypochlorites and hydrogen peroxide and ultra violet light.
- Articles which are disinfected in the food industry include machinery, food contact surfaces, cleaning equipment and the hands of food handlers.
- Chemical disinfectants must be made up and used according to manufacturers' instructions and not kept for long periods since they become inactive. They require time to work, up to 30 minutes contact may be needed.
- Soap and hot water is often stated to be the best and cheapest disinfectant and

is particularly useful in hand washing. This term is often misused and confused with sterilisation.

Dispensers (soap) Tablets or bars of soap are known to support bacterial growth and liquid soap in a dispenser is thus preferred. The soap may be bactericidal and should be non-perfumed to avoid taint.

Dogs
- These, nor any other live animal, should not be allowed in food rooms due to the wide range of diseases they may carry.
- There is also danger of physical contamination of food from hairs or any substance present on the feet or fur of the animal.
- Local bye laws exist in the UK which prevent members of the public from taking dogs into food premises (guide dogs excepted).
- Examples of canine-transmitted diseases include leptospirosis, hydatid tapeworm, fungal infections, salmonellosis and toxocariasis.

DoH *See*: Department of Health.

Domestic premises Use is sometimes made of domestic kitchens to prepare food for functions and cases of food poisoning have occurred which involved food thus prepared. Such premises may be unsatisfactory because
- equipment is not likely to be made to handle the heavy use for which commercial units are designed
- refrigeration may be inadequate
- the layout of the kitchen will not be so as to minimise cross-contamination
- separate hand-washing and equipment sinks are not normally present
- the room is used by non-food handlers and pets.

16% of all outbreaks of food poisoning in England and Wales 1992-1994 were associated with domestic premises, mainly caused by *S. enteritidis* PT4 from poultry and eggs. *See*: Design of equipment/ food premises.

Doner kebab A spit-roasted minced meat product (lamb or sometimes beef), machine or hand-moulded onto a spit before cooking, and removed in slices by carving.
- Correct temperature control during preparation and cooking is vital since bacteria present will be all through the kebab and not solely on the outside.
- Destruction of pathogens depends on thorough cooking and a high temperature must be achieved at the centre, making sure the grill is not turned down or off at any time.

- Since the product may be handled during preparation, personal hygiene must be of a high standard and raw kebabs refrigerated before use.
- Care should also be taken with salad materials used, especially since they are often prepared in bulk and in advance.

Door handles Often contaminated after contact with hands, a particular example being the internal door handle in a WC compartment. Handles should be included in cleaning schedules.

Doors Like all other surfaces in food rooms, doors should be finished with an impervious (non absorbent) surface so that they may be readily cleaned. Kick plates may be necessary at the bottom to prevent access to rodents and the door should fit well leaving no gaps.

Doubling time Alternative term for generation time.

Drainage
- An essential service requirement for all premises. It needs careful design and planning (in consultation with local authorities) to ensure conformation with building regulations.
- Grease traps may need to be installed to prevent blockage of the system by congealed fats; they need periodic emptying and are best located outside food areas.
- All sinks and sanitary equipment are connected to the drainage system via a trap, the function of which is to prevent odours entering the room and to provide a barrier against rodents.
- Some items of equipment such as peeling machinery may have filter traps to prevent large quantities of debris entering the drainage system.
- Floors in food rooms are often laid with a gentle slope (1 in 60) to a half-round drainage channel, which is covered by a grating, or alternatively to a trapped inlet.

Dried food *See*: Dehydration.

Drip Water lost from frozen food as it thaws, resulting in loss of quality since the liquid lost originated inside cells. The amount of drip is proportional to the time taken to freeze the food, quick freezing in under one hour producing least drip. In meats quick freezing time is not feasible for large items (such as entire carcasses) although a high ultimate pH reduces drip considerably. Smaller food items such as peas may be frozen very rapidly, tend to suffer less drip and are of high quality. Drip from thawing meat and poultry may contain pathogenic organisms.

Drinking water Must be provided for employees at all places of work including food businesses. The responsibility for ensuring that water is fit to use (potable) rests initially with the water supply company. After it has left the tap it may become a food (for example under the Food Safety Act 1990), and may become the responsibility of the person operating the food business.

Drinks Subject to much the same hygiene problems as foodstuffs particularly where there are high-risk components such as milk. Water is a known vehicle of foodborne diseases such as typhoid fever.

Droplet infection The transmission of infection by small liquid droplets which carry micro-organisms. The liquid (mucus, from the nose, mouth or throat), will carry bacteria, and if allowed to contaminate open food, may result in an outbreak of food poisoning. *See*: Personal hygiene, Sneeze screens, *Staphylococcus aureus*.

Droppings The faeces of rats, mice, insects and other animals. These are often the first visible sign of infestations and have characteristic sizes and shapes from which identification of pests may be made, e.g. the droppings of the black rat have a curved appearance. The presence of different sizes of rat droppings usually means that the infestation involves several generations.

Drosophila **(fruit fly)** Small flies which feed on decaying fruit, sour milk and fermenting foods such as wine and vinegar, apparently being attracted by smell. There are several varieties including *D. melanogaster*, *D. funebris* and *D. repleta* , all of which lay large numbers of eggs which become maggots and eventually pupae before the adult flies emerge.

Drugstore beetle (*Stegobium paniceum*) A winter-hardy pest of stored cereal products and pharmacies, also called the biscuit beetle. It is a small, reddish-brown insect with a hooded thorax and is covered with short yellow/brown hair. It frequently infests domestic premises with the larvae (brown, 5mm long) burrowing through packaging materials to infest food.

Dry goods stores
- Non-perishable foods and some preserved foods such as cans and dehydrated products are best kept in a well-ventilated room at between 10-15°C.
- The construction and equipment used should be of the same standard as

for food rooms.
- In order to allow effective cleaning to take place, storage should be off the floor.
- A stock rotation system must be in place and sound containers used to prevent pest infestation.
- Humidity is best at around RH 60%.
- Store rooms should be well-lit and ventilated.

Drying (after washing up) If the final rinse temperature is hot enough (over 82°C) then air drying may result. This avoids the use of potentially contaminated cloths. *See*: Cleaning, Washing up.

Drying of hands Suitable facilities for this are required so that the important personal hygiene function of hand-washing may be completed. Several methods exist, including hot air, single use (disposable) and roller towels, all of which have advantages and disadvantages.
1. Hot air dryers, if used correctly are very hygienic but tend to be slower than other methods, causing misuse and non-use if a queue develops. A back-up system using disposable towels is often installed in case the dryer fails.
2. Disposable paper towels are very effective as long as the supply is sufficient and disposal is satisfactory.
3. Mechanical roller towels are good as long as they are replaced as required and the mechanism does not malfunction.
4. A length of ordinary towelling on a roller quickly becomes contaminated and is not suitable for use by more than a few people.

Dublin bay prawn (*Nephrops norvegicus*) Also called the Norway lobster, langoustine or scampi. A large (20 cm) lobster-like crustacean coloured orange/pink after boiling. *See*: Shellfish.

Duck eggs Known to have been the vehicle of species of *Salmonella* in a number of cases of food poisoning. The shell is porous and micro-organisms may penetrate before and after laying. Raw or lightly cooked duck eggs are not generally regarded as being safe. *See*: Eggs, shell (duck).

Ducks *See*: Poultry.

Due diligence
- A legal term under the Food Safety Act 1990. It indicates the need for producers of food to take all reasonable precautions to avoid food safety problems and is a defence in law.

- Doing nothing is not enough - some positive action is required. A system of controls must be set up, implemented and monitored; this includes:
- hygiene of staff, premises and equipment
- specifications for raw materials
- storage conditions
- all preparation and production operations to be considered
- compliance with all legal standards
- labelling, description and advertising
- staff training
- dealing with customer complaints
- documented hazard analysis systems such as HACCP, ASC or SAFE among others are employed
- all precautions which can reasonably be taken must be taken
- circumstances dictate what is reasonable, for example a large cook-chill production unit has to take more precautions than a small sweet shop because of the far greater risks involved to a larger number of people
- monitoring and review of control measures must occur.

See: Appendix: Food Law, HACCP.

Duodenum The first part of the small intestine.

Dust May be both a physical contaminant of foods and also a source of soil-borne organisms such as *Clostridium* and *Bacillus* species, both of which are frequent causes of outbreaks of food poisoning.

Dustbins *See*: Refuse (storage and disposal), Waste (control and disposal of).

Dysentery (amoebic/bacterial) Inflammation of the large intestine resulting in diarrhoea and other symptoms including nausea and pain. There are two types of organism responsible for the disease: bacterial and protozoan.
See: Amoebic dysentery, Bacillary (bacterial) dysentery, *Entamoeba histolytica*, *Shigella*.

EC (European Community) An economic/political organisation of European Countries including France, Germany and the UK. It has developed from a trading group and generally has increasing powers over a wide range of activities in its Member States. The aim of some members is to eventually achieve both economic and political union in a 'United States of Europe'. In terms of food hygiene and related matters this could mean that standards would eventually be similar across the whole community, for example in composition of foods, labelling, the use of additives and food safety. Many EC Directives and regulations have been issued with this end in view but harmonisation is likely to take some years.

EC Directive The European Community issues Directives on matters such as food hygiene, safety at work and trade, which Member States comply with by legislation. The overall aim is to ensure similar regulation in all member countries by certain dates. EC Directive 93/43 is concerned with food safety and deals with, among other items, hazard analysis systems. Directive 93/43/EC is the driving force behind food hygiene regulations and codes of practice of Member States.

Echinococcus granulosus/veterinorum A tapeworm parasite of dogs, the cystic stage of which may infect humans and food animals. Many human cases are caused by eating food contaminated with dog faeces. *Echinococcus* disease is prevalent in North Africa and Asia.

E. coli A commonly used abbreviation for the bacterium *Escherichia coli*.

Eggs Raw eggs, as with any other raw food of animal origin, may cause *Salmonella* infections. Until the late 1980s, raw hens' eggs were considered to be a very safe food, provided the shell remained intact; there was always the chance that contamination from outside of the shell surface (e.g. from faecal contamination from the hen), or elsewhere (e.g. through washing or packaging) could occur, if the shell was cracked or during the act of breaking.

In the late 1980s a number of outbreaks of food poisoning occurred, which were associated with the consumption of lightly cooked eggs. The bacterium *Salmonella enteritidis* phage type 4 was found to be the organism responsible; it was found in the yolk of unbroken eggs and it is now known that it is possible for the organism to be in the egg when laid. Such contaminated eggs are produced by birds which themselves contain the organism. The feeding meal given to the birds is thought to have been responsible for the infections; heat pasteurisation of such meal is considered sufficient to destroy the organisms.

It is now considered advisable to avoid recipes which use raw eggs for uncooked dishes. Such dishes, as well as lightly cooked egg dishes should not be given to vulnerable groups, in particular the elderly, infants, the infirm and possibly pregnant women.

Raw eggs should be handled and stored in the same way as any other raw food of animal origin. They should be refrigerated after purchase (as *Salmonella enteritidis* does not grow below 8°C), and stored separately in egg boxes. Eggs should be handled hygienically in the kitchen; hands should be washed before and after handling shell eggs, with the use of cracked or dirty eggs avoided. Cooked egg dishes should be eaten as soon as possible after cooking; if not they should be stored in a refrigerator.

Pasteurised liquid eggs are available in the catering industry and wherever possible they should be substituted for raw eggs, particularly if they are to be consumed by any individuals in the high risk groups. However it needs refrigerated storage and protection from contamination, since it is a product which readily supports the growth of micro-organisms. Commercially produced mayonnaise and other sauces are safe as they are prepared using pasteurised eggs. They are also acidified, which prevents the growth of *Salmonella enteritidis*.

- **Use of eggs:**
1. Eggs with cracked shells should be avoided.
2. Refrigerate during storage and handle hygienically.
3. Do not use raw eggs for the production of foods which are not to be subsequently cooked, such as mayonnaise or mousse. Commercially produced mayonnaise made from pasteurised eggs is available.
4. Young children, the elderly, the ill and pregnant women should not eat raw or lightly cooked eggs.
5. Egg yolk used for glazing pastry readily supports the growth of micro-organisms. It requires refrigeration when not in use, and care needs to be taken to protect it from cross-contamination, and to prevent it from contaminating other foods, surfaces and equipment.

- **Cooking of eggs:**

All eggs and foods containing eggs should be cooked thoroughly. They should be cooked throughout to 60°C or above; the yolk and white should both be firm.
The following recommendations are suggested for the cooking of eggs, but such cooking times and temperatures cannot be guaranteed to ensure total safety of the product. There are many variables to be considered, such as the initial numbers of organisms in the eggs, and the initial temperature of the egg. It is best to bring the egg to room temperature before cooking.
1. boiled in the shell: 7 minutes completely submerged in boiling water
2. scrambled: at least one minute at 121°C
3. poached: at least 5 minutes in boiling water
4. fried: frying pan at 121°C

"sunny side up" at least 7 minutes uncovered, or at least 4 minutes covered
"over easy" at least 3 minutes on one side and at least 2 minutes on the other.

- **Spoilage of eggs**:
Some of the following spoilage effects are noticeable with the naked eye, others are only shown by candling.

1. Fresh eggs
Cracks in the shell, leaks, stained or dirty spots on the outside, blood clots, and clear spots in the yolk (the latter two can only be seen through candling).

2. During storage
a) Microbial changes to an undamaged egg require initial penetration of both the shell and the internal membranes; bacterial spoilage may take up to several weeks at refrigerated temperatures.

Effects include various 'rots', caused by a large variety of bacteria (e.g. green, colourless and black rot); they all produce 'off' flavours, and the black rot produces the putrid foul-smelling 'rotten egg' smell (caused by *Pseudomonas fluorescens, Alcaligenes* and *Proteus* species).

Fungal spoilage includes 'pin spot' moulding of various colours (yellow, green, blue, black and pink) on the surface of the shell and just inside it. Such spoilage moulds include *Penicillium, Mucor* and *Sporotrichum* species. This is often followed by further fuzzy mycelial growth on the surface, followed finally by fungal rotting after the mycelium has penetrated the egg through the pores or cracks in the shell, typically by *Cladosporium* and *Sporotrichum*.

Note: Eggs will be more likely to spoil if moisture is allowed to accumulate on the shell. This may be prevented by maintaining a constant temperature during storage, and keeping the eggs covered.

b) Non-microbial spoilage includes the loss of moisture leading to weight loss, thinning of the white of the egg, and the weakening of the egg yolk membrane. When opened, affected eggs show thinned whites and the yolk may flatten or even break.

- **Egg white (albumen)** is not a good medium for microbial growth due to the following reasons:
1. the low content of non-protein nitrogen
2. the unavailability of certain vitamins through combination with proteins

80 Eggs, (duck)

3. the lack of 'free' iron, which is needed by micro-organisms for enzyme activity
4. its (high) pH of 9.6.
All of these help protect eggs from microbial attack during proper storage.

Eggs, (duck) Duck eggs are known to contain significant numbers of *Salmonella* organisms. Ducks live in and around ponds with their nests nearby, and so their nests tend to be in muddy places. This high moisture environment favours penetration of the shell by micro-organisms. The shells of duck eggs are porous when laid, unlike those of hens' eggs which have a waxy coating. The duck is a scavenger and it shares its surroundings with many other wild animals, including possibly rats. There is a high chance that the bird itself may become infected with a variety of bacteria, including species of *Salmonella*.

As a consequence, duck eggs must be treated with caution. Refrigerated storage is essential, and they should always be cooked thoroughly.

EHEC Enterohaemorrhagic *E. coli*. A strain of verocytotoxin- producing *E. coli*, including *E. coli* 0157:H7. See: *Escherichia coli*.

Electromagnetic radiation Radiation including X-rays, gamma rays (food irradiation), ultra violet (flying insect killers), infra red (some cooking equipment), visible light and radio waves.

Emergency prohibition notice and order Under the Food Safety Act 1990
- if the condition of a food premises is thought to be a serious and imminent health risk it may be closed immediately on the judgement of an EHO or other authorised officer
- a notice to this effect is conspicuously displayed on the premises
- the closure must be confirmed by court order within three days.

Common reasons for issue of such orders include:
- pest infestations
- very dirty conditions.

Other legal action may also follow. The order remains in place until the enforcement authority issues a certificate stating that the health risk has been eliminated. The person running the business must apply for this certificate. There is a right of appeal at all stages.

Emulsion A suspension of small droplets of one liquid in another. Butter is a water-in-oil emulsion while water after washing up is an oil-in-water emulsion.

Enamel Metal or ceramic ware coated with a glaze containing toxic chemicals such as antimony or cadmium may cause chemical food poisoning if used with acid foods. Non-food grade enamel ware should not be used.

Endospore
- A non-growing, heat-resistant structure (round or oval) that some bacteria are able to form inside the vegetative (growing or multiplying) cell.
- Formed when environmental conditions become unfavourable, such as very high temperatures, lack of nutrients or low moisture.
- Structure is complex: an outer spore coat, cortex, and inner spore membrane surrounding the protoplast (the living contents of the cell).
- They are able to withstand strong chemicals, such as acids, disinfectants, and the destructive effects of radiation.
- Endospore-forming bacteria are distributed widely in nature, but are primarily soil inhabitants.
- Endospores of two groups of bacteria, the *Bacillus* and *Clostridium* groups, are of importance in the food industry.
- Endospores may survive for many years, for example in the soil, as the endospore coats make them resistant to dehydration.
- The most important potential danger associated with endospores in food preparation concerns their ability to withstand most normal cooking procedures.
- They can for example survive up to five hours in boiling water; vegetative cells in comparison are destroyed in a few minutes at this temperature.
- Any spore-former, such as *Bacillus cereus* and *Clostridium perfringens* will form endospores as soon as the temperature starts to rise significantly.
- They will survive cooking unharmed and will revert to the vegetative stage in a matter of minutes as soon as the temperature falls to below 63°C, so careful treatment of foods after cooking is essential.

Endotoxins
- Poisonous substances released from bacterial cells and some other microorganisms such as fungi.
- They are not released from the cell during its life, only after the cell wall has been damaged, or following death and subsequent fragmentation of the cell (e.g. in the intestinal tract), or during spore formation.
- Endotoxins may take some time to cause symptoms in the human body due to the time it takes for their release.

- Typically they are found in Gram-negative bacteria, such as *Escherichia coli* and *Salmonella* but also in *Clostridium perfringens* (a Gram-positive bacterium).
- Endotoxins are not easily destroyed by heat and are responsible for such symptoms as diarrhoea, local tissue shock and fever.
- Aflatoxin (a mycotoxin) is an endotoxin produced by some fungi.
- Endotoxins are lipopolysaccharides (lipid attached to a carbohydrate), sometimes attached to protein, and are part of the structure of the cell, usually part of the outer membrane.

End seam In canning, the join between the lids (end plates) and body. The dimensions of the seam are important and are routinely measured to check that the seam is effective. *See:* Canning.

Energy in cleaning Three types of energy are involved in most cleaning methods.
1. Kinetic or physical energy provided by machine or person.
2. Heat energy, normally supplied by hot water.
3. Chemical energy, supplied by detergents, sanitisers and disinfectants.
See: Cleaning.

Entamoeba histolytica A single-celled organism (a protozoan) which causes the water-borne and food-borne disease known as amoebic dysentery (or amoebiasis). It produces ulceration and bleeding of the intestinal wall, with blood and slimy mucus in the faeces, fever and chill. All ages are susceptible to infection, and fatalities are rare. Within the intestine, and in the faeces of affected individuals the organism exists in two forms.

1. The amoeboid (vegetative) state, which is easily destroyed when released from the body (and so is unlikely to spread the disease).
2. A resistant cyst form, that is easily transmitted in water, food, or even by houseflies. It is not destroyed by the chlorine used in the water treatment process. A new infection follows the swallowing of cysts in contaminated food or water, which set up an intestinal infection by then taking up their amoeboid form.

- The severity of the disease depends on the number of intestinal lesions produced and the extent of damage to the lining of the intestine.
- Many victims lack any symptoms and so act as carriers of the disease.
- Those with symptoms may have mild, but prolonged diarrhoea or they may have moderate diarrhoea containing blood and mucus; rarely, abscesses may occur in the liver and/or other organs. Onset time is highly variable.

- The disease may last for months; it sometimes flares up after travellers have returned from countries where the disease is common, such as SE Asia, parts of Africa, China and Mexico.
- Transmission is by faecal contamination of drinking water and foods, but also by direct contact with dirty hands or objects, and also by sexual contact (so is not infrequently found among homosexual men).
- There is a significant reservoir of infection in the United States.
- Modern medical treatment is effective.
- Good public health measures such as efficient sewage and water treatment control the disease.

Enteric fever A general term used to describe both typhoid fever and paratyphoid fever, both of which are exclusively diseases of man.

Enterics *See*: Enterobacteriaceae.

Enteric viruses *See*: Enteroviruses.

Enteritis Inflammation of the intestines, sometimes a symptom of food poisoning.

Enterobacter aerogenes A Gram-negative bacterium, which is one of the coliform group of organisms; it is found in the intestinal tract and is an opportunistic pathogen. It is also commonly of plant origin. This organism, together with *Escherichia coli* and *Klebsiella*, are frequently used as indicators of faecally contaminated water.
Note: This organism was formerly known as *Bacillus aerogenes*, and later, *Aerobacter aerogenes*.

Enterobacteriaciae A group of Gram-negative bacteria that inhabit the gastrointestinal tract of man and animals. Some are resident organisms and others are present only when causing disease. Included in this group are *Escherichia coli*, and the *Enterobacter, Shigella* and *Salmonella* groups.
See: Coliforms, Individual named organisms.

EIEC Enteroinvasive *E. coli*. *See*: *Escherichia coli*.

Enterotoxins
- A general term for poisonous waste products which act on the lining of the intestine or stomach, causing diarrhoea or vomiting.

84 Enterovirus

- They are resistant to heat, surviving for 30 minutes at 100°C; the bacteria which produce them are often much less heat-resistant (e.g. *Staphylococcus aureus*) and the presence of bacteria in contaminated food is not essential for illness to occur. Endotoxins and exotoxins are both examples of entero toxins.

Enterovirus A term used to describe any virus which can be transmitted by faeces. They can be spread from person to person by direct contact or by water and food contaminated by faeces. They may be found in both fresh water and sea water. Included in this group are the viruses that cause poliomyelitis and hepatitis (HAV).

Entry (power of) *See*: Power of Entry.

Environmental Health Officer (EHO) An authorised officer of a UK local authority who is empowered to enforce various laws and perform certain functions including:

>food hygiene
>health and safety
>pollution
>housing
>infectious disease control
>and many others.

The modern EHO was previously called Inspector of Nuisances, Sanitary Inspector and Public Health Inspector and is required to have a professional qualification (diploma or degree) before appointment. The EHO on occasions works with HSE inspectors and Trading Standards Officers. They have power of entry and may visit premises at any reasonable time, take photographs, samples, detain food, take formal and informal action and offer advice.

Enzymes
- Biological catalysts, protein-based, having great importance in the bio chemistry of all living organisms. After harvest or slaughter, enzyme action continues.
- They can cause food spoilage and decay.
- Most work best at body temperatures and neutral pH.
- Their action decreases as temperature falls or rises.
- They continue to work in refrigerators (1-4°C).
- They work very slowly in freezers (minus 18°C).
- They are destroyed (denatured) by heat, e.g. as a result of blanching or

cooking.
- A low pH denatures them e.g. in vinegar.

Note: A catalyst speeds up the rate of a reaction without itself being affected, so it may be reused again and again.

EPEC Enteropathogenic *E. coli*. *See*: Escherichia coli.

Epidemiology The study of environmental and other factors, with regard to when and where diseases occur and how they are transmitted in human populations.

Equipment (design and construction) Equipment likely to come into contact with food must be made so that it can be effectively cleaned. Food grade stainless steel and some plastics are ideal materials for many items as long as the method of cleaning is satisfactory. *See*: Chopping boards.

Ergotism A fungal disease in humans caused by eating rye contaminated with an alkaloid mycotoxin released by *Claviceps purpurea*. Symptoms include convulsions, hallucinations and may result in death. The disease is also known as St. Anthony's fire. *See*: Aflatoxin.

Erwinia Food spoilage bacteria causing vegetable spoilage, such as soft rots in fruits and vegetables, e.g. *Erwinia carotovora*.

Escherichia coli (E. coli) A Gram-negative coliform organism found in the gut of man, farm animals and domestic pets. Most of the strains are harmless; it normally serves a useful function in the body by suppressing the growth of harmful species of organisms, and it also synthesises vitamins. However some strains do cause a variety of illnesses, due to
1. the release of an enterotoxin, which causes a cholera-like illness
2. invasion of the intestinal lining, causing a dysentery-like illness, and
3. a different mechanism that is not understood.
- It causes food poisoning by infection, with an incubation period of anything from 8 to 72 hours (depending on the strain), with the illness lasting from one to seven days.
- Symptoms include abdominal pain, watery or bloody diarrhoea, vomiting and sometimes fever; it usually requires a large infective dose, therefore requiring poor temperature storage after contamination, or a high initial contamination dose.
- It grows best between 10 and 40°C.

- It is commonly found in raw foods of animal origin. Foods commonly involved are meat, poultry and fish, and their products. It is not a spore-former, so it is easily destroyed by heat, e.g. by proper cooking of foods, or by pasteurisation.
- Generally it is more of a problem for infants and young children; most of the severe outbreaks have occurred in hospitals, nursing homes and nurseries. For infants, breast feeding is the best preventative measure. Strains of *E. coli* are also able to cause food spoilage.
- Its presence is an indicator of poor hygiene or improper processing. Control involves cooking food thoroughly, chilling food rapidly in small quantities, good personal hygiene, and efficient sewage and water treatment. An addition score of 20 points is added in the Inspection Rating Scheme if there is a significant risk of food being contaminated with *E. coli 0157* or *Clostridium botulinum.*

There are four recognised classes of enterovirulent *E. coli*, collectively referred to as the EEC group (Enterovirulent *E. coli*).

1. Enteroinvasive *E. coli* (EIEC)
Rarely responsible for causing illness in the UK. It may produce a mild form of bacterial dysentery. All age groups are at risk, and symptoms are similar to those of VTEC. These strains are closely related to *Shigella* species. Any food contaminated with human faeces (from a sufferer) either directly or indirectly (e.g. from contaminated water) may be responsible for spreading the illness. No specific foods have been implicated.

2. Enteropathogenic *E. coli* (EPEC)
Causes sporadic cases and outbreaks of diarrhoea in young children, usually those under 2 years of age (hence is often referred to as 'infantile diarrhoea'). Can cause watery or bloody diarrhoea; 50% mortality rates have been recorded in third world countries. The incidence is higher with bottle fed babies, hence the use of contaminated water is suspected. Although often associated with raw meat and poultry, any food exposed to faecal contamination is likely to be responsible. Countries with poor sanitation practices have the most frequent outbreaks. It can also be spread by person to person by the faecal oral route (e.g. in nurseries).

3. Enterotoxigenic *E. coli* (ETEC)
The major cause of gastroenteritis world wide (known as 'traveller's diarrhoea') affecting all age groups. It frequently causes diarrhoea in infants in less developed countries and in visitors there (hence 'traveller's diarrhoea'). It is not considered a serious foodborne disease in countries having high sanitary standards and practices. Contamination

of food often derives from water contaminated with human sewage and from infected food handlers.

4. Verocytotoxin producing *E. coli* *(VTEC)*
The commonest serotype in the UK is *E. coli* 0157:H7. This is a highly virulent strain, requiring relatively few organisms to cause harm in humans. It survives well in frozen storage, but thorough cooking can be relied upon to kill it. The toxin produced is very similar to that of *Shigella dysenteriae,* the usual cause of bacterial dysentery. The toxin binds to molecular receptors on the cells that line the gut, damages them and causes bleeding. (This strain is described also as 'enterohaemorrhagic', hence it is also referred to as Enterohaemorrhagic *E. coli* or EHEC.) The organism can then enter the blood stream; it not uncommonly causes kidney damage.
The reservoir of infection is the gastrointestinal tract of cattle and possibly other domesticated animals.
The range of contaminated foodstuffs is diverse; beef and beef products (e.g. undercooked beef burgers), milk and vegetables have all been associated with cases or outbreaks. Contamination of meat may occur during the slaughtering process and if meat is eaten rare or inadequately cooked, or if there has been cross-contamination with another food, then infection can occur. Person to person spread can occur by the faecal-oral route, particularly in nurseries, infant schools and households.

VTEC causes haemorrhagic colitis (bleeding into the bowel leading to bloody diarrhoea) and about 5% of cases suffer kidney damage (haemolytic uraemic syndrome, HUS) , including kidney failure (which may be permanent). There were 792 cases in the UK in 1995, an increase of 93% in previous years.

A major outbreak occurred in North Lanarkshire, Scotland, in late 1996, centred around a butcher's shop. The total number of cases exceeded 490, with 18 deaths, all adults. It was the largest ever outbreak of infection with this organism in the UK.

An outbreak at a farm in Berkshire was traced to river water contamination of drinking water via a plumbing defect in the farm's irrigation system.

A very large outbreak was reported from Osaka, Japan, early in 1997 involving over 5,700 persons who had probably eaten sprouting cress seeds mainly in school lunches. *See:* Pennington Report.

ETEC Enterotoxigenic *E. coli. See: Escherichia coli.*

Ethanoic acid *See:* Acetic (ethanoic) acid.

European Food Poisoning and Food-borne Disease A WHO report for 1990-1992 shows rising figures generally with salmonellosis the most prominent disease and eggs the food most often involved in outbreaks. A high level of *Campylobacter* reports emanated from Holland. Private houses were the most frequent location with poor temperature control the most common reason.

Eukaryotic A type of cell possessing a true nucleus, separated from the surrounding cytoplasm by a nuclear membrane. It is possessed by the single-celled protozoa, the algae, fungi, plants and animals.

Eustrongylides **species** Roundworms (nematodes) infesting many species of fish with water birds playing a part in the life cycle. Larvae in humans affect the intestines by burrowing causing severe pain. The condition is thought to be rare.

Evaporated milk A canned product similar to condensed milk, but having no sugar added.

Exclusion of food handlers
- Food handlers suffering from food poisoning should not be allowed to enter food rooms until medical clearance is obtained.
- In the case of most food poisoning this may be when symptoms have subsided and bowels have been normal for 48 hours.
- Any confirmed typhoid cases must show a period of negative faecal samples (for example 6 over 14 days) before being allowed back into food areas.
- Persons suffering from hepatitis A should be excluded during the seven days following appearance of symptoms since they may pass on the disease during this period.
- Any person returning to work after illness should be especially careful about personal hygiene standards.
- Many other conditions such as heavy colds, boils, septic cuts, whitlows and styes may also warrant exclusion, each case being judged on its merits.

Excrement Term commonly used to mean faeces.

Excreta The normal discharges from the body, i.e. faeces, urine and sweat.

Excreter An individual who, whether suffering from a disease or not, persistently passes disease-causing organisms from the body in the faeces and/or urine. *See:* Carrier.

Exotoxins
- Poisonous substances released by micro-organisms such as *Staphylococcus aureus, Bacillus cereus* and *Clostridium botulinum*.
- They are actively released from the bacterial cell during its growth in food before its consumption, often producing symptoms within hours of eating contaminated food. Pain and vomiting are common.
- Most exotoxins are fairly easily destroyed by heat; e.g. the exotoxin of *Clostridium botulinum* (which causes the disease known as botulism and affects the nervous system) is destroyed in 30 minutes at 60°C. Most are inactivated at 60 to 80°C.
- The exotoxin of *Staphylococcus aureus* (which affects the digestive system) is responsible for many outbreaks of bacterial food poisoning, and can survive over 30 minutes at 100°C.
- Tissue damage can be severe and at a great distance from the bacterial cells which produced it. Exotoxins are proteins produced by the cytoplasm of bacteria, both Gram-positive and Gram-negative cells.
- Effects are exerted in a variety of ways:
  1. inhibition of protein synthesis in cells
  2. interference with nerve impulse transmission (at synapses)
  3. disruption of membrane transport
  4. plasma (cell) membrane damage.
- Divided into three categories on the basis of the site affected: neurotoxins (nerve tissue), enterotoxins (intestinal lining), and cytotoxins (general tissues).

Exponential growth The increase in numbers of cells by a constant doubling of cell numbers, i.e. 1, 2, 4, 8, 16, 32, 64, 128, 256 and so on. Such an increase in numbers leads to extremely large population numbers in a fairly short period of time.
As a rough guide one bacterium, given good growth conditions, will easily produce one billion(10^9) cells in ten hours. (It is also known as Logarithmic growth.)
See: Bacterial growth curve.

Extraction systems (food room use) Hoods or canopies placed over cooking equipment collect fumes and water vapour which are extracted through ducting by fans. Filters may be provided to trap grease which would otherwise build up in the inaccessible interiors of ducting. Deep cleaning of ducts is essential due to the risks of pests and fire. Design of ventilation and air conditioning systems is an expert task. *See:* Ventilation.

Factory Inspector Common term for a UK enforcement officer appointed by the

Health and Safety Executive (HSE) having duties under a large variety of safety law. *See:* Environmental Health Officer (EHO).

Facultative A term used to describe the ability of a micro-organism to grow under a variety of conditions. Facultative means optional and the term is often used to indicate the ability of a micro-organism to live in both the presence or absence of oxygen.

Faecal-oral route A common way of spreading disease through faecal matter carried on the hands. Such matter, which will certainly contain many forms of bacteria, and possibly protozoa, can easily contaminate food. In young children, it can be ingested directly, through sucking fingers etc. As a means of spreading disease, it can easily be prevented by good personal hygiene, particularly hand-washing (with soap and hot water) after using the lavatory, changing or handling babies' nappies etc. There are many diseases which are frequently spread by this means, including amoebic dysentery, bacillary (bacterial) dysentery (shigellosis) various strains of *E. coli*, cholera, paratyphoid and typhoid fever and poliomyelitis.

Faeces Excrement discharged from the bowel, normally semi-solid in consistency. It is a ready source of bacteria (including pathogens), protozoa, and the eggs of parasites including tapeworms. Insects, rodents and shellfish feed on faeces, ingesting organisms which may be passed on, possibly contaminating food. Laboratory analysis of faeces is often carried out to identify specific micro-organisms.

Faggot A meat product made from spiced chopped liver, spleen and lung, (offal) with cereal binder. It is wrapped in a fatty abdominal membrane (omentum) and cooked. Since it is a high-risk food it must be subject to strict temperature control and treated in the same way as other meat products and cooked meats.

Family (outbreak of food poisoning) Two or more cases in the same household not connected with any other cases.

Farcy *See:* Glanders.

Fasciola hepatica A liver fluke affecting many animals including cattle, sheep and humans. Symptoms in humans are non-specific but the livers of food animals may be unfit if the infestation has badly thickened the bile ducts (so-called 'pipy' liver). Cases of the disease fascioliasis have been reported after eating wild watercress grown in water contaminated with sheep or cattle faeces.

Fascioliasis The disease caused by the liver fluke, *Fasciola hepatica*.

FAST (Food Authentication by Spectroscopic Techniques) Laboratory techniques using spectroscopy and nuclear magnetic resonance (NMR) to analyse foods. Differences between Greek and Spanish olive oils are detectable as well as the characteristics of different types of coffee bean.

Fats
- Substances found in varying quantities in a number of foodstuffs including meat, butter and margarine.
- Nutritionally they provide large amounts of energy.
- They are broadly grouped into saturated and unsaturated fats, the latter reported to be less likely to be involved in causing heart and circulatory diseases.
- Fats generally do not support the growth of bacteria but are prone to develop off-favours and odours during storage, thus becoming unfit.
- They are chemically similar to oils, most having three fatty acids attached to a glycerol 'backbone' molecule. The major difference between fats and oils is their melting points.
- Saturated fats (few double bonds) tend to be hard animal fats, while unsaturated and polyunsaturated fats tend to be of vegetable or marine origin.

See: Fatty acid, Rancidity.

Fatty acid A hydrocarbon chain, up to 35 carbons in length, ending in a carboxyl group, -COOH. The bonds between carbons may be single or double, the more double bonds the more unsaturated the chain. Unsaturated fatty acids are more reactive and foods containing these may spoil faster than those with saturated fats, consequently, for example frozen beef has a longer life than frozen pork.
See: Hydrogenation, Rancidity, Smoke point.

Favism An anaemic disorder caused by consumption of undercooked broad beans (fava beans), or an allergic reaction to its pollen.

Feeding stuffs Animal feeds have been known to be contaminated with various pathogens. The practice of recycling carcass meat as feed stock, if it has not been sterilised, has been proved partly responsible for the increase in *Salmonella* infection in intensively reared poultry. *See:* BSE.

Fenitrothion A general purpose organophosphorus substance often used as a residual insecticide to control cockroaches.

Feral Means 'wild' and is applied to pigeons and cats to distinguish them from domesticated individuals.

Fermentation
1. A chemical reaction involving the conversion of sugar into alcohol by the action of yeasts (*Saccharomyces*) and accompanied by the release of carbon dioxide gas. Mainly found in wine-making and brewing although fruits may ferment by the action of naturally occurring yeasts.
2. A preservation process in which lactic acid is produced by various micro-organisms; sauerkraut and yoghurt are typical products. The flavour enhancer, monosodium glutamate is also produced by bacterial fermentation of soya beans.
3. A laboratory method of identifying bacteria such as *Clostridium* species.

Fever A bodily reaction to infection involving a rise in temperature.

Filth testing US technique for detecting insect fragments and animal (including rodent) hairs in foodstuffs.

Fimbriae Small unbranched extracellular appendages possessed by some bacteria. There are two forms, long and short. The long fimbriae are involved in sexual reproduction; the short are more numerous and are thought to enable bacteria to stick to a surface or to other cells. This latter property is related to the ability of bacteria to cause disease. Fimbriae are also known as pili.

Fines Under current UK food legislation, in a magistrates court, a maximum fine of £5 000 is possible for most offences but there is provision for unlimited fines for more serious offences. *See:* Food Safety Act 1990.

Fingernails *See:* Nails.

Finnan haddock A cured and smoked fish, often dyed yellow.

Firebrats (*Thermobia domestica*) A greyish speckled wingless insect with long antennae, a relative of the silverfish (*Lepisma saccharina*). It infests bakeries and kitchens and other warm places, feeding mainly on cereals (also crumbs and other food scraps). This insect has the odd habit of biting holes in inedible fabrics. There is no evidence of it carrying pathogens, but it may become a nuisance and a physical contaminant rather than a serious health risk.

First Aid The main functions of first aid are to treat minor injuries and also to prevent more serious occurrences from worsening until medical help is obtained. Suitable and sufficient first aid materials, such as plasters (those for food use should be waterproof, non-food coloured and may have metal detector strips) and bandages should be provided in all workplaces including food businesses, the exact amount being determined by the numbers of people employed and the nature of work done. Trained first-aiders and sometimes medical staff are also needed where large numbers of people are employed, or where dangerous work is carried out.

Fish
- As protein-containing foods, fish and shellfish are included in the high-risk category and must be subjected to strict temperature control and proper handling.
- Raw fish and shellfish must be separated from other foods to avoid cross-contamination.
- Fresh fish deteriorates rapidly and may be stored at 0°C, preferably in ice, for periods of up to two weeks depending on the variety.
- Cooked fish or shellfish must either be refrigerated (1 to 4°C) or kept hot (above 63°C).
- Unfit fish have a dull lustreless surface appearance often with beads of mucus, dark coloured blood around the gills, sunken eyes, and limp bodies.
- Several parasites (including tapeworms) are carried in fish, but these are normally destroyed when fish is cooked, smoked or frozen.
- Fish which is to be eaten raw should be frozen at minus 18°C for at least 24 hours.

Spoilage of fish is by enzymes, bacteria and oxidation. Examples include

- *Pseudomonas* and *Acinetobacter-Moxarella* bacteria are common residents on fish and become invasive after death.
- Histamine may be formed by bacteria from histidine in oily fish, particularly whitebait and mackerel, leading to scombrotoxin food poisoning.
- pHu (ultimate pH) above 7, usually from exhausted fish with a low glycogen content leads to rapid spoilage.
- Evisceration (gutting) extends keeping qualities by reducing the numbers of enzymes and bacteria present.
- Oily fish spoil, sometimes rapidly, by oxidative rancidity of unsaturated fatty acids.
- Cold water fish may have a psychrophilic bacterial population which causes spoilage under chill conditions.
- The malodourous substance trimethylamine (TMA) is often a first sign of spoilage, the fish smelling strongly of ammonia. Certain species such as skate and dogfish produce this early in decomposition

- The first sign of enzymic spoilage, after a few days, is loss of flavour and tastelessness.
- Storage times at minus 18°C range from 4 months for fatty fish, 6 months for some shellfish and 9 months for flatfish.

Fish and shellfish are capable of carrying many parasites, pathogenic bacteria and poisonous substances including: *Anisakis simplex*, *Chloromyscium thrysites*, Ciguatera, *Clostridium botulinum* ,*Dibothriocephalus latum*, *Escherichia coli*, Mercury, *Phocanema*, Sarcotases, Scombrotoxin and *Vibrio parahaemolyticus*.
See: Furunculosis, Paralytic shellfish poisoning. Details are under individual entries.

Flagella (singular flagellum)
- One of the two unbranched threadlike extracellular appendages found in the bacteria (the other being fimbriae).
- Many bacteria are capable of active movement (actively motile) in liquid surroundings, this being achieved by the possession of these structures.
- They are composed of a special contractile protein (flagellin) and are so small (20 to 30 micrometres in length), that special staining techniques must be employed in order to see them under the light microscope.
- The flagellin is arranged in a coiled helix and each flagellum is attached to the cell, inside the cell wall, to a basal body. These are thought to initiate and co-ordinate contractions of the flagella.
- In movement, the flagella rotate like propellers, and pull the bacterium through the water in a helical path.
- The number and distribution of flagella varies amongst the bacteria. Some forms possess a single flagellum only, some have them distributed over the whole cell while others have one or more tufts of them.
- They are commonly found in the bacillus and spirillum forms.
- Some non-flagellate forms can also demonstrate motility, this being achieved by flexing of the cell.

Flat sours Organisms such as *Bacillus stearothermophilus* and *Bacillus coagulans*, which attack carbohydrates in low and medium acid canned foods (such as meats, soups and vegetables) cause spoilage ('sour') but not gas production ('flat'). Since no gas is produced the can vacuum is unaffected. These bacteria are both thermophiles and facultative anaerobes. Slow cooling of foods after heat treatment produces favourable temperatures for their growth (50 to 70°C), as does storage of cans at high ambient temperatures. *See:* Canning.

Flatulence Distension (swelling) of the stomach or intestines by excessive accumulation of wind or gas. It is a common symptom of many forms of food poisoning/ food-borne illnesses.

Flavobacterium A group (genus) of Gram-negative bacteria commonly found in the soil. They may be responsible for contamination of water supplies and are spoilage agents of a wide range of foods, including beer (during production), shellfish, poultry, eggs, butter and milk. They may cause discoloration on the surface of meats. They are obligate aerobes and some members are psychrotrophic and so are able to grow at refrigeration temperatures. Some have been found growing on thawing vegetables.

Fleas Small insects capable of jumping great distances; they are parasitic on warm-blooded animals. Over 1 000 species are known, examples being the dog flea (*Ctenocephalides canis*), the cat flea (*Ct. felis*) and the human flea (*Pulex irritans*). Most fleas will attack other hosts, of particular note being the rat flea (*Xenopsylla cheopis*) which is the vector of plague.

Flesh fly (*Sarcophoga carnaria*) A grey coloured blowfly with a chequered thorax sometimes infesting refuse bins.

Flies Insects belonging to the order of Diptera (two wings) and affecting foods in many ways.
- The families *Muscidae* (housefly) and *Calliphoridae* (blowfly) are most important since they are vectors of disease and cause food spoilage.
- Flies regurgitate (vomit) partly-digested food during feeding and may transmit bacteria to food in this way.
- They can only feed on liquid food and use the regurgitation technique to liquefy solid food.
- Maggots developing from eggs grow in many foods, particularly meat.
- The characteristic 'fly spots' seen where flies have been feeding are the dried liquid faeces of the insects.
- All types may carry bacteria on their feet and bodies.
- Physical contamination of food is possible with bodies, pupae, egg cases and fragments of flies.
- The fruit fly (*Drosophila*) feeds on sweet foods and fermenting wines and beers.

Control of flies and other flying insects can be achieved by
- screening open windows with mesh
- using plastic strip doors
- keeping refuse bins lidded

- keeping refuse areas tidy
- using ultraviolet flying-insect killers
- using fly paper away from food.

The use of insecticides in food rooms is a specialist task; fly sprays are not recommended because of the danger of food contamination.

Floors As with other parts of food areas, floors must be constructed so that they are capable of being cleaned effectively, durable, and non-slip. A gentle slope (1:60) to the drainage point is desirable as is a coved join between wall and floor.

Many finishes are available at different costs. Examples include:
- terrazzo and granolithic (Grano) floors very durable but smooth terrazzo (a marble-like appearance) is likely to be too slippery for food area use
- grano floors use crushed granite laid in a concrete base and are resistant to most substances found in food areas
- tiled surfaces are adequate if the joints between tiles are properly grouted
- epoxy resin mixed with aggregate is an effective but expensive floor finish
- welded heavy-duty vinyl sheeting is a cheap but often not long-lasting solution.

Flora (body) A term used to describe the population of micro-organisms living in and on a human or animal body. It includes those found both on the outer surface (skin, hair, fur, feathers) and those which inhabit the 'inside' of the animal (nose, mouth, throat, gastrointestinal and urinary tracts). The term includes both resident and transient groups. (The word 'flora' is used due to the original misclassification of bacteria as plants.)

Flour mite (*Acarus siro/Tyroglyphus farinae*)
- A common pest of stored cereal products and domestic food stores. They are less than 0.5 mm in length and have a colourless body with reddish/yellowish legs.
- They do not breed in conditions of low humidity (less than 75% RH) or in foodstuffs with water contents less than about 13%.
- The most effective control measure is to ventilate food stores and keep cereal products dry.
- Mites generally are light-shy and will move slowly from bright light, resembling a moving dust when present in large numbers.
- There is a characteristic smell of mint from crushed mite bodies.
- Another mite (*Cheyletus eruditus*) is parasitic on the flour mite and mixed infestations are often encountered.

Flow diversion valve An automatic device used in pasteurisation and sterilisation plant (e.g. for milk/liquid egg) to return under-heated products to the start of the process. The valve diverts liquid if its temperature has not reached the required levels.

Fluidised bed freezing A method of quick-freezing in which small items such as peas are frozen while suspended in currents of cold air passing through holes in a perforated plate. The bed may be inclined so that food travels along by gravity. Food is individually frozen with the advantages to the consumer that it may be 'poured' from the pack in any desired quantity and that final quality is high.

Flukes Parasites of the bile duct, blood and lungs of various animals including humans. *See: Fasciola hepatica, Schistosoma.*

Fluoroacetamide A highly toxic substance used as a rodenticide in sewers. Unsuitable for use in food areas.

Fluorescent Whitening Agents (FWAs) Used to create a bright white effect in food packaging and may migrate onto the surface of food. Some FWAs may have harmful properties but the amount contaminating food from this route is thought to be very low and not potentially harmful.

Fly papers As a control measure for wandering flies these may prove effective but must not be located near open food. They are also unsightly and may cause adverse reaction from customers or others. Often used near to refuse, in stores or in passageways between rooms.

'Fo' value The number of minutes heating at 121°C needed to kill a particular micro-organism. Examples include:
    Clostridium botulinum, Fo = 3
    Bacillus stearothermophilus, Fo = 6.
This information is of use in canning and other forms of heat preservation. The measurement depends on the slope of the thermal death time curve.

Fomites Inanimate objects such as clothing, bedding, cutlery and crockery, which may distribute pathogens.

Food In Britain this is legally defined and includes everything normally thought of as food and also drinks, additives, ingredients and chewing gum.
See: Appendix: Food law.

Food Advisory Committee (FAC)
MAFF (UK) committee reporting on a wide range of topics including composition and labelling. Genetically modified foods such as cereal grains are currently being considered.

Food-borne disease/Food-borne infection
- Small numbers of pathogenic organisms use food as a vehicle only and may not multiply in it.
- Symptoms produced are often different to food poisoning although diarrhoea and vomiting sometimes occur.
- The organisms may enter the bloodstream and cause infection and incubation periods are often much longer than for food poisoning.
- These diseases may also be spread by non-food items.

Typhoid and paratyphoid fevers, brucellosis, listeriosis, dysentery, hepatitis, cryptosporidiosis, giardiasis, cholera, campylobacter enteritis and tuberculosis are all examples of non-food poisoning diseases which may be carried by food. *See:* Individual entries.

Food business Commercial or non-commercial activities which produce food for human consumption. Schools, hospitals, clubs and other non-profit making organisations are included in UK law defininitions.

Food-contact surfaces Work surfaces which come into contact with food.
- They should not affect the food in any way. Be smooth and impervious to allow for proper cleaning and be non-absorbent.
- Food grade stainless steel and certain plastic materials are considered to be most suitable.
- The use of wood is unsuitable for all but raw meat preparation although a genuinely effective alternative has yet to appear.
- As a general rule, food-contact surface should be cleaned and disinfected after each use with raw or high-risk foods.

Food handler A somewhat self-explanatory term with many possible categories including food production workers, chefs and bar staff. The hygiene training of food handlers should be related to the risk they pose to food. For example, a person working in a hospital cook-chill production unit may need more knowledge of food hygiene than a person only employed to stack shelves in a supermarket. *See:* Exclusion, Training of food handlers.

Food hygiene The term hygiene is derived from the name of the Greek goddess of health, Hygeia. Food hygiene includes

- all aspects of health related to the consumption of food
- the prevention of food poisoning
- legislation
- design of equipment and premises
- personal hygiene
- staff training
- pest control
- food preparation practices
- cleaning systems
- storage of foodstuffs
- refrigeration and heating (temperature control)
- refuse and waste handling
- monitoring
- quality control.

Food Labelling Regulations, 1996 A full entry for these is to be found in Appendix: Food Law.

Food Law Modern UK food law has developed over a period of time, well in excess of 100 years and is currently enshrined in the Food Safety Act 1990. Previous major Acts (not with the same title) are dated 1984, 1956 and 1938. Some of the first food laws in England during the 1800s concerned the adulteration of foods such as bread (with chalk and alum) and milk (with water), although religious food laws date back several thousand years.

Periodically the law is modified because of:
- changes in the food chain
- developments in technology
- the appearance of new trends in food poisoning
- pressure from various groups.

EC harmonisation of European food law is currently underway. Food law in the USA is covered in the appendix. *See:* Appendix: Food Law.

Food (open) Unwrapped or unpackaged food. It should be kept covered or effectively screened during delivery or while exposed for sale.

100 Food poisoning

Food poisoning A general term loosely applied to diseases which result in a disturbance of the gastrointestinal tract, normally affecting the stomach and intestines.

ACMSF definitions, 1992 (adopted by WHO):

Food poisoning - 'any disease of an infectious or toxic nature caused or thought to be caused by the consumption of food or water'. This includes all food and waterborne illnesses whether or not gastrointestinal symptoms occur but excludes allergic reactions and food intolerances.

Outbreak -'an incident in which two or more people thought to have a common exposure experience, similar illness or proven infection (at least one of them being ill)'.

General outbreak - 'an outbreak affecting members of more than one private residence, or residents of an institution'. The majority of general outbreaks in England and Wales during the period 1992-1997 were from salmonellas and SRSV (less outbreaks from *Clostridium perfringens* and *Shigella* species) with poultry, eggs, red meat and meat products being the commonest vehicles.

```
            Direct
    ┌──────────────────┐
    ▼                  │
┌─────────────┐   ┌──────────┐   ┌────────────┐   ┌────────┐   ┌─────────┐
│Food Poisoning│  │High-risk │──▶│Time/Warmth │──▶│ People │──▶│ Illness │
│   Bacteria  │   │   Food   │   └────────────┘   └────────┘   └─────────┘
└─────────────┘   └──────────┘
    ▲                  │
    └──────────────────┘
          Indirect         **Food Poisoning Chain**
```

Outbreaks restricted to residents of a home are called 'family outbreaks'.

Food poisoning is mainly caused by
- bacteria or their toxins
- viruses
- metals
- chemicals
- poisonous foods.

Symptoms of food poisoning include
- nausea
- vomiting
- diarrhoea
- fever
- abdominal pain.
- The causes of food poisoning such as bacteria do not affect the taste, smell or appearance of the food concerned.
- Those most at risk include the very young, the elderly, people who are ill and women during pregnancy. Severe cases may be fatal.
- The most commonly reported food poisoning bacterium in many countries is the *Salmonella* group.
- The cost of treating inpatients for infectious intestinal disease in hospitals in England during 1991-1994 has been estimated as being in excess of £83 million. The figure includes elements related to public sector, society and individual costs.
- In Britain and other countries, almost as many cases of *Campylobacter* (a food-borne disease) occur annually.
- Global under-reporting of food-borne diseases and food poisoning is thought to be up to 100 times too low

See: High-risk foods, Incidence of Food Poisoning, Temperature control.

Food premises All parts of the food business, including: delivery, storage, preparation, cooking, food service, washing up, toilets, refuse disposal and any other relevant areas are included as part of the food premises.

General requirements include
- adequate drainage
- water supply
- sanitary conveniences
- wash-hand basins (with related items)
- first aid materials
- accommodation for clothing
- separate facilities for washing food and equipment
- adequate lighting and ventilation
- cleanliness
- good repair
- facilities for keeping certain foods at specified temperatures
- suitable storage.

See: Appendix: Food Law, and individual entries for above items.

Food preservation Deterioration and then spoilage of food starts from the point of harvest or slaughter due to the actions of several groups of micro-organisms including bacteria, moulds and yeasts and also enzymes. The aim of the various preservation processes is to halt this decay and so make available food which would otherwise be lost. Food may also be eaten out of season and surpluses may be kept for use in times of shortage. Some methods keep food in a condition closely resembling the fresh state, while other methods cause great changes to occur.

The history of food preservation dates back several thousand years (e.g. sun drying) and new techniques (such as irradiation) are constantly being developed. Examples of food preservation include AFD, use of additives, bottling, canning, chemicals, chilling, cook-chill, cook-freeze, dehydration, freezing, irradiation, osmotic methods (salting/sugar), pickling, sous vide and vacuum packing.

Food preservation (nutrient losses) Vitamins of the B group (particularly B1, thiamine) as well as vitamin C (ascorbic acid) are destroyed in varying amounts by heat in some preservation processes including canning and dehydration. The losses may be considerable, for example 100% loss of vitamin C occurs in some canned peas. Other vitamins are affected to a lesser degree.

Food processing Alternative term for food preservation and also used to indicate that a foodstuff has originated from large-scale production. The same term is used in small scale cookery to describe mechanically prepared foods.

Food Safety Act 1990
- The main piece of food legislation in UK law covering many aspects of food and food hygiene.
- The Act defines the legal meanings of many terms including 'food', 'sale' and 'food business'.
- It sets out offences including those of selling food 'not of the nature, substance or quality', and food 'injurious to health'.
- It deals with false labelling and description of foods as well as the wider offence of not complying with food safety requirements.
- The defence of 'due diligence' is contained in the Act.
- The power of the EHO is extended in terms of Improvement Notices and Prohibition Orders.
- Many regulations have been made under the Act including registration of food premises, general food safety and temperature control.

See: Appendix: Food Law.

Food Safety (General Food Hygiene) Regulations 1995 Introduced a risk-based

approach to food safety requiring the identification and control of food hazards and training and/or supervision of food handlers. There are specific points relating to prevention of contamination of foods, ventilation systems, water supply, reporting of communicable diseases in food handlers, handling of waste and many others. The regulations are supported by Industry Guides which illuminate the Regulations in respect of Catering, Retail and other branches of the food industry.
See: Appendix: Food Law, HACCP.

Food Safety (Temperature Control) Regulations 1995 State the temperatures of hot and cold high-risk foods. Generally these should not be kept in the range 8-63°C.
See: Appendix Food Law, Danger zone, High-risk food, temperature control.

Food spoilage Deterioration of the quality of food, not to be confused with food poisoning. The common food poisoning organisms such as *Salmonella* do not normally cause spoilage to occur. *See:* Bacteria, Enzymes, Food preservation, Moulds, Organoleptic assessment, Yeasts.

Food Standards Agency The James Report in 1997, which consulted around 2 000 organisations, dealt with food safety in the UK and amongst other observations concludes that the public has lost confidence in the food supply, secrecy affects decision-making, political and industrial interests conflict with food safety and co-ordination of policy is poor. The report recommends that an independent Food Standards Agency should be set up based on the model of the Health and Safety Commission/ Executive (HSC/E). The Agency should co-ordinate national food policy including the microbiological, chemical and nutritional aspects of food, standards and labelling, developing policy, proposing and drafting legislation, food law enforcement and responsibility for public education and information. It should have powers "from the plough to the plate" and work with local authorities to produce a new organisation with national, regional and local structures including a national inspectorate. The time scale for setting this up is expected to be in the region of three years.

Food Standards Committees Advise Ministers on compositional standards in foods, for example on meat content in pies, allowable levels of additives and labelling of foodstuffs. A large number of regulations governing all types of food have been made in this way having taken into account the requirements of manufacturers, EHOs, the general public and other parties, including Trading Standards.

Forced convection oven A method of reheating (regenerating) quantities of chilled or frozen foods using a fan-assisted oven in which the same temperature is achieved throughout the oven. Often used in conjunction with cook-chill and cook-

Foreign bodies *See:* Physical contamination.

Formic acid (including calcium and sodium formates) Preservatives not permitted in Britain.

Freeze drying *See:* Accelerated freeze drying.

Freezers (temperature of)
- Commercial and domestic deep freeze equipment operates in the temperature range minus 18 to minus 30°C, the lower temperatures being found in deep freeze stores.
- Frozen food has a shelf life of up to a year since low temperatures greatly reduce the activity of spoilage organisms and enzymes.
- Some bacteria in frozen food are killed but many survive, become dormant, and will start to multiply once thawed.
- Temperature monitoring is important since at around minus 10°C spoilage organisms start to grow.
- Deliveries of frozen food must be checked to ensure that food is still frozen; it has become common practice to reject deliveries above minus 18°C, although minus 12°C is sometimes judged to be the absolute limit for acceptance of deliveries.

See: Danger zone, Star markings, Thermometers.

Freezers (use of)
- Food should be placed in the freezer immediately on delivery.
- Freezer space should be sufficient to prevent overloading.
- 'Display type' freezers have a maximum load line, which should not be exceeded.
- The freezer should be located away from heat sources such as cooking or heating equipment and not exposed to direct sunlight.
- Opening of doors on upright models affects temperatures inside.
- A system of stock rotation must operate.
- Damaged packaging of frozen food may lead to freezer burn.
- Generally, most meats, fruit and vegetables may be kept for 9-12 months and other foods 3-6 months, following manufacturers' instructions.
- Deep freezers are not designed to produce good quality frozen raw food but may successfully freeze cooked items.
- Re-freezing of thawed food even if this has been cooked is not advisable, since the numbers of bacteria (bacterial load) increase through each freezing and thawing cycle.

Freezing (effect on bacteria) Significant numbers of food poisoning bacteria are not killed by freezing and spores remain virtually unaffected. Some organisms, principally those involved in food spoilage, are active at well below 0°C. Micro-organisms return to the vegetative (growing/reproducing) state once the food is thawed.
See: Psychrotrophs, Thawing.

Freezer burn The unprotected surface of frozen food dries out (desiccates) giving a whitish, spongy appearance. The problem is often found in meat and is the result of ice crystals turning into water vapour by sublimation. Effective packaging is the answer to this problem.

Fresh fish tapeworm (*Dibothriocephalus latum*) Parasitic on freshwater fish and salmon, it is also known to affect humans. The cysts in the fish appear as white growths.

Frozen food (thawing and cooking of)
- Small items of food may be cooked direct from frozen.
- Large items such as joints of meat and poultry must first be thawed otherwise the heat of cooking will be wasted in melting ice and the final temperature will be too low.
- Thawing in a refrigerator takes longer than at room temperature but the numbers of bacteria present after thawing will be less; if cooking is adequate then most bacteria are killed in any case.
- Ideally, a thawing cabinet or cool room (10-15°C) away from other food should be used.
- Microwave and other electrical methods may be satisfactory, as long as thawing is even and localised, so that hot and cold spots do not develop.
- Any liquid from thawed food may contain large numbers of bacteria and should not be allowed to contact other food.
- All equipment used in thawing must be disinfected before further use.
- As with other cooking, the final centre temperature should be at least 70°C.

See: Cross-contamination, Thermometers.

Frozen food (production of)
Low temperature preservation of foods has been performed for thousands of years although the familiar modern products are a recent development. Quick freezing causes ice to form within the cells of the food as small crystals. With slow freezing, water is withdrawn from cells, forms larger ice crystals and is lost as drip. Technically, freezing stops bacterial growth because of a reduction in available water (a_w for ice is 0.85) but has little effect on spores and toxins. It is achieved by a variety of

methods.

See: Available water, Birdseye (Clarence), Blanching, Blast freezer, Cook-chill, Cook-freeze, Cryogenic freezing, Fluidised bed freezing, Plate freezer, Zone of maximum ice crystal formation.

Fruit Generally there are few food hygiene problems with fruits as they are low protein and sometimes high acid foods. Deterioration during storage is prevented by storing unwrapped in cool conditions and ensuring adequate air circulation. Occasional outbreaks of chemical food poisoning have resulted when acidic fruit juice has dissolved metals into foods. They are subject to surface contamination, so washing of dessert fruits is recommended. Fruits are susceptible to several types of spoilage.

Fruit fly (*Drosophila*) Several species including *Drosophila repleta, D. funebris* and *D. melanogaster* feed on fruits, vegetables, wine, vinegar and faecal matter. Used, unwashed milk bottles have provided breeding grounds for these flies.

Fruit taint Fatty foods, for example meat and butter, readily absorb odours from oranges and other fruits. Correct packaging and storage conditions prevent this.

Frying A cooking method involving heat transfer through hot oil or fat, rapidly achieving high surface temperatures in foods. There is a risk that the centre temperature may be inadequate to destroy any pathogens present.

Fugu fish (*Tetraodontiformes*)
- The internal organs and skin, but not the flesh of pufferfish can contain levels of tetrodotoxin sufficient to produce rapid and violent death. Some types of newts, frogs, octopus, starfish, angelfish and crabs also contain the toxin which is produced by the common marine bacteria such as *Vibrio, Pseudomonas* and *Photobacterium* species.
- Numbness of the lips and tongue, appears 20 minutes to three hours after ingestion. This spreads to the extremities and may be followed by sensations of lightness or floating, headache, nausea, diarrhoea, and/or vomiting. Paralysis increases and death occurs in 4 to 6 hours.
- Estimates as high as 200 cases per year in Japan with 100 deaths have been given.
- It is a delicacy prepared in special restaurants by highly trained and licensed chefs.
- An outbreak in Italy in 1977 resulted in three deaths after imported, mislabelled, frozen pufferfish was eaten in mistake for angler fish (this can be cooked to resemble scampi) and an outbreak in the USA was reported in 1996.

The problem is compounded since the level of toxin appears to be at its highest at the very time that this fish is traditionally consumed in Japan. *See:* Puffer Fish.

Fumaric acid An organic acid used as a preservative in packet mixes and other foods. It has an antioxidant action.

Fumigation Buildings or parts of building may be filled with toxic substances such as methyl bromide or hydrogen cyanide to eliminate pests such as cockroaches. The procedure is hazardous, requiring expert operators and safe systems of work. The Environmental Health Department and Health and Safety Executive need to be informed prior to treatment. Fumigation often does not kill insect eggs and reinfestations are sometimes reported some months after when these have hatched.

Fumonisin A toxin produced by the mould *Fusarium,* mainly in maize and thus possibly in corn products such as popcorn, corn snack crisps, tortillas, corn syrup and various thickening agents. The effects on humans are not fully known.

Fungi One of the five Kingdoms of living organisms. They are a very large group and consist of forms which vary from the unicellular (the yeasts), through the multicellular moulds and mildews, to the large multicellular types such as the mushrooms. Such large types look like plants, and indeed the fungi were originally misclassified as such. However, the fungi are incapable of photosynthesis, a fundamental property of plants. Many fungi are edible, but there are some poisonous forms such as the Death cap mushroom.

- The majority of fungi are saprophytes living in soil or water, where they decompose plant material.
- They acquire their food by absorbing solutions of organic material from their surroundings, and so are often responsible for decomposing matter.
- They are responsible for much spoilage of foods.
- Many fungi are pathogenic to plants (such as the rusts and mildews), causing economic losses; a few forms are pathogenic to animals, including humans.

See: Aflatoxin, Food spoilage, Mycotoxins.

Fungicide Substance capable of killing fungi, an example being benzoic acid.

Furunculosis
1. A highly infectious and contagious disease of freshwater fish caused by the

bacterium *Bacillus salmonicida*. Affected fish have ulcerating boils or furuncles under the skin and are unfit for human consumption.
2. The term also describes an outbreak of boils in humans, caused by staphylococci.
See: Lesion (skin), Personal Hygiene, Pus.

Galvanised steel Mild steel coated with a thin layer of zinc is protected from corrosion and termed 'galvanised'. Zinc is dissolved by acid foods and has caused food poisoning, an example being the result of fermentation of cider apples in a so-called 'tin' bath.

Game Certain wild animals, mainly birds (such as pheasant, grouse and partridge) but also including hares, which are not eaten fresh but traditionally are 'hung' for some days to develop flavour and tenderise the flesh. This is achieved by the action of bacteria and enzymes, the final state being termed 'high'. Other meats in this condition would probably be considered unfit to eat. There is a legally defined season for hunting of game which may only be sold by licensed dealers.

Gannymede system A heated tray conveyor belt system of meal assembly often used in institutional catering such as hospitals.

Garchey system A method of refuse disposal in which waste water is used to carry rubbish by gravity from high-rise buildings.

Gas flushing A technique for modifying the atmosphere inside a pack by closing in a current of gas such as carbon dioxide or nitrogen. It is used to control the growth of aerobic spoilage organisms.

Gastronorm A modular oven for roasting and baking used in commercial kitchens.

Gastroenteritis A general term applied to diseases which cause inflammation of the stomach and intestines. Symptoms usually include one or more of the following: nausea, vomiting, abdominal pain and diarrhoea.

Gastrointestinal tract Another name for the digestive system, which essentially consists of the stomach and intestines.

Gelatine A high-risk meat product which has been involved in salmonella food poisoning due to contamination, followed by storage at too low a temperature. Gelatine melts at less than 40°C and if it is kept around this temperature, conditions are ideal for the growth of any bacteria present. When molten it should be kept at a temperature of above 63°C, and after use (for example as a glaze) it should be cooled to gelling point as rapidly as possible.

General outbreak (of food poisoning) An often widespread series of cases involving at least two people in different families.

Generation time The time taken for bacteria to double in number by binary fission. It depends upon all growth factors and is often quoted with particular reference to temperature. Many *Salmonella* species have a generation time of around 10 hours at 10°C. *E. coli* have been known (given ideal conditions) to double in number in as little as 10 minutes. *See:* Bacterial growth curve, Danger zone.

Genus A classification name (plural: genera) given to groups of species that are very similar. The first letter is always written in the upper case (i.e. a capital). For example: *Bacillus, Clostridium* and *Salmonella* are three genera of bacteria; *Aspergillus* and *Penicillium* are two genera of moulds. Together with the species name, it forms the scientific name of the organism.

Gerber test A laboratory method for determining the amount of fat in milk.

German cockroach *(Blattella germanica)* A brownish-yellow insect up to 15 mm in length, also called the 'steam fly' due to its preference for warm conditions. It is found in kitchens, bakeries and centrally heated buildings such as hospitals but it is also prevalent in many hot countries. The adult is active and agile and capable of rapid movement. It is also able to climb glossy surfaces. Any food may be infested, the insect is also gregarious and often found in large numbers.
See: Cockroaches.

Germicide Any agent designed to kill 'germs' (micro-organisms).
See: Bactericide, Fungicide, Virucide.

Giardia lamblia
- A flagellated enteric protozoan which has been shown to be an important cause of endemic and epidemic diarrhoea. The number of cases of the disease (giardiasis) in Britain has shown a fivefold increase from 1970 to 1990. It is the most frequent cause of non-bacterial diarrhoea in North America. Incidence of infection is higher in children than in adults, but all ages are susceptible.
- It is found in the gastrointestinal tract of humans and animals. The life cycle of the organism has two stages, a free-living stage, and the cyst, which is the environmental survival form and the infective stage of the organism.

- Infection occurs after ingesting a small number of the cysts.
- Duration of illness is normally one to two weeks, but there are reported cases of chronic infections lasting months to years.
- Transmission is from person to person, with food borne transmission rare. With young children, the faecal-oral route is common. Spread within families is frequent.
- The free-living forms are destroyed by the acid contents of the stomach. About half of the people swallowing the cysts develop diarrhoea within one week of ingestion of the cyst. Other symptoms include abdominal cramps, bloating, flatulence and nausea. Vomiting and fever are less common. Symptoms persist for several weeks, with cysts being released in the faeces.
- Infection is acquired from contaminated water or direct contact with faeces-contaminated individuals or objects. Cool, moist conditions favour survival of the cysts.
- *Giardia* is sensitive to chlorination, but the cysts survive standard concentrations of chlorine used by most wastewater treatment plants. Higher levels of 4 to 6 mg/dm^3 are required.

Glanders A notifiable disease of horses, affecting mucous membranes of the nostrils, which may fatally affect humans. The causative organism is the Gram-positive bacterium *Bacillus mallei*. The disease is also known as farcy.

Glass (contamination by) A serious physical contaminant of foodstuffs since affected food is clearly injurious to health. In food premises, glass must be carefully controlled. Examples include automated scanning of foodstuffs to detect glass fragments, 'non-shatter' lighting, wired glass in doors and windows and the banning of glass items from production areas.

Glass washing Large quantities of glassware, for example in restaurants or the licensed trade, are best washed by a specifically designed machine with a final polish, if required, with disposable paper towels. *See:* Cleaning, Washing up.

Gloves Disposable gloves may be worn by food handlers to protect against staphylococcal contamination. Gloves can, however, become a vehicle for cross-contamination. Food-use gloves are less likely to cause physical contamination if brightly coloured (blue).

Glycoalkaloids Form the green colour in potatoes exposed to light.

Glyphosate resistance A genetic modification, using bacterial genes ('Roundup-

Ready' genes, 'Roundup' being a common glyphosate formulation together with 'Tumbleweed') in soya beans and rapeseed against the herbicide glyphosate which is used to kill weeds amongst these crops. There is limited data on the toxicity of glyphosate on humans but ill-effects are thought to be low.

Goats *See: Brucella abortus*, Meat, Milk.

Goitrins Cyanide-containing compounds present in the cabbage family (*Brassica*). They may aggravate thyroid problems by interfering with the uptake of iodine which is used by the thyroid gland to manufacture the hormone thyroxine.

Golden spider beetle (*Niptus hololeucus*) A widespread pest in many countries; the adult (less than 10 mm long) is covered in golden hairs and resembles a spider. Cereal products and other foods are affected and the beetle may also feed on textiles.

Good housekeeping A self-explanatory term often translated as 'A place for everything and everything in its place'. This should be part of the general cleaning and maintenance operations of all food businesses and has several benefits including discouraging pests, increasing safety and promoting a positive image.

Grain beetle or Grain weevil (*Sitophilus granarius*) A small brown weevil, up to 5 mm long and having a characteristic snout. It is very widely occurring and contaminates many stored cereals and cereal products.

Gram stain A laboratory procedure used to dye bacterial cells. It is used as an aid to identification. The process involves applying two stains (or dyes) one after the other. Due to differences in the composition of their cell walls, all bacteria retain one or other of the two stains. The test is easy to perform, taking just a few minutes. Depending on which of the two stains is retained, bacteria are classified as either Gram-positive or Gram-negative. Knowing how pathogenic bacteria react to the Gram stain is of value in determining a course of action in cases of infection; e.g. antibiotics vary in their effectiveness against Gram-positive and Gram-negative organisms, and all sporing bacteria are Gram-positive.

Gravy Made from meat juices, so it is a high-risk food. Temperature control is therefore important; it must be kept refrigerated (1-4°C) or hot (over 63°C).

Grayanotoxin A toxin (diterpene) naturally occurring in flowering plants such as rhododendrons which affects honey. It is also known as rhodotoxin. *See:* Honey.

Great Plague The bubonic plague caused by the bacterium *Yersinia pestis* carried on the rat flea which swept Europe in the Middle Ages, causing the death of one third of the population.

Grease trap In drainage systems, a device to trap grease and thus prevent it solidifying or congealing and causing blockages. These should be located outside food rooms and cleaned at regular intervals.

Green mould rot A type of food spoilage. *See: Cladosporium.*

Growth curve (bacterial) *See:* Bacterial growth curve.

Growth requirements (bacterial) Micro-organisms which cause food poisoning must be able to grow in food. In order to grow they need the following:
1. Food
Bacteria will grow in most foods, but they will grow best in foods rich in protein, e.g. meat and meat products, fish, poultry, eggs and egg products, milk and milk products. *See:* High-Risk Foods.
2. Warmth
Human pathogens grow best at body temperature (37°C), but they will grow and reproduce at temperatures both above and below this temperature. The effective range is 5 to 63°C. *See:* Danger Zone.
3. Moisture
Like all living organisms, bacteria need moisture in order to survive. If a food is dehydrated bacteria are unable to grow or reproduce. However, as soon as such foods are rehydrated, bacteria will start to grow and reproduce. Hence rehydrated foods must be treated in exactly the same way as fresh foods. *See:* Dry Goods Stores, Food Preservation.
4. pH
Most bacteria prefer a pH of around 7.0 (neutral). However, some bacteria are able to grow down to around pH 4 (acid). *See:* Acid Foods (classification), Pickling.
5. Gaseous requirements
Some bacteria need oxygen to survive (aerobes), but others cannot grow in its presence (anaerobes). Some can grow under both conditions (facultative organisms).
6. Time
Given ideal conditions, bacterial cells can grow and reproduce in as little as ten minutes. This means that extremely large numbers of bacteria may be produced in a short period of time. *See:* Mean Generation Time.

Growth requirements (fungal)
1. Food
Require less nitrogen for growth compared with bacteria; they are nutritionally more efficient, and so can grow on such things as leather. In general, sugars are best for yeasts; moulds grow well on a wide range of foods, both simple and complex.
2. Temperature
Generally less heat tolerant than bacteria, but they do grow better at lower temperatures. Optimum temperature is from 25 to 30°C, maximum temperature for growth is in the range 35 to 47°C. Some can grow at 0°C or less.
3. Moisture
They are more able to grow on foods with too little moisture to support bacterial growth. Yeasts require more moisture than moulds. Most fungi are more resistant to high osmotic pressure than are bacteria, and so readily grow in e.g. jams.
4. pH
Fungi usually grow better in an acid pH, yeasts in particular around pH 4 to 5.
5. Gaseous requirements
All moulds growing in foods require oxygen (aerobes). Yeasts can grow in both the presence and absence of oxygen (facultative organisms). If oxygen is present, carbohydrates are broken down to carbon dioxide and water; if it is absent, carbon dioxide and alcohols are produced. This fact forms the basis of the baking and brewing industries respectively.

Gut An alternative name for the intestines.

Gyromitrin A toxin occurring in some mushrooms. *See:* Mushrooms.

Habits (personal) Unconscious actions involving contact between fingers and other parts of the body, for example the nose, the unguarded cough or sneeze, licking the fingers to pick up paper for wrapping food etc. Such actions may cause bacteria or other contaminants to be passed onto foods.

HACCP *See:* Hazard Analysis Critical Control Points.

Haemagglutin (Lectin) A toxic substance found in various pulses including red kidney, butter and haricot beans.

Hair Stray hairs may become physical contaminants of food and may also be contaminated with *Staphylococcus aureus* from the scalp. A total hair covering, using a hair-net where necessary, should be put on before entry into food rooms.

Haloduric 'Salt-tolerant'. Certain staphylococci are haloduric and so will live (but not multiply) in salty foods such as ham and also on salted wooden chopping boards. It is not a property of most food poisoning bacteria.

Halophile 'Salt-liking'. Some organisms are able to multiply in high concentrations of salt.

Ham
- A cooked, cured pork product involved in many cases of food poisoning due to inadequate temperature control after cross-contamination.
- Ham is sometimes contaminated by hand/machine contact during slicing or food preparation.
- Contact between ham and raw meat should be avoided.
- It is particularly prone to contamination by staphylococci from food handlers, due to the bacterium being able to tolerate the high salt content of the product.
- All other cold cooked meats share these risks.

Hand-contact surfaces A self-explanatory term; such surfaces (e.g. work surfaces and door handles) require disinfection to ensure that any bacteria transferred to them by the hands are not passed on to food or other items.
See: Cleaning schedules, Food-contact surfaces.

Handkerchiefs Become contaminated with bacteria such as *Staphylococcus aureus* and after use the hands should be thoroughly washed. It is questionable if the use of these should be allowed in food rooms since the user may not be in a fit condition to handle food if suffering from a heavy cold. Generally single-use disposable tissues are preferred but pose a physical contamination problem.

Handles *See:* Hand-contact surfaces.

Hands
- The hands of a food handler are probably the most dangerous part of their body.
- Hands may become covered with bacteria after handling raw foods such as meat and poultry.
- They are often the vehicle in cross-contamination as well as being reservoirs of bacteria such as *Staphylococcus aureus*.
- Fingernails should be kept short and not bitten.
- Nail varnish (a possible physical contaminant) should not be worn.
- Perfumed hand creams may contaminate foods.
- Cuts must be covered with a suitable waterproof dressing.

- Jewellery is restricted to a plain wedding ring which cannot collect food scraps and harbour bacteria.
- Infections such as septic cuts or whitlows must be reported and contact with food or related equipment avoided until medical clearance is obtained.
- Frequent hand washing is vital, for example before starting to work with food and between handling different foods such as raw and cooked.

Hand-washing Food handlers are required to wash their hands on many occasions including:
- before entering the food room and starting work
- after using the toilet
- after smoking
- when refuse or waste has been handled
- after leaving the food room for a break
- after handling any raw food
- after any other occasion that they have become contaminated.

Soap, hot water, a separate basin, suitable drying facilities and a nail brush should be provided and a notice requesting hand-washing should be clearly visible.

Harbourage A term used to mean shelter for pests. Examples of harbourage for rats and mice include cavity walls, roller boxes for shutters, spaces behind and within equipment, suspended ceilings and badly stored foodstuffs.

Hard cheese Cheeses such as cheddar, parmesan and emmenthal, produced by a process including pressing, in which the moisture content is 30-40%. Storage of these is at 10°C during ripening and 5-10°C afterwards. Any cooked products containing cheese must be kept out of the danger zone of temperature. Occasional outbreaks of staphylococcal food poisoning have been reported with cheese made from unpasteurised milk.

Hardness of water Caused by various dissolved substances such as calcium and magnesium salts. Hard water will not allow water to lather with soap, causes scum formation and results in deposits on heating equipment affecting safety and efficiency. Hardness may be temporary (caused by hydrogen carbonates) which may be removed by boiling, or permanent (caused by sulphates) which must be chemically removed by water softeners such as Calgon or Permutit.

Hard swell A can of food, the ends of which are permanently protruding due to gas production; also called a 'blown' can.

Hazard Analysis Critical Control Point (HACCP)

Hazard Analysis Critical Control Point (HACCP) A system of risk assessment and control measures developed by NASA, Pillsbury and the Navick laboratories to ensure zero defects in food for uses including space travel. It relies upon constant feedback and information flow from control points within the production system and is proactive rather than reactive. All stages of food production are examined from raw material to end user with non-food items such as staff, premises and equipment also considered. A comprehensive knowledge of food hygiene is required to do assessments which are best performed by teams some of whose members are actually involved in food production.

A **hazard** is the potential to cause harm and may be microbiological (such as the presence of *Salmonella* organisms), physical (such as glass, parts of machinery, human hair etc.) chemical (such as substances used in cleaning, metals or pesticides).

A **critical control point** (CCP) is a step in the system at which loss of control would lead to an unacceptable health risk and one which will not be remedied later in the system.

There are several stages through which the system is developed with the use of an on-site verified flow diagram central to the overall system.

1. Identify the hazards.
Microbiological, chemical and physical hazards are considered.

2. Establish Critical Points during purchase, delivery, storage, preparation, production, cooling, reheating, display and sale. Examples could include setting a minimum time and temperature for cooking or devising a cleaning method which would leave surfaces free from contamination.

3. Controls.
Many control measures and checks are possible including

- high specification raw materials from reputable suppliers
- checking of goods inward by designated persons
- using low risk ingredients
- temperature control during storage and cooking
- training of staff for example in the use of temperature measuring apparatus
- stock rotation
- separate high-risk foods areas
- producing minimum quantities
- organised cleaning regimes,
  and many others.

4. Monitoring and corrective actions.

Monitoring makes sure that the control targets or limits are met and corrective action will ensure that staff know exactly what to do if a control is not met. For example if food in a refrigerator starts to rise in temperature it should be clear to staff what corrective action they must take. Corrective actions could be disposal of the food or an instruction to inform a senior person immediately. Automation of some controls and monitoring is possible and monitoring may be on the job and immediate (such as a temperature or cleanliness check) or off the job (such as a hygiene swab of equipment or bacterial count in food).

5. **Documentation** should be completed so that records are available for managers and operational staff within the business as well as inspectors. A record system may be part of a basis for the legal defence of due diligence if prosecution occurs.

6. **Review** periodically to establish if CCPs are correct, if other CCPs are needed, if any changes in the system from supply of materials to end use have occurred or if there are any non-conformities such as deviations from recipes or methods. Staff training will need to be reviewed and a regular review will be needed to make sure that the documented system reflects reality.

The advantages of HACCP -
- prevents hazards from contaminating food
- based on sound scientific principles
- provides rapid feedback so that problems may be 'nipped in the bud'
- permits more efficient and effective control since records allow managers, inspectors and investigators to test compliance with laws and standards over a period of time
- places responsibility for ensuring food safety appropriately on the food manufacturer or distributor.

A full HACCP system is complex and may focus upon each ingredient. It is more suited to manufacturing than catering, for which other methods such as ASC and SAFE may be more appropriate.

Problems from the small business point of view have been identified including
- the system is too complex to initiate and operate
- advice has been conflicting
- all existing controls must be scrapped
- language and literacy problems.

For most businesses a simple system is understood by all food handlers is preferable to acomplex system which is unclear.

118 Head covering

Head covering *See:* Hair.

Health and Safety at Work etc Act 1974 A major piece of UK legislation dealing with all aspects of safety at work. It applies to employers, employees and members of the public. Employers have major responsibilities and must ensure that workplaces are safe and that staff receive adequate training and information about hazards at work. The Act and its many Regulations is jointly administered by the Health and Safety Executive and Local Authorities depending on the type of workplace.

Health and Safety Commission and Executive (HSC and HSE)
1. The HSC is an independent body established under the 1974 Act (see previous entry) consisting of representatives from employers, trades unions and professional bodies, for which the Secretary of State answers to Parliament. The HSC has responsibilities including research, administering health and safety legislation, advising, preparing new legislation for consideration and investigating safety issues such as accident prevention.
2. The HSE is essentially the enforcement agency of the HSC operating 'in the field'. HSE inspectors are divided into several specialist divisions (such as pollution) and work from regional centres. Generally HSE inspectors are involved with factories, mines and quarries, construction sites, other dangerous occupations and educational establishments. HSE also publishes a large amount of information relating to all aspects of safety.

Health Inspectors Popular term used for Environmental Health Officer and derived from the pre-1974 title of 'Public Health Inspector'.

Healthy carriers Persons who excrete food poisoning or other disease-causing organisms without ever having shown symptoms. They may pass a disease unknowingly through food to other people. *See:* Carriers.

Heat treatment of milk and other foods Milk may be made safe by pasteurisation, sterilisation or ultra heat treatment (UHT), all of which destroy pathogenic organisms. Canning is the most common heat treatment preservation process for other foods although cooking could also be considered as such. *See:* Milk.

Heavy metals *See:* Metals.

Hepatitis A Virus (HAV)
- Hepatitis A (HA) or Type A viral hepatitis is an infectious disease of the liver and is caused by a group of viruses.

- It causes epidemic or infectious hepatitis because of its mode of transmission. It is usually spread by the faecal-oral route (and probably urine) but not infrequently outbreaks occur through the transmission of the virus in water, food and milk.
- Foods involved have included cold meats, sandwiches, salads, raw and steamed shellfish, bakery products and iced drinks, all contaminated by infected persons.
- Young children (under 6 years of age) commonly develop no symptoms, but older children and adults do. It is usually a mild illness with a sudden onset of fever, malaise, abdominal discomfort followed by several days of jaundice.
- The incubation period is anything from 10 to 50 days, depending on the number of infectious particles ingested, with the illness lasting from 1 to 2 weeks. Sufferers become most infective just before jaundice develops. Mortality rate is very low.
- Outbreaks are common in institutions; recovery from illness usually confers lifelong immunity.
- Proper hand washing before food preparation and serving will effectively prevent such outbreaks.

An outbreak in 1989 involving more than 50 persons centred on a village shop selling bread, rolls and sandwiches was noted, together with a 1990 outbreak involving shellfish and a 1991 outbreak from prawn vol-au-vents at a private party (all in England).

Hepatitis B Virus (HBV) A viral disease spread through mucous membranes and carried in body fluids such as blood. It is only very rarely known to be food-borne. This virus is not related to HAV.

Hepatitis E Virus (HEV)
- Causes hepatitis E, or enterically transmitted non-A non-B hepatitis. (Other names include faecal-oral non-A non-B hepatitis.)
- Symptoms are the same as those in hepatitis A disease. Incubation period varies from 2 to 9 weeks, and the illness normally lasts about two weeks.
- Transmitted by the faecal-oral route. Waterborne (usually associated with contaminated drinking water) and person to person spread have been demonstrated.
- The disease is often seen in people aged 15 to 40 years of age, and pregnant women are exceptionally susceptible to a severe form of the disease, in which there is a high mortality rate.

Herbivore An animal that feeds exclusively on plants, examples include cattle and sheep.

Herbs and spices The flavour of some of these may mask deterioration in foods. Cloves and mustard are known to be bactericidal and other herbs have medicinal uses. These are amongst a number of foods which are successfully irradiated.

Herring Fish often smoked and cured to make various products including kippers.

Hexamine (Hexamethylenetetramine, E239) Fungicide used in some fish and cheese.

Hide beetle (*Dermestida*, *Dermestes* and *Anthrenus* species) Small oval/round beetles (2 to 5 mm in size) with patterned bodies. They infest dry protein material including leather goods, biscuits, dead animals and birds, mummies and occasionally food stores. The larvae can cause considerable damage by boring.

'High' Term used to describe the state of game such as pheasant after hanging for some time at ambient temperatures. The growth of bacteria and the activity of enzymes during this period develops flavour and tenderises the meat due to partial breakdown of protein. Non-game items in this condition would probably be judged as unfit.

High Pressure Preservation Pressures between 700-900 MPa at 45°C for 15 minutes inactivate vegetative cells.

High-risk foods Foods which support the growth of bacteria, particularly pathogens, when conditions are favourable and which are intended for consumption without treatment which would destroy such organisms.
These foods commonly contain protein and include:

- cooked meats, fish and eggs (and substitutes for any of these) and any product containing them (such as pies)
- cooked cheese, cereals (e.g. rice), pulses and vegetables
- soft cheeses ripened with moulds or micro-organisms
- smoked or cured fish
- smoked or cured meat which has been sliced
- desserts containing milk, with pH 4.5 or more
- prepared vegetable salads including those with fruit
- sandwiches
- cream cakes.

All of these foods should be kept under strict temperature control, generally out of the danger zone (8-63°C). There are exemptions under UK law to allow time for sale

and service of some foods and to cover other eventualities.
See: Appendix: Food Law.

Histamine A substance (amine) produced at the site of allergic reactions. A Danish report published in 1997 suggested that 80% of food poisoning from seafood and fish are not due to bacteria but are caused by histamine and other biotoxins.
See: Allergies, Scombrotoxin.

Home catering *See:* Domestic premises.

Homogenised Literally, the same composition throughout; used to describe milk whose cream has been converted into small globules which remain in suspension and do not separate into a top layer. The process involves forcing milk through a fine nozzle under pressure and is used before sterilisation and UHT processes.

Honey
- May contain sufficient levels of naturally occuring bacterial spores to affect infants under 12 months old.
- Pyrrolizidine alkaloids (PAs), natural intoxicants which cause liver damage in humans, are present in many wild flowers and may occur in low levels in honey.
- The condition 'Honey Intoxication' is produced when honey produced from the nectar of rhododendrons which contain grayanotoxin is eaten.
- The condition is rarely fatal and generally lasts for no more than one day causing dizziness, weakness, excessive perspiration, nausea, and vomiting shortly after ingestion.
- The disease is dose-related and more severe symptoms such as convulsions are possible.
- Reports from Turkey, Austria and the USA suggest the problem is worldwide and related to indigenous toxic species of rhododendron, not all species being toxic.

Hot air hand driers A modern and effective method of hand drying eliminating the risk of person to person contamination. A disadvantage is their slowness which may discourage their use. They are best used with a backup system such as disposable paper towels in case of failure.

Hot cabinets (Hot cupboards) Equipment consisting of a heated metal cabinet with shelves for keeping food hot while awaiting service. Food in these should be at above

63°C and the cabinet temperature over 80°C. Such cabinets are not suitable for reheating food, their use being to hold the temperature of hot high-risk foods above the danger zone. For plate warming a temperature of 60°C is satisfactory. *See:* Bain marie.

Hot food High-risk foods should be kept above 63°C to prevent the growth of food poisoning bacteria or the germination of spores. This temperature is lower than the service temperature for many foods, this being above 70°C.
See: Appendix: Food Law, Thermometers.

Hot water A requirement in food rooms for washing hands unless no open food is handled. *See:* Appendix: Food Law.

HSC and HSE *See:* Health and Safety Commission and Executive.

HTST 'High Temperature Short Time'. A method of pasteurisation often used for milk in which 72°C is held for at least 15 seconds followed by immediate cooling to 10°C.

Humidity (Relative Humidity, RH) The amount of water vapour present in air at any one time, expressed as %RH. 100% humidity indicates that the air is saturated and cannot hold any more water vapour. Excess humidity (over RH 70%) is uncomfortable to work in since the body cannot lose heat by sweating, and it may cause condensation problems affecting buildings and stored foods. For dry food storage rooms, RH range of 30-70% is satisfactory, whereas raw meat and most fruit and vegetables need RH of 90%. Humidity is measured with a hygrometer.

Humectant Substance which absorbs water from the atmosphere and prevents food from drying out, for example glycerol (glycerine) in icing.

Hung *See:* Game.

Hydatid disease/cysts The tapeworm *Echinococcus granulosus* lives in the gut of dogs, cats, foxes and other carnivores. It is a small tapeworm (1cm long) whose eggs are eaten by an intermediate host including humans, cattle, pigs and sheep. The eggs produce cysts in many organs including the liver and brain. Direct contact with dogs or through food contaminated with dog faeces (such as uncooked vegetables) have been shown to be common ways for humans to contract this disease.

Hydrogenation The process of saturating some double bonds in unsaturated oils by passing hydrogen gas through the heated oil under pressure in the presence of powdered nickel as a catalyst. Many margarines are made in this way.

Hydrogen peroxide A substance with a bactericidal effect increasingly used in cleaning agents such as disinfectants. It is biodegradable, producing oxygen and water but is not as powerful as hypochlorites.

Hydrogen sulphide A gas with an offensive odour produced during decomposition of eggs and during cooking of cabbage and other vegetables.

Hydrogen swell Internal corrosion of cans resulting in a gas build up which produces 'blowing'. It mainly affects canned fruits containing acids which attack the tinplate and react with the mild steel of the can.

Hydrometer A flotation device for measuring the density (specific gravity) of liquids including wines, beers, fruit juices, sugar syrups and milk with the object of determining some element of composition, for example alcohol content of wine, and solids in milk.

Hydrophilic Literally 'water-liking', a term used in detergency.

Hydroxybiphenyl, E231 *See:* Biphenyl.

Hypha A single slender filament composed of a number of cells; the unit of structure of most fungi. *See:* Moulds, Mycelium.

Hypochlorite
- Salts of hypochlorous acid containing the radical -OCl and used as disinfectants due to the action of chlorine released from them.
- Chlorine is bactericidal and is effective against some spores.
- At a concentration of over 100 ppm a fresh sodium hypochlorite solution will disinfect an aesthetically clean surface in 2 to 3 minutes.
- If the surface is dirty then disinfection may not be achieved unless the strength of the solution is increased; there is a limit to this since the chemical affects both the skin and metals.
- Solutions are often supplied at a concentration of 10% and require dilution before use, with rinsing after use to avoid taint.
- Strong hypochlorite solutions may damage the skin, eyes and fabrics and should be carefully handled.
- If mixed with other cleaning agents such as scouring powders, chlorine gas may be released, the inhalation of which could be fatal.

Ice

Hypochlorites are anionic and should not be mixed with cationic substances. There is concern over the biodegradability of hypochlorites and related environmental effects, but they have wide use domestically and commercially, being readily available, effective and cheap. *See:* COSHH, Contact time.

Ice Has been involved in cases of food poisoning (including salmonellosis) from ice cubes in drinks. Ice-making machines should be well maintained to avoid problems. Under UK law, ice is included within the legal definition of food. *See:* Growth requirements (bacterial), Psychrophiles.

Ice-cream
- A high-risk product whose production and sale is closely controlled by law in the UK.
- Ingredients may include milk, eggs, sugar, thickening agents and water, many products having a large percentage of air ('overrun').
- Pasteurisation and sterilisation times and temperatures are legally defined with cooling to 7°C within 90 minutes.
- The final product may be stored at minus 18°C but special ice-cream refrigerators operating at minus 12°C are also used for short-term storage (one week); the texture is best at around this temperature.
- If ice-cream thaws it must not be refrozen.
- Scoops for portioning ice-cream from bulk should be washed and disinfected between each service. A 1995 survey in England and Wales showed contamination of ice cream scoops with several organisms including *E. coli* being detected.
- With soft ice-cream it is vital to clean the machine regularly according to manufacturers' instructions.

Ichneumon flies Minute two-winged parasitic insects which attack pests of stored products by laying eggs into larvae or caterpillars. Their presence is an indication that pest infestation is at a high level.

IEHO Outdated term, Institution of Environmental Health Officers, replaced by CIEH.

Ileum The last part of the small intestine. The lower part contains resident bacteria which rarely cause disease.

Illness in food handlers
- Infectious diseases such as food poisoning, typhoid fever, gastroenteritis

Incineration of food **125**

- and others must be reported to the local authority.
- A decision is made as to whether or not the food handler may continue working.
- Faecal samples may be taken to identify the cause of the disease.

See : Exclusion.

Imitation cream Subject to the same problems as cream.

Immersion freezing *See:* Cryogenic freezing.

Imported foods Regulations governing these are found in many countries including all parts of the UK. Port Health Authorities employ EHOs whose duties include food inspection and the examination of health certificates required for some imports.

Impression plate A technique used to inoculate an agar plate by pressing the material to be tested, e.g. a cloth or part of an overall, directly onto the surface of an agar plate.

Improvement notice
- Under the Food Safety Act 1990 and other laws, a formal notice stating works to be done to bring premises or practices up to standard may be served on the proprietor of a food business if the 'minded to' notice is disregarded or agreement not reached.
- The notice is normally served after an inspection by an EHO or other authorised officer.
- The notice is subject to appeal and at least 14 days must be given to do the work required; extensions to this time may be applied for.
- If the notice is not complied with then prosecution or prohibition may result.

See: Informal notice, "Minded to" notice, Prohibition orders.

Incidence of food poisoning and food-borne disease In Great Britain there has been a general upward trend in reported cases of food poisoning and food borne-disease in the period 1970-1996. Total reported cases have more than doubled to around 60 000 but the number of non-reported cases, most of which may be relatively minor, is likely to be far in excess of this figure. Various estimates of up to 10 million total cases per year in the USA with 2-4 million cases of salmonellosis (7 000 deaths from *Salmonella* per year) alone. Food-borne diseases and food poisoning have risen almost 200% in Germany from 1965 to 1990. *See:* Food poisoning.

Incineration of food Unfit food may be destroyed by this method.

Incubation period The time between consumption of contaminated food and the appearance of any signs or symptoms. The precise time varies from hours to days and sometimes weeks, and depends on a number of factors, including the micro-organism involved, the number of infecting micro-organisms (the dose), and the resistance of the host. *See:* Onset Period.

Incubator A thermostatically-controlled cabinet used to grow cultures of micro-organisms at known temperatures.

Incubatory carrier *See:* Carrier.

Indian-meal moth (*Plodia interpunctella*) A pest principally of dried fruits and nuts, prevalent in California, Australia and Mediterranean countries. It also attacks chocolate and cereals and is cold-hardy, being able to survive British winters. *See:* Moths.

Indicator organisms Organisms whose presence is tested for when assessing water safety. Such organisms must:

1. be consistently present in substantial numbers in human intestinal wastes
2. survive in the water for at least as long as pathogenic organisms
3. be detectable by simple tests.

The usual indicator organisms are the faecal coliform bacteria such as *E. coli*. *See:* Presumptive water (coliform) test.

Indictable offence Serious offences normally heard in a Crown Court.

Induction training Training for new employees covering the most important principles of food hygiene and other matters such as safety, company policy and terms of contract. New employees may also require a period of close supervision.

Industry Guides Guides such as the Catering Industry Guide to Good Hygiene Practice give advice regarding the interpretation and implementation of food legislation and explains what should be done in food businesses to comply with regulations. Levels of training, premises construction, use and suitability of equipment and personal hygiene are covered in detail. Other guides for retailers, manufacturers and others are planned.

Informal notice
- A letter sent by an EHO following an inspection of a food premises stating

defects and remedies.
- The notice has no legal status and is only used for non-urgent matters but if no action is taken then stronger measures such as an improvement notice may result.
- As the name suggests this notice is a form of 'friendly persuasion' and is favoured by some as a means of getting problems dealt with without being too heavy-handed.
- Another school of thought suggests that it is a waste of time since it may be ignored because of its lack of legal weight.

Infection (food poisoning by) A food-borne illness caused by the ingestion of food contaminated with living bacterial cells. There are two types of food infections:
1. those in which the pathogens use the food as a medium for growth and actively grow and multiply in the food; such illnesses are usually referred to under the general term 'Food Poisoning'
2. those in which the food does not support the growth of pathogens, but simply serves as a carrier for them; illnesses of this type may be referred to under the general term 'Food-borne Diseases'.

Infections (food-borne) *See:* Infection (food poisoning by).

Infections (waterborne) In the food industry water has many functions and is used
1. as an ingredient
2. to wash ingredients
3. to heat/cool food
4. to clean.

In each case it is important that the water is free from pathogenic and spoilage organisms. A large number of pathogenic organisms may be carried by water.

Contamination by water
a) Direct, for example by drinking water. A variety of micro-organisms may be spread by this route, including viruses (such as the hepatitis A virus, the poliomyelitis viruses and the enteroviruses), bacteria (such as the organisms responsible for causing typhoid fever and cholera) and protozoa (such as the organism causing amoebic dysentery).
b) Indirect, for example through contamination of a food product, such as faecally-contaminated shellfish and plant crops. There is also the possibility of infection by a variety of worms such as cestodes, nematodes and trematodes in raw or undercooked fish.

Infectious disease *See:* Communicable disease.

Infestation The presence of pests such as insects or rodents in or on food, premises or persons.

Inoculate To transfer micro-organisms to, for example, a sterilised growth medium. After inoculation, the medium is placed in an incubator for one to two days to allow the micro-organisms to grow. *See:* Culture Media, Incubator.

Inoculum A sample of micro-organism culture used to start a new culture.

In-place cleaning *See:* CIP.

Insecticides Chemical formulations or natural substances used to kill insects. Examples include pyrethrum and diazonium compounds. Food room use must be strictly controlled by professional operators. *See:* Cockroaches, DDT, LD_{50}.

"Insect-o-cutor" A trade name for a type of electrical flying insect killer using ultra violet radiation to attract pests.

Insects A large class of invertebrates having head, thorax and abdomen, two antennae, three pairs of thoracic legs and normally two pairs of thoracic wings. Examples include flies, beetles and cockroaches.

Inspections of food premises
1. May be performed by authorised officers such as EHOs at any reasonable time, obstruction being an offence.
2. Regular and systematic walking tours of food premises using a prepared check list are a useful supervisory and management tool to ensure that standards are being maintained.

Intestinal flora (organisms)
- Bacteria heavily populate most of the digestive system.
- The stomach and small intestine contain fairly small numbers, due in part to the acid nature of the gastric juice.
- The large intestine however contains enormous numbers of bacteria; it has been estimated that there are over 100 billion bacteria per gram of faeces.
- Up to 40% of the weight of faeces consists of wet microbial cells, both living and non-living.
- In the adult lower bowel most of the organisms are commensals, but there will also be low numbers of potential pathogens, such as salmonellas and *Clostridium perfringens*.
- The larger numbers of these organisms excreted by infected people or

carriers may lead to an outbreak of disease, especially if their personal hygiene is poor.
- The non-pathogenic bacteria assist in the enzymic breakdown of foods and some produce useful vitamins, such as vitamin K.

Note: The word 'flora' is used due to the original misclassification of the bacteria as plants.

Intoxication (food poisoning by) A food-borne illness caused by the consumption of food containing a chemical toxin (poison). The toxin may be a natural product found in certain plants or animals, or it may be a toxic substance excreted by a micro-organism such as a bacterium or a fungus.

Invasiveness *See:* Aggressiveness.

IVS (Intervening ventilated space) Such a space, ventilated to the outside, should exist between a room containing a WC and another room.

Iodophors Iodine-containing sanitisers used principally by beverage manufacturers and dairies in CIP systems. They tend to be expensive but are effective in a wide range of conditions. Formulations are non-ionic and buffered with phosphoric acid at pH 3-5.

Iron A common metal used for making cooking vessels and the mild steel plate of cans. When dissolved by acid foods, there is a risk of metallic food poisoning and also unpleasant tastes.

Irradiation
- A method of food preservation developed as a result of research during the 1960s.
- Radiation at levels around 10 kGy (gamma and X rays) or 10 MEv (electrons) from a radioactive source or generator will kill micro-organisms and insect pests.
- High doses (sterilising doses) of radiation cause severe changes to the taste of foods making them unacceptable to consumers and current practice is to use lower levels to reduce the total bacterial load.
- Low doses are also used to prevent potatoes, onions and other vegetables from sprouting.
- Many foods such as chicken, shellfish, strawberries and spices preserved by this method have been on sale world-wide for some years. Only one facility

is currently licensed in the UK, Isotron plc in Swindon. A maximum dose of 10kGy on wide variety of spices and condiments is used.

Main problems
- The process does not affect spores or toxins and is not a substitute for good food hygiene practises.
- Much concern has been expressed about the possibilities of induced irradiation in consumers, mutation of bacteria and the increased risk of survival of some pathogens since spoilage organisms are more easily destroyed.
- There is no simple reliable test to detect irradiated food although tests using gas chromatography, thermoluminecence (for herbs and spices), electron spin resonance (for dry foods such as seeds) are available to detect food which has been irradiated. There is also a microbiological technique based on the reduction of the aerobic plate count (APC) after irradiation.
- Consumer studies have shown that many people would be reluctant to eat irradiated food for various reasons including safety issues.

Jam Fruit product preserved by sugar and having a shelf-life of up to a year if unopened. Mould growth may cause spoilage. Refrigerated storage after opening is often recommended, especially with low sugar, preservative-free jams.

Jejunum Part of the small intestine.

Jewellery When worn by food handlers this creates several risks including
1. trapping food particles upon which bacteria may breed
2. the possibility of physical contamination if any part falls into food
3. various safety hazards.

It is common practice for food handlers to be allowed to wear only a plain wedding ring.

Juvenile hormone A synthetic hormone used in insect control (Pharaoh's ants and cockroaches) which when eaten by the young insect prevents their development into adults. The hormone is species-specific and should not affect other life forms.

Kickplate A panel fixed to the bottom of a door to minimise damage. It may be made of a number of materials, such as plastic, but if metal is used it is more durable and it helps proof against rodent pests. This latter property is further enhanced if it makes a close fit on closing.

Lactic acid **131**

Kidney bean *See:* Red kidney beans.

Kipper A cured, dyed and smoked herring. *See:* Curing, Fish, Smoked foods.

Kitchen design *See:* Design of food premises.

Knacker's yard A slaughterhouse dealing with animals not intended for human consumption.

Koch, Robert (1843-1910) A German physician and microbiologist, whose seminal studies of anthrax, tuberculosis and cholera showed them to be bacterial diseases. He is regarded by many as the first true bacteriologist.

Kosher Food prepared according to Jewish traditions.

Labelling It is an offence under English law to label, describe, advertise or present food in a way that is likely to mislead, based on the expectations of an ordinary person.

Examples include
- Making a false claim (describing a cheap cut of meat as fillet steak or using a picture of a dairy cow on a food containing no milk).
- Failing to declare information.

All types of printed material including wrappers, circulars and menus, together with radio, TV and any other form of advertising are covered by these requirements.

Very detailed regulations were made by the UK Government in 1996 requiring the name of the food, an ingredients list, shelf life, instructions for use, percentages of any specially emphasised ingredient, special storage conditions and the name and address of the manufacturer, seller or packer. Several schedules giving lists of approved additives, food names governed by law and nutritional information are included. There are also a host of specific labelling requirements for some foods such as wine and canned fish, the situation being extremely complex. *See:* Appendix: Food law.

Lactic acid An organic acid produced in foods by bacteria including *Lactobacillus* and *Streptococcus* species.
1. In cheese-making lactose is fermented to lactic acid, the resultant lowered pH being suitable for the clotting action of the enzyme rennin.
2. In slaughtering food animals, a rested animal which has a high level of glycogen in its muscles produces better quality meat. This is because glycogen is converted

(post-slaughter) into lactic acid, which tenderises meat by breaking down the fibres of the proteins collagen and elastin. Meat with a low pH keeps longer since bacterial growth and enzyme action are inhibited. *See:* Dark cutting meat.
3. In yoghurt and similar products lactic acid is produced from various sugars including lactose, the low pH causing coagulation of the milk protein casein and gives the product its characteristic taste. If the pH falls to less than 4.5, these products do not support the growth of common pathogens.

LACOTS (Local Authorities Co-ordinating Body on Food and Trading Standards) The overall mission is to 'promote consistency and good practice in the enforcement of trading standards and food safety legislation throughout the United Kingdom' by producing advice such as Codes of Practice to local authorities, representing local government at national and international level, liaising between local government and trade bodies and developing information systems.

Lactobacillus Gram-positive bacteria which ferment sugars including lactose to produce lactic acid. The most common is *L. bulgaricus* (*L . acidophilus, L. jugurti, L. lactis* and *L. helveticus* are also used in yoghurt making). Some species are sugar-tolerant and cause spoilage in sweet cured hams. In canned meat products a green appearance may result from the growth of these organisms.
See: Streptococcus species.

Lag phase *See:* Bacterial growth curve.

Lacquer band In the treatment of infestations by insects such as cockroaches, a band of lacquer or varnish containing an insecticide is painted around areas such as pipework. The insect walks over the lacquer and picks up the insecticide on its feet and body. The insecticide is ingested after grooming and/or carried back to the nest.

Larva (insect) A developmental stage in the life cycle of some insects, between egg and pupa, for example the maggot of flies. (Plural = larvae.)

Latent heat Heat which must be added or removed to change the state of a substance, temperature being unchanged. For example a large amount of heat must be removed to convert water into ice at freezing point. Thawing of frozen foods often takes longer than would be expected since melting of ice to form water requires the input of large amounts of heat.

Lavatories *See:* Sanitary conveniences.

LC$_{50}$ The concentration of a substance, such as an insecticide or rodenticide, which will kill 50% of those exposed to it. More often used is the unit LD$_{50}$.

LD$_{50}$ The dose of a substance which will kill 50% of those exposed to it and thus is used a measure of acute toxicity and as an indication of harmful effects to others at risk. The substance dieldrin, while very effective against insects, is also toxic to mammals having an LD$_{50}$ of less than 100 mg/kg body weight in rats while pyrethrum, a common flykiller, has an LD$_{50}$ of over 800 mg/kg and is thus 'safer' for mammals. *See:* LC$_{50}$.

Lead
- A heavy metal which may contaminate food from water pipes, exhaust fumes, paints and some pottery glazes.
- A Council of Europe report in 1995 indicated that lead intake in humans is derived from a range of sources including foods such a mussels, airborne contamination of fruit and vegetables, wine, lead-soldered cans, lead water pipes and lead crystal glasses.
- Lead is a cumulative poison whose effects, including deterioration of the brain, may not be apparent for many years.
- The maximum 'safe' level in foods is around 1 ppm but an even lower figure may be more desirable.

Lectin *See:* Red kidney beans.

Legislation *See:* Appendix: Food Law.

Leptospira Bacterial organisms having a coiled appearance including those causing Weil's disease and Canicola fever, both being examples of leptospirosis. The organisms are carried by several animals including dogs and rats. Both diseases are waterborne.

Lesion (skin) An area of damaged skin, such as a graze, cut or burn. Such damaged tissues readily support the growth of bacteria and so there is a high risk of the wound becoming septic. They should be covered with a suitable waterproof dressing. *See:* Appendix: Food Law, Personal Hygiene, Pus, *Staphylococcus aureus*.

Leuconostoc Gram-positive food spoilage fermenting bacteria causing rot in vegetables. They are both salt and sugar tolerant. They are found in slimy sugar solutions, fermenting vegetables and in milk and dairy products. Some are able to spoil wine.

Leucosis (avian)

Leucosis (avian) A disease of the liver in poultry causing emaciation. Affected birds are unfit for human consumption.

Licensing and registration of food premises
- In Britain certain types of food business, such as slaughterhouses, those making ice-cream, and those dealing with certain aspects of milk production and sale, are registered with the local authority who may refuse to issue or renew the licence if operations are unsatisfactory.
- General registration of most food premises, so that EHOs know what food businesses exist or are planned, is now in force in Britain.

See: Food Safety Act 1990.

Lighting
- This should be suitable for the task and the person performing it.
- It is difficult to set absolute figures although 500 lux (measured at the work surface) is sometimes quoted as a good general figure for kitchens.
- Detailed work may require up to 2 000 lux.
- The requirements of individuals vary considerably.
- Too much light is as bad as too little and the number, choice and placement of light fittings is a specialist task. There is an HSE Guidance Note (HSG 38) on lighting at work.

Advantages of good lighting
assists cleaning
discourages pests
improves performance and safety
creates a comfortable work environment.

Artificial lighting is more controllable than natural light, but the latter may be more pleasant although heat from solar gain is a potential problem.

Lima beans Contain considerable quantities of cyanide-containing substances which must be removed by boiling in an open pan so that poisonous hydrogen cyanide gas may escape. Special low cyanide varieties of these beans have been developed for agriculture and only these are permitted to be grown, for example in the USA.

Lindane Common name for the insecticide gamma BHC; its use is banned in some countries, including Britain.

Linear flow In the design of kitchen and food production units, the flow in one direc-

Linear flow

tion from raw materials to finished product.

- Cross-contamination is minimised by separating clean and dirty processes.
- More efficient cleaning.
- Linear operation can be smoother and more economical in time and effort.

A typical line of progress in a kitchen would be:

```
Delivery
   ↓
Storage
   ↓
Preparation
   ↓
Cooking
   ↓
Assembly
   ↓
Service
```

Note: *The flows of people, equipment and utensils (including disposable and re-usable containers) and waste must also be considered*

Equipment and work areas need to be carefully arranged so that linear flow is considered as far as is practicable. The flow of foodstuffs, persons, equipment and wastes need to be considered. *See:* Design of equipment and food premises.

Lipophilic Literally 'lipid-liking', lipids being fats and oils. A term applied to the tails of detergent molecules.

Liquid egg A product consisting of mixed whole eggs used for convenience in bakeries. It has been implicated in outbreaks of food poisoning and is pasteurised (65°C for 2 minutes with immediate cooling to 3°C, to pass the alpha amylase test) to reduce the numbers of pathogens such as salmonellas. Being a batch product, one contaminated egg could affect the rest.

Listeria monocytogenes A bacterium, commonly referred to simply as *Listeria*, which is widely distributed in nature.
- It has been found in, sewage, decaying vegetable matter, soil, insects, birds, ruminants (e.g. cows), humans, all types of farm animals and domestic pets. A survey in Spain during 1995 showed over 70% of farm hens with *L. monocytogenes*.
- In humans it causes the disease known as listeriosis.
- Young children, the elderly, the sick and pregnant women are most at risk.
- Nausea, vomiting and diarrhoea may be the only symptoms of illness. However they may precede the more serious symptoms of septicaemia (blood poisoning), meningitis, and infections of the uterus or cervix in pregnant women, with the possibility of miscarriage and stillbirth resulting (the mother usually survives). Usually before such symptoms an influenza-type illness occurs.
- Incubation period is from 8 days to 3 months.
- Antibiotic treatment is effective.

Important considerations

1. The optimum temperature for growth is 37°C, but it grows at all temperatures down to 2.5°C. It is capable of multiplying in refrigerators. It is a fairly hardy organism, resisting the harmful effects of freezing, drying and heat which would kill other non-sporing bacteria.
2. Foods which have had problems with this organism include commercial chilled foods, such as prepared salads, sandwiches, pates, cooked meats and ready-to-eat meals which just require reheating.
3. Milk, ice cream, raw and smoked fish, and soft white cheeses with a crusty rind (such as Brie and Camembert) have also been suspected. The EU level in soft cheese is absence in any 25 gram sample.

4. Its presence in cooked food is an indicator of poor hygiene practices during manufacture, distribution or sale. Detection of *Listeria* species is a frequently used critical control in environmental samples used to check cleaning regimes taken during food production.
5. Salad foods should be washed before use.
6. Cook-chill products must not be eaten after the 'use-by' date has expired.
7. Reheating foods must be thorough and to a centre temperature of at least 70°C.
8. Refrigerators should be kept below 5°C and defrosted regularly.

The organism is Gram-positive, non-spore forming and has a thermal death time of 10 minutes at 58-59°C.

Numbers of cases in the UK have declined since the late 1980s with 108 cases in 1992 compared with almost 300 at its peak in 1987-1988. During 1993, 33 cases were reported in NW France among people eating rillettes (a pork product). Four miscarriages, two stillbirths and two deaths were attributed to the outbreak. A major outbreak of 279 cases, with 63 deaths, was noted in 1992 in Eastern France from the consumption of pork tongue in aspic (langue de porc en gelee).

Outbreaks from raw vegetables include a Canadian coleslaw outbreak following storage of cabbage overwinter. Several log increases of the organism in lettuce held between 5-22°C for 14 days were noted.

French research showed that storing dairy products, smoked ham and minced beef at 8°C lead to a decrease of between 50-80% in the time needed for bacterial growth compared with growth at 4°C.

Research (New Zealand) suggests that low pH of meat is important in controlling growth of *Listeria* in raw meat and products and cottage cheese remains unaffected probably because of its low pH according to a USFDA report in 1996.

An outbreak in the USA was reported in 1997 due to consumption of factory-produced chocolate milk.

Lister, Joseph (1827-1912) Professor of Surgery at the University of Glasgow around 1860 who developed the use of carbolic acid (phenol) as an antiseptic in operations. It resulted in a dramatic reduction in post-operation infections.

Listeriosis The disease caused by the bacterium *Listeria monocytogenes*.

Liver fluke (*Distoma lanceolatum/hepaticum*) Trematodes affecting the bile ducts of pigs, sheep and cattle. They are similar in size and shape to flattened wood lice and their presence causes bile ducts to enlarge, giving the so-called 'pipy' liver. Badly affected livers are unfit.

138 Load line

Load line A marking found on display refrigerator and freezer cabinets indicating maximum recommended capacity. If the level is exceeded the temperature of the food at the top may be above a safe level. *See:* Danger zone.

Local Authority Administrative areas in Great Britain including District, Borough and City councils which deal with various matters including environmental health. Officers including EHOs are appointed by the Local Authority.

Lockers In food businesses, storage for outdoor clothing must be provided. If storage is in a food room, a locker or cupboard is required.

Log phase *See:* Bacterial growth curve.

Lovibond comparator A device using coloured discs, graduated in intensity, which may be compared with the colour of an experimental test sample. The technique is widely used for example in the analysis of milk (resazurin test) and water (chlorination and pH).

Low-acid food Foods over pH 5.0, including meats, fish and many vegetables. *See:* Acid foods (classification of), Canning.

Lupin seeds Seeds of *Lupinus angustifolius* cause an allergic reaction in some people due to the presence of an alkaloid. Lupin seeds are made into flour, fermented or used whole.

Lux A measure of illumination, one lumen per square metre. The lumen is a measure of light received or emitted.

MacConkey agar An enriched agar medium on which coliforms readily grow. It can be used for the isolation of coliforms from water samples.
See: Presumptive water (coliform) test.

MacConkey broth An enriched and differential broth medium (containing lactose and a pH indicator) used to demonstrate the presence of coliform bacteria in water.
See: Presumptive water (coliform) test.

Made-up dishes These contain several ingredients and are thus liable to a greater risk of contamination both from the ingredients and handling. An example is a meat or fish pie. Proper temperature storage, together with thorough cooking are essential.

MAFF (Ministry of Agriculture, Fisheries and Food) One of two Government Ministries in Britain involved in food matters. *See:* Department of Health.

Maggot Larva of insects such as flies.

Maize weevil (*Sitophilus zea-mais*) Common tropical pests often imported with maize (corn).

Malachite Green An anti-fungal agent used in trout farming but has safety questions including possible carcinogenicity.

Malic acid An organic acid present in apples, and also manufactured. It is used to lower the pH of some canned soups.

Malta fever Another name for the disease brucellosis. *See: Brucella abortus.*

Margarine A high-fat product similar to butter made with various oils and fats. It is a low-risk food, but it is perishable, so subject to spoilage. Refrigerated storage is recommended.

Mastitis Inflamed udder in cows, often affecting milk quality. It is the result of a bacterial infection.

Mayonnaise Mayonnaise made with raw egg should not be made or consumed. There is a proven risk of salmonella food poisoning, caused by *Salmonella enteritidis* phage type 4. Commercially produced mayonnaise, made with pasteurised egg, is available.

MBM Mammalian meat and bonemeal.

Meals-on-wheels A system of delivering hot meals by road in vans equipped with heated containers. Temperature control is the main problem since there may be some hours between loading and delivery.

Mealworm Larva of the mealworm beetle (*Tenebrio molitor*).

Mean generation time The time taken for a population of bacterial cells to go through its life cycle, i.e. to double in numbers. Such times are usually short for prokaryotic cells, compared to eukaryotics, and for smaller cells compared to larger cells. (Bacteria are small prokaryotic cells.) For most bacteria the mean generation time (also known as doubling time) is from one to three hours, but some have been shown to double in number in as little as ten minutes. Reproduction is by binary fission.

Measles
1. A notifiable viral disease of humans.
2. A term used in the meat trade to describe the cysts (bladderworms/cysticerci) of the tapeworms affecting pigs and cattle.
See: Beef tapeworm, Pork tapeworm.

Measly beef/pork Meat affected with the cysts of tapeworms. *See:* Beef tapeworm, Pork tapeworm.

Meat
- A high-risk food when cooked due to its high protein content.
- Both raw and cooked meats should be stored in a refrigerator.
- Raw meat (nor anything with which it has been in contact) should not be allowed to come into contact with cooked foods, or other foods eaten raw.
- If possible raw meat should be kept in a separate refrigerator to avoid cross-contamination.
- Raw meat or poultry must never be stored above other foods to avoid drip contamination.
- The surface of a piece of raw meat from a healthy animal may be contaminated with micro-organisms introduced during slaughter or butchery.
- The inside of a piece of meat will normally have no harmful bacteria.
- Apart from the risk of tapeworm, rare-cooked meat such as steak is safe as long as the temperature has reached a level sufficient to kill any surface organisms.
- Minced meat is likely to contain bacteria all the way through and must be thoroughly cooked

See: Beefburgers, Growth requirements (bacterial), Pennington Report, Poultry.

Meat products
- Items containing meat such as pies, pasties, sausages, rissoles and many others.
- These are more likely to cause hygiene problems than meat itself since they contain multiple ingredients which are handled considerably during preparation.
- Contamination may be introduced and spread throughout the product.
- They should be stored under refrigeration and thorough cooking is essential.

See: Centre temperature, stock rotation.

Mercury **141**

Meat Inspector An authorised officer, with a professional qualification, who inspects all food animals before, during and after slaughter to ensure that they are fit for human consumption. In some countries including parts of Europe, meat inspection is performed or supervised by veterinary surgeons.

Meat thermometers A device used for measuring the centre temperature of meat during cooking. The use of such is the only reliable way to ensure that the centre has reached a sufficiently high temperature (minimum 70°C) to ensure that bacterial cells (other than spores) have been destroyed. Washing and disinfecting of the probe are essential after use, to prevent cross contamination. *See:* Thermometers.

Mechanical dish washing *See:* Two-sink system.

Mediterranean flour moth *(Anagasta kuhniella)* An insect pest of stored cereals affecting milled cereals, nuts and many other foods including dried fruits.

Medical questionnaire A pre-employment document requiring information from prospective food handlers as to any relevant medical condition such as food poisoning or infectious diseases affecting themselves, family or other personal contacts.

Medical screening Faecal samples may be required from food handlers who are suspected of having certain infectious conditions such as food poisoning.
See: Exclusion of food handlers.

Melons A large and unusual outbreak of food poisoning (caused by the bacterium *Salmonella chester*) occurred in the USA in 1991 due to melons contaminated on their surface rind.

Meningitis A serious disease, with inflammation of the membranes (meninges) of the central nervous system (brain and spinal cord). It is one of a number of possible complications for sufferers of listeriosis, particularly in new-born children.

Mercury
- A metal capable of entering the food chain and causing serious effects such as brain damage and foetal deformities in humans.
- Fish, by eating plankton, may take up mercury from industrial waste pollution, this being the cause of the serious outbreak of mercury poisoning in Minamata Bay, Japan (1980s). Cats died after eating contaminated fish; chickens' eggs were found to contain the metal (through feeding the chickens with scraps which included fish) and human breast milk was also found to be contaminated.

Mesophile A term used to describe those micro-organisms that have a preferred midrange temperature for growth of 20 to 45°C. It includes most of the common spoilage and disease-causing organisms.

Mesosome A membranous organelle in some bacteria, formed by infolding of the cell membrane. It is thought to be the site of production of adenosine triphosphate (ATP), which is the useable form of energy in cells.

Metal detectors Devices employed in food factories to detect physical contamination from metal fragments, parts of machines etc. First aid plasters may have an internal metal strip (similar to that used in bank notes) to aid their detection.

Metals Several toxic metals, including aluminium, antimony, cadmium, copper, iron, lead, mercury and zinc have all been known to cause food poisoning.

Certain species of fish such as plaice and rays have up to four times higher natural levels of lead and cadmium; 1mg/kg for lead and 0.1 mg/kg for cadmium is thought to be acceptable. Lead levels in drinking water should be a maximum of 10ug/litre and generally less than 1mg/kg in foodstuffs with very low levels in infant foods. The WHO level for mercury is set very low at 0.005 mg/kg bw/week.

Long term exposure to cadmium leads to kidney failure and demineralisaton of bone. The tolerable weekly intake is 60-240 ug/day. The main food sources are vegetables and cereals which have a suggested EU safe limit of 0.1 mg/kg. The level of cadmium and other metallic residues in sewage sludge used agriculturally is also limited by UK Government advice. *See:* Individual entries.

Methyl bromide An insecticidal gas toxic to the human nervous system.

Methylene blue test One of a number of indirect methods used for the estimation of bacterial numbers in, for example, milk, cream and ice-cream. Methylene blue is blue in the presence of oxygen and colourless in its absence. This test shows how quickly any bacteria present in the milk use up the oxygen; the faster the dye loses its colour, the faster the oxygen is used up, and the more bacteria are presumed to be present in the milk.

Mice
- One of a number of rodent pests which live in or invade buildings.
- The house mouse (*Mus domesticus*) is the most common and is attracted to all foods and water.

- It does not move far from its nesting site to feed.
- A single breeding pair under good conditions may produce 2 000 offspring within a year.
- Mice may carry pathogens on their bodies, and excrete them in their urine and droppings.
- They also spoil food with droppings and spillages.
- Other varieties such as field mice occasionally enter food premises.

See: Pests, Proofing of buildings, Rats.

Microaerophile A micro-organism that prefers a much lower oxygen concentration (2 to 10%) for respiration compared to normal atmospheric concentration (20%). See: Campylobacter.

Microban One of a number of trade names (others include Triclosan used in food conveyor belts and Irgasan used in toiletries and creams) given to the antibacterial substance 5-chloro-2-(2,4-dichlorophenoxy)-phenol. Originally used in medicine, it is now incorporated into footwear, chopping boards, containers, textiles and other items used in the food industry. A log reduction of bacterial numbers in 1-2 hours is claimed.

Microbicide See: Germicide.

Microbiology The branch of biology which deals with the study of micro-organisms.

Microbistat A general term for an agent which is able to stop or inhibit the growth of micro-organisms, but does not necessarily kill them. Specific agents are called bacteriostats, fungistats, virustats.

Micrococcus
- A group of bacteria widespread in nature, found in soil, dust and fresh water.
- They are often found on inadequately cleaned utensils and equipment.
- They are not pathogenic, but they are responsible for spoilage of various foods.
- They are aerobic organisms, some are psychrotrophic (growing well at under 10°C), and are halophilic (favour an environment with a high salt concentration).
- This latter property means that they can cause spoilage of processed meats, such as ham and bacon, as well as red meat stored at 10 to 15°C.
- One type *(Micrococcus varians)* is common in milk, dairy products and animal carcasses, as well as in dust and soil. It is thermoduric, and so can survive pasteurisation, and so is able to cause spoilage of milk.

- Some are pigmented (yellow, orange or red), and discolour the surface of foods on which they grow. For example, *Micrococcus luteus* produces yellow discoloration on meat.

Microcystin A common toxin from blue-green algae.

Microwave ovens A method of cooking which offers the advantage of greater speed in some cases. In terms of food hygiene there is nothing magical about microwaves; they do not kill bacteria directly but are merely a means of heating food. Many problems with microwave ovens are the result of not following the manufacturers' instructions regarding power and times.

- Microwaves are high frequency radiations, produced by a magnetron, which causes food molecules to vibrate generating heat.
- Microwaves penetrate up to 40 mm in food and heating may be very fast, although some foods heat up more quickly than others.
- Water absorbs microwave energy faster than ice and this may cause localised cold spots in foods.
- Heat from microwave cooking, if sufficient, will kill micro-organisms but spores and toxins are likely to remain unaffected.
- Commercial microwave equipment is normally of heavier duty than its domestic equivalent.
- A major use of microwaves is in the reheating of pre-cooked food; the standing time allowed for in some recipes is important so that the food is heated to a safe temperature.
- Microwave defrosting can be very quick but the correct setting and time must be strictly followed.
- Microwave disinfection may be effective on wooden chopping boards which may reach a surface temperature of 95°C after 3-4 minutes at high power but not on plastics which reach only 40°C. The technique depends on a combination of factors including microwave power, board size, exposure time and initial bacterial load.

See: Cling film, Cold spots, Defrosting, Runaway heating.

Mildew A type of fungus which is similar to a mould. There are two types:
1. Downy mildews, so called since they form a downy growth on the surface of the host. Many are severe plant pathogens, many are saprophytes or weak parasites. They are able to form spores to carry them over unfavourable conditions. They require a moist habitat and grow best in rainy or humid weather. They are very common fungal infections frequently found on grapes, beans, melons, peas and potatoes.

See: Phytopthora infestans.

2. Powdery mildews, so called due to the powdery appearance of the surface of the leaves infected. All are obligate plant parasites. They grow on leaves, flowers and fruits of apple, grape, cherry and many other plants. In the early stages of infection, the mycelium looks like a delicate cobweb.

Milk
- Milk and most milk products are protein foods and readily support the growth of pathogens.
- They are considered to be high-risk foods, exceptions being hard cheeses and acid products (pH less than 4.5).
- Raw milk is known to be likely to contain a variety of pathogens, so it is subjected to a number of forms of heat treatment, including pasteurisation, sterilisation and UHT.
- Milk and its products must be subjected to strict temperature control, either refrigerated or kept hot as appropriate.
- Brucellosis, food poisoning and tuberculosis amongst others have all been traced to milk.
- Returnable milk bottles used as containers for other substances have caused problems (creosote, paint and paraffin have been noted) as have bottles containing the eggs of flies.
- Outbreaks of campylobacteriosis have been attributed to birds pecking through foil tops of milk bottles.

Streptococcus zooepidemicus invasive infections, with a high fatality rate, have been noted in England during the period 1984-1994 from the consumption of raw milk. The reservoir of this organism is farm animals, especially horses.
See: Appendix : Food Law, Dehydration, Individual product entries (Butter, Cheese, Yoghurt etc).

Milk and Dairies Law In many countries there is a considerable amount of law covering production, composition, distribution, heat treatment and labelling of milk and many of its products including other related foods such as eggs. *See:* Appendix: Food Law.

Milkstone A hard phosphate-based deposit occurring in the pipe work and heat exchangers of milk processing plant. It may harbour bacteria and is removed by an acid cleaning solution *See:* CIP.

Milky hake A condition of hake, caused by a protozoan (*Chloromyscium thyristes*) which causes a softening of the flesh. Affected fish are aesthetically unfit for human consumption.

Minced meat A meat product with a high risk of contamination throughout, since surface organisms on the original larger pieces of meat are spread throughout the product, including the centre. Items containing minced meat, such as beef burgers, need to be cooked to a centre temperature of over 70°C to ensure their safety.
See: Meat, Meat products.

'Minded-to' notice (UK Law) A document that is sent to the proprietor of a food business stating that unless a food safety problem is resolved by discussion within 14 days, an improvement notice will be served. It is a 'last chance' strategy.

Mineral water, bottled Commonly contaminated with *Pseudomonas aeruginosa*, a non-pathogenic organism with contamination by moulds reported world-wide. The highest bacterial counts are usually from coloured containers which may filter out UV light. Other contaminants including benzene have also been reported.

Mist netting Very fine mesh used by licensed pest control operators to trap birds. Protected species are released and others (pests) killed.

Mites (*Acarina*) Many species are known, some of which affect food. All are very small (around 0.5 mm in length), and tend to be pale-coloured often appearing pearly-white under the microscope. The flour mite (*Acarina siro*) is most common; it also affects other foods and causes a sour and 'minty' taint. *See:* Cheese mite (*Tyrophagus casei*)

Mollusc Shellfish such as cockle, clam, scallop, oyster etc. having soft bodies usually encased in hard shells. All are high-risk foods and have been known to be responsible for outbreaks of food poisoning. Strict temperature control is essential.

Monilia A mould responsible for food spoilage. It appears as a pink growth on bread, causes brown rot of apples and it can spoil cereals and flour.
Note: The organism has also been described under the genus *Neurospora*.

Moths
- Many species of these insects attack food, mainly stored products including flour, nuts and dried fruit.
- Adults and larvae may eat and contaminate food.

- Larvae also spin dense threads of webbing which causes food spoilage and have been known to interfere with the action of milling machinery.
- Large infestations may result in grain heating (from the body heat of the insects) which in turn causes convection currents resulting in moisture movement and hence mould growth in damp regions.
- Control of moths rests initially on good housekeeping, proper storage and stock rotation.
- Fumigation of infested goods is also possible while insecticide-impregnated strips may control flying adults to some degree; badly affected foods are unfit for human consumption.

Motility of bacteria The vast majority of bacteria are unable to move around on their own. They rely on air, water, people, animals, food etc. to carry them from one place to another. Some forms however possess flagella, which enables those which live in a watery environment to move around within their immediate surroundings.

Moulds
- A group of fungi, most of which are aerobic (require oxygen).
- They consist of a network of fine threadlike filaments called hyphae, which collectively form a massed growth called a mycelium.
- They often appear as white cottony growths, e.g. on fruits, grains and vegetables.
- The coloured spores of mature moulds are responsible for the characteristic colours which become apparent.
- They obtain their food by absorbing solutions of organic material from their environment.
- They reproduce very quickly, by the production and release of spores, particularly under warm, moist conditions.
- Commonly responsible for the spoilage of a wide variety of foods, they are the most common cause of spoilage of bread and most bakery products.
- Some species are known to produce toxins, known as mycotoxins.

See: Aflatoxin.

Mucor A white filamentous mould affecting food, causing spoilage, the spores of which are commonly found in household dust.

Mucous membranes Membranes which line body cavities, such as the entire respiratory system, including the mouth and nasal passages, the urinary, reproductive, and digestive tracts. They secrete a viscous (thick) fluid called mucus, which helps prevent the surfaces from drying out. *See: Staphylococcus aureus.*

Mushrooms Natural toxins produced by some mushrooms and toadstools (German 'Todesstuhl', death's stool) cause food poisoning. The toxins are not destroyed by cooking, canning, freezing or processing. Recognising the toxic varieties is an expert task. Symptoms are extremely variable, depending on the toxin consumed and include organ failure, profuse sweating, coma, convulsions, hallucinations, excitement, depression, nausea, vomiting, abdominal cramping, diarrhoea and death. As an example of the possible outcome of eating a poisonous species, the Death Cap *(Amanita phalloides)* mushroom produces a toxin (Amatoxin) causing liver, kidney and heart damage with death often within a few days.

If edible mushrooms are eaten raw they may be washed or peeled to remove surface contamination.

Mussels *See:* Shellfish.

Mutualism A kind of symbiosis where both organisms benefit. An example is the bacterium *E. coli* in the gut of humans. It produces vitamin K and some B vitamins, which are absorbed and used by the human body. The bacterium receives shelter and obtains all its necessary nutrients from its immediate surroundings. Many of the resident bacteria in the large intestine demonstrate this kind of relationship. Such organisms may become pathogenic when, for example following injury to the intestine, large numbers of *E. coli* may pass through the peritoneum (a membrane which lines the abdominal cavity), into the peritoneal cavity. Severe peritonitis (inflammation of the peritoneum) may occur, which can be fatal.

Mycelium The entangled cottony mass of hyphae, which forms the basic structure of the fungi. It is visible to the naked eye. In some forms it makes an organised structure, e.g. the stalk of a mushroom.

Mycobacterium bovis A Gram-positive bacterium, a pathogen mainly of cattle and other animals. It causes bovine tuberculosis, which can be transmitted to humans by contaminated milk or food. Pasteurisation and testing of dairy herds for tuberculosis has greatly reduced the incidence of this disease in humans.

Mycobacterium tuberculosis A Gram-positive pathogenic bacterium which causes the infectious disease tuberculosis, mainly in humans. The organism is resistant to drying and chemical agents and it can survive for six to eight months outside the body. It is one of the most common communicable diseases in the world. Transmission is usually via inhalation, but it can be food-borne (for example in milk), transmitted through the gastrointestinal tract or by direct contact with infected material.

Mycology The study of fungi.

Mycotoxins Toxins produced by some fungi. *See:* Aflatoxin.

Myristicin A toxin and hallucinogenic substance found at low levels in nutmeg.

Mussel *See:* Shellfish.

Myxomatosis A disease of rabbits affecting eyes and lungs. It is not known to affect humans, but affected carcasses are unfit.

Nail brush May be provided for personal washing facilities. Plastic brushes with nylon bristles are recommended so that they can be disinfected. Since they are a possible vehicle of contamination they should be cleaned and disinfected frequently. At the end of each day they should be stored dry, not in disinfectant solutions. *See:* Hand washing.

Nails The nails of food handlers should be kept short and clean. Nail varnish should not be worn since it may chip off and contaminate food. Biting the nails is potentially hazardous since it may spread staphylococci from the mouth to the fingers, and ultimately to food. *See: Staphylococcus aureus.*

NAMAS (National Measurement Accreditation Service) Certain laboratories, including those analysing foods, may be accredited as to their quality assurance and thus use the term NAMAS in describing themselves. Facilities and techniques will be at high level with wide-ranging, sophisticated and specific analysis methods being used. There is an official list of accredited food control laboratories held by MAFF.

Nanophyetus **species** The North American and Russian flukes (trematodes) or parasitic flatworms causing bowel disturbances, abdominal pain and nausea. The disease is endemic in Russia from the consumption of raw or underprocessed freshwater fish and occasionally salmon.

Narcotising (effect) Substances in a bait, such as alpha chloralose, have been used to render birds unconscious. The method is used to control feral pigeons and starlings; any protected species are released whereas the unwanted birds are killed. It has been used in city areas and around airfields with limited success and mixed public reaction. Alpha chloralose may prove fatal to small animals such as mice, particularly at low temperatures. It achieves its narcotising effect by inducing a type of hypothermia.

National Health Service (Amendment) Act 1986 This piece of UK legislation removed Crown Immunity from NHS premises in respect of food and safety. Food production in hospitals etc. is subject to food hygiene law.

Nature, substance or quality Under the UK Food Safety Act 1990 it is an offence to sell food which prejudices the purchaser by being either inferior, harmful or defective in some other way. The legal term 'prejudice' implies that the person has suffered in some way.

'**Nature**' is applied to food which is different to that requested, such as supplying margarine instead of butter.

'**Substance**' applies if, for example, compositional standards are not met or if foreign bodies are contained in food.

'**Quality**' applies, for example, if food has deteriorated.

Prosecutions are taken by local authorities and it has sometimes happened that cases were lost because the wrong term was used.

Nausea A feeling of sickness, often preceding vomiting.

Nematodes Small worms inhabiting the respiratory systems of food animals. *See: Ascarides, Strongylus* species.

Neurotoxic shellfish poisoning (NSP) Caused by the dinoflagellate *Ptychodiscus brevis* which in North America affects clams, oysters and other shellfish. The disease causes numbness in the mouth and general symptoms of food poisoning and is not normally serious or prolonged. (The same organism is responsible for the 'red tides' of Florida.) *See:* Algae, Paralytic shellfish poisoning.

Neurotoxin A toxin (poisonous substance) affecting the nervous system, often seriously. Several organisms produce such toxins. They are also a feature of some types of food poisoning from shellfish, including 'paralytic shellfish poisoning'. They are usually ingested as pre-formed toxins. Examples include staphylococcal enterotoxin, *Clostridium botulinum* toxin, ciguatoxin (ciguatera) from dinoflagellates, and tetrodotoxin from puffer fish. An outbreak of food poisoning affecting over 100 people with 31 deaths was reported near Bombay in 1996 in persons eating vegetable curry left overnight at ambient temperature. The owner of the cafe and the cook both died. Symptoms suggested either botulism or alkaloids from native plants were responsible.

Nisin A controlled antibiotic used as a preservative in cheese and canned foods.

Nitrate (Saltpetre)

1. Both potassium and sodium nitrates are used in cured products such as bacon. Both are converted by a reduction reaction to nitrites by enzymes and micro-organisms during the process. Nitrates are also used as preservatives in cheese and pizzas.
2. Used as a fertiliser in agriculture. Excess nitrate may enter the water cycle and cause illness. The EC suggested limit for lettuce and spinach of 2 500 - 4 500 mg/kg depending on the time of year of the harvest.
3. A case of nitrate poisoning whose rapid symptoms included dizziness and greying of the skin, occurred in Manchester, England in 1996 due to the use of high levels of sodium nitrate and nitrite in Jewish sausages. Large intakes of nitrate interfere with the oxygen-carrying capacity of the blood. *See:* Nitrite, Nitrosamine.

Nitrite The characteristic pink colour of cured meats is due in part to a chemical reaction between nitrite and myoglobin, producing the substance nitrosomyoglobin. Potassium and sodium nitrite act as preservatives and are known to slow the growth of the bacterium *Clostridium botulinum*. *See:* Nitrate, Nitrosamine.

Nitrogen (liquid) *See:* Cryogenic freezing.

Nitrosamines Reactions between protein and nitrite can produce small quantities of these substances, which have been shown by some researchers to be carcinogenic.

Non-ionic detergents Uncharged molecules used in low-foam preparations and some special cleaning agents. *See:* Detergents.

Normal flora A term used to describe a micro-organism that is normally to be found in or on an animal (such as on the skin or in the gastrointestinal tract) without causing disease.
(The term 'flora' is a legacy of the original misclassification of the bacteria as plants.)

Norwalk virus (Norwalk agent) A food-borne virus-like particle causing a mild form of gastroenteritis. All age groups who ingest the virus and who have not, within the previous 2 years, had an infection with the same (or related strain) of virus are susceptible to infection. Around 180 000 cases occur annually in the US; fatalities are rare. The incubation period is normally 1 to 2 days, with the illness lasting from 1 to 3 days. The symptoms typically include nausea, vomiting, abdominal cramps and diarrhoea. Transmission is by the faecal-oral route, and water is the most common source of outbreaks. Shellfish and salad ingredients are the foods most often implicated in outbreaks. Foods associated are raw or insufficiently cooked shellfish (clams and oysters) e.g. in the US (Louisiana) in 1992, 250 cases and in 1993, 70 cases, all associated with the consumption of raw oysters. Foods other than shellfish are usually contaminated by food handlers. *See:* Food-borne disease, Viruses.

Notices (informal, 'minded to', improvement and emergency prohibition)

1. The so-called **'informal notice'** is a letter sent after an inspection by an authorised person (e.g. an EHO) indicating any matters which need attention and stating that a re-inspection will take place after a specified period. Such a letter has no legal backing but is used as a low-key method of getting food premises up to standard. It is not used if the situation is serious.

2. An **improvement notice** is a legal document served to the proprietor of a food business following an inspection by an authorised person. It states what is wrong, what must be done to put matters right and gives time (not less than 14 days) for any work to be done. There is a right of appeal which must be stated on the notice. If the notice is not complied with then a prosecution can result. Before an improvement notice is served the local authority must inform the person running the food business of its intention to serve this notice. This is the so-called **'minded to'** notice which invites a discussion about the problem within a specified time.

3. The **emergency prohibition notice** is issued when a serious health risk exists and may be used to close food premises immediately. It must be confirmed within three days by a court issuing an emergency prohibition order otherwise compensation may be claimed.

See: Prohibition notice/order.

Notifiable disease In Britain, the occurrence of a number of dangerous diseases must be notified to the Medical Officer of Environmental Health so that appropriate control measures may be taken to limit their spread.

Examples involving food include anthrax, cholera, diphtheria, food poisoning, hepatitis, tuberculosis and typhoid fever.

There are many others such as malaria and smallpox which are spread by other means.

Notification of diseases in food handlers Food handlers who are diagnosed as suffering from
- food poisoning
- typhoid fever
- paratyphoid fever
- dysentery
- other contagious illnesses

must be reported to the local authority and may be excluded from food-related work. Food handlers must themselves report any suspected food poisoning to their manager or supervisor who must in turn inform the local authority. *See:* Exclusion of food handlers.

Nuclear region (zone/body) One of a number of names (also nucleoid, nucleophore) for the bacterial equivalent of the nucleus of a eukaryotic cell. Bacterial cells are prokaryotic and so lack a true nucleus.

Nucleoid/Nucleophore *See:* Nuclear region.

Nutrient agar A nutrient broth solidified by the addition of agar. *See:* Agar-agar.

Nutrient broth A liquid culture medium used extensively in laboratories for bacteriological work. It is a complex medium made of meat extracts.

Obligate The word means compulsory/no choice. The term is most often used to describe an organism's gaseous requirements.
1. Obligate aerobe: an organism that must have free oxygen present in order to live.
2. Obligate anaerobe: an organism that cannot live in the presence of free oxygen.

Obligate intracellular parasite A parasite that can only actively grow and reproduce inside a living host cell of another species. Such organisms can survive for variable periods of time outside the host cell. *See:* Viruses.

Ochratoxin A (OA) Produced by *Aspergillus* and *Penicillium* moulds. It may be carcinogenic and has been associated with kidney damage and as such a very low safe limit of 100 ng/kg body weight intake is suggested. Cereals and coffee are mainly affected but meat may also become contaminated via feedstuffs.

Offal Internal organs such as liver and kidney of food animals. These must be treated in the same way as meat since they are high-risk foods.

Oils (cooking)
- These deteriorate during use, especially if overheated, giving rise to off-flavours in food.
- The substance acrolein, having a bitter taste and unpleasant smell, is released by very hot oils.
- Cooking temperatures in the range of 160-180°C are used, for example in deep fryers, so there is a risk that the surface of large food items will be cooked while the centre temperature remains too low to destroy pathogens.
- Oils are also subject to rancidity.
- Oils should be changed regularly, owing to the production of molecules which are suspected of being carcinogenic.

Onset period The time between consumption of contaminated food and the appearance of the first signs or symptoms of illness. This term is often used with reference to ingestion of preformed toxins. *See:* Incubation period.

Ootheca The name given to the egg case of the cockroach.

Open food Unwrapped or unpackaged food, which should be covered during delivery, storage and service to protect it from contamination.

Open wound Any uncovered area of damaged or broken skin such as a spot, pimple, boil, burn, cut, graze or other skin lesion. The covering of such lesions with a suitable waterproof dressing desirable since they provide excellent conditions for the growth of bacteria which may otherwise escape and contaminate food.

Opportunist pathogen A generally harmless organism in its normal habitat. It can become pathogenic in a host who is seriously injured, weakened or ill, or who is under treatment with broad spectrum antibiotics or immunosuppressant drugs. A person's normal flora (bacteria) can become opportunist pathogens under the above conditions.

Optimum pH The pH at which a species of organism grows best. It is not necessarily the maximum pH for growth. As an example, most salmonellas grow best at around pH 7 but will also grow at higher or lower values. *Salmonella* species have been reported in fruit juice at less than pH 4.5. *See:* Growth requirements (bacterial/fungal).

Optimum temperature The temperature at which a species of organism grows best. It is not necessarily the maximum temperature for growth. Most human pathogens grow best at 37°C, but the range of temperatures for growth may be between 8-63°C. These figures are reflected in the Food Safety (Temperature Control) Regs 1995. *Listeria monocytogenes* is known to multiply at even lower temperatures. *See:* Growth requirements (bacterial/fungal).

Organoleptic assessment
- The use of the senses of taste, smell, sight and texture to judge the quality of foods.
- Hearing is occasionally used, as in the characteristically dull sound produced by shaking a bag of unfit shellfish.
- Commercially, this is carried out by trained taste panels who are known to achieve a high degree of reliability.
- Some individuals have remarkable abilities to detect the presence of chemicals such as pesticides in foods, and have been employed in the food industry in this capacity.

Oriental cockroach (*Blatta orientalis*) The most common species of cockroach in Britain, originally being a tropical insect. It is a dark brown insect up to 30 mm in

Outdoor catering 155

length with antennae of similar length. Females lay around sixteen eggs in a brownish capsule (ootheca) up to 15 mm long, the eggs not hatching until external conditions are suitable. *See:* Cockroaches.

Osmosis The diffusion of water from a region of high concentration (i.e. a weak solution) to a region of comparatively low concentration (i.e. a stronger solution), through a differentially permeable membrane. The preservation of foods by the use of salt and sugar utilise this phenomenon. *See:* Food preservation.

Outbreak of food poisoning Two or more cases, a case being any single person suffering from the condition. Outbreaks occur anywhere food is prepared including domestic and commercial premises, institutions and occasional venues such as outside catering. The most common reason for outbreaks in general is lack of temperature control, often made worse by preparing food too far in advance. *See:* Food poisoning.

Outdoor catering The provision of food, often for large numbers of people, in a situation often not purpose-designed, poses many food hygiene problems. Typical events include
- music concerts
- weddings
- barbecues
- sports events
- country fairs
- fetes.

Precautions include
- planning and consultations between organisers and environmental health professionals before the event to identify problems and their solutions
- provision of suitable storage facilities including refrigeration
- hygienic delivery of foods and equipment
- prevention of cross-contamination
- temperature control of high-risk foods
- personal hygiene facilities
- suitable food hygiene training for staff
- services such as water supply
- refuse disposal.

Temporary facilities should not be allowed to become permanent. In general the construction and use of equipment is the same as that for any other food business, with exceptions mainly applying to premises including such items as the short-term use of wooden duck boards as a floor surface in tents.

Overlap A measurement of end seams in canning.

Oysters Since these may be eaten raw they are a frequent cause of food poisoning from various organisms including species of *Aeromonas, Salmonella, Shigella*, algae (DSP, NSP, PSP) and many others. *See:* Shellfish.

Oxygen requirements (of micro-organisms) *See:* Aerobes, Anaerobes, Facultative, Growth requirements (bacterial/fungal).

Ozone A gas which has been reported to double the storage time of loosely packed small, fresh fruits, such as strawberries, raspberries and grapes. It is used at concentrations of 2 to 3 ppm.

Packaging Materials such as cardboard boxes which may have been contaminated should be removed before foods are placed into storage. Physical contamination from packaging materials including binding and staples is possible so removal should be away from food. *See:* Freezer burn, Wrapping materials.

Paint Paint is an acceptable surface for certain areas of food rooms including walls, ceilings and doors etc. If food-quality washable paint is properly applied it is non-absorbent and may be easily cleaned. However, the finish may be short-lived and flaking can become a problem, which may result in physical contamination of food.

Paragonimus westermani A human lung fluke affecting persons eating raw or under-cooked crabs.

Paralytic shellfish poisoning (PSP) Mussels and other bivalves feeding on poisonous organisms (the dinoflagellates, a type of alga, found in plankton) sometimes become contaminated with toxins (saxitoxin) which affects the human nervous system (hence called neurotoxins). The problem is most likely during warm weather when planktons 'bloom' (as a result of rapid growth) and cause a visible 'red tide'.

Cooking may not destroy the toxins which produce an almost immediate numbing of the mouth and pharynx (throat) with a tingling sensation spreading to the upper body and arms within six hours. Other symptoms include dizziness, headache, thirst and loss of motor co-ordination. The condition is often fatal, death being due to paralysis of the respiratory system. Several species of alga, *Alexandrium tamarense, Gonyaulax catanella* (North America and Japan), *G. tamarensis* (USA and Europe) and *Pyrodinium bahamense* (South America and SE Asia) have been identified as causal agents.

Parasite An organism that lives in or on a living host. It obtains nutrients and shelter from the host and so the host is damaged. Such organisms therefore cause harm to the host, resulting in disease.

Parasitism A form of symbiosis in which one species (the parasite) benefits and the other (the host) is harmed.

Paratyphoid fever (enteric fever)
- Caused by *Salmonella paratyphi* A,B and C.
- Reservoir of infection is usually the gastrointestinal tract of humans, both cases and carriers.
- Transmisson is mainly food-borne from consumption of food contaminated with faeces by a human case (sufferer) and occasionally from a symptomless excreter.
- Water contaminated with sewege has also been found to be responsible, both through drinking and through washing fruit and vegetables.
- Person to person spread has occurred in poor hygiene conditions, especially where overcrowding occurs.
- Outbreaks often occur following natural disasters such as floods and earthquakes.
- Efficient sanitary control by sewage removal and treatment and water purification are the best control measures.
- Milk-borne outbreaks have occurred.
- Paratyphoid fever is less severe than typhoid fever and is rarely fatal.
- Symptoms begin with chills and resemble those of normal salmonellosis.
- Incubation period is from one to three weeks.

See: Food-borne disease, Milk, Typhoid fever.

Parev ice Kosher ice-cream, containing no milk fat but at least 10% other fat.

Pasteur, Louis (1822-1895) French chemist, professor at Strasbourg and later Lille, whose work with fermentation showed that spoilage organisms could be destroyed by heat. In 1877 he produced revolutionary evidence proving that the disease anthrax was caused by micro-organisms and so helped lay some of the foundations for modern microbiology and medicine. *See:* Koch, Pasteurisation.

Pasteurisation Technique named after Louis Pasteur which uses heat to destroy micro-organisms in a product, so extending its shelf-life. The process is not severe, for example milk is heated to 72°C for 15 seconds (80°C for ice-cream). This is sufficient to kill pathogens but some spoilage organisms survive as do toxins and spores. *See:* HTST, Ice-cream, Liquid egg, Thermoduric, Thermophilic, Sterilisation.

Pastry products   Pies, pasties, quiches and similar items which contain high-risk foods such as meat, egg or cheese must be kept refrigerated to limit the growth of pathogens and moulds. Some of these products have a very short shelf-life of only a few days. *See:* Appendix: Food Law, Temperature control, Use-by date.

Pathogen   A micro-organism capable of causing disease. Pathogenicity is dependent on two main factors:
1. the ability to produce potent toxins
2. the aggressiveness (invasiveness) of the agent.
A successful pathogen need not possess both properties.

Patulin   A possibly mutagenic mycotoxin, produced by *Penicillium expansum* and other fungi, associated with brown rot in apples and mould growth on peaches, pears and vegetables. Damaged foods are most at risk. A suggested safe level is 50ug/kg.

Peanuts
- Susceptible persons may have a severe allergic reaction to peanuts producing anaphylactic shock. Fatalities have occurred within minutes of exposure due to swelling of the throat and blocking of the airway. Other symptoms include vomiting and abdominal pain after smelling, eating or touching peanuts.
- Often preceded by eczema and egg allergy in young children. Increased consumption of peanuts during pregnancy and lactation may be linked with infant allergy.
- Mandelonas (almond flavoured peanut product) used as almonds in Canada were reported in one outbreak. Food manufacturers and restaurants now commonly label dishes containing peanuts.
- Peanut allergy may be so severe that merely smelling substances such as peanut butter may provoke a reaction as may the further use of oil used to cook peanut products such as nutburgers. *See*: Aflatoxin.

Pediococcus A group of Gram-positive bacteria which have a number of important growth characteristics. They
- are microaerophilic
- grow in the temperature range 7 to 45°C

- are slightly halophilic
- produce lactic acid as a result of fermentation.

They can cause spoilage of food due to their ability to grow at low temperatures and their ability to ferment sugars can ruin brined vegetables and beers. Some members (such as *Pediococcus cerevisiae*) are used for meat preservation by fermentation, as in such products as smoked sausage and salami. The bacteria are inoculated into the meat, where they release preservative organic acids inside the food.

Penicillins A group of antibiotics produced either by the mould *Penicillium* or they may be made synthetically in the laboratory.

Penicillium Moulds producing characteristics of some cheeses. *P. roqueforti* is used in several blue-veined cheeses while *P. camemberti* coats both Brie and Camembert. These moulds may also cause spoilage of other foods. Some species produce the antibiotic penicillin.

Pennington Report Following an outbreak of *E. coli* 0157: H7 food poisoning in Lanarkshire, Scotland from late 1996 to early 1997 which resulted in 20 deaths (see entry on *E. coli*) an expert group under Professor Hugh Pennington made many recommendations regarding all stages of meat production. These recommendations included the following

- hygiene training for all workers in the food chain (from the farm onwards)
- supervisors and operators of one-person high-risk businesses to be trained at an intermediate level
- food hygiene training as part of the school curriculum
- stricter slaughterhouse hygiene including cleanliness of animals pre-slaughter
- effective control over hides and intestines
- better transportation standards
- licensing of butchers shops
- separation of cooked and raw meat at all times
- separate staff for cooked and raw meat
- separate utensils and equipment for raw and cooked meats
- full adoption of HACCP by the food trade
- stricter enforcement of regulations
- a review of the procedures for handling outbreaks
- further research into *E. coli*.

The report revealed that 40% of manufacturers and wholesalers of cooked meat had not carried out a hazard analysis, less than 50% of butchers do not have a temperature probe and that 90% of businesses are visited annually by EHOs.

Perishable foods All foods deteriorate eventually but this term is normally applied to those with a short life and includes the high-risk foods and some fruits and vegetables. *See:* Appendix: Food Law, Best-before date, Storage, Use-by date.

Personal hygiene The means by which food handlers prevent contamination on or within themselves from gaining access to food. People working with food must have a good standard of general health and adopt good habits and standards. There are a large number of obligations, including wearing clean overclothing, not smoking and reporting food poisoning as well as an overriding obligation not to cause contamination of food. The following areas all come under the umbrella term of personal hygiene:
- coughs and sneezes
- drying facilities
- fingernails
- undesirable habits (such as nose-picking)
- hair/beards/moustaches
- hands and hand-washing
- jewellery
- medical screening
- nail brushes
- overclothing
- skin and skin lesions
- smoking and snuff
- waterproof dressings.

Pests and pest control
- The prevention, detection and destruction of insects, animals and birds which attack foodstuffs.
- Common pests include rats, mice and cockroaches, all of which are known to carry pathogens such as salmonellas.
- Pests also spoil a great deal of food and cause damage to buildings.
- Generally speaking, the control of pests is a specialist task; DIY is often not successful.
- Control measures are normally physical (prevention of entry of pests, trapping) or chemical (use of pesticides).
- The presence of pest infestations is one of the largest single causes of emergency closure of food premises.

See: Cleaning, Design of food premises, Good housekeeping, Individual entries for pests (e.g. Rat), Proofing, Storage.

Pesticides Chemical substances used to kill pests. Poisons used to control rodents (for example warfarin) must be used in food rooms with extreme care by specialists. Pesticide residues on agricultural produce should be washed off fruits and vegetables before use. A recurrent problem is the eventual resistance of pests to chemical attack and the subsequent search for new control measures. Pesticides may also affect other organisms including humans. *See:* DDT, LC_{50}, LC_{50}, Individual entries for pests (e.g. Cockroach).

Petri dish/plate A flat circular glass or plastic dish, which has a close-fitting lid. Containing various types of agar gels, they are used extensively for the cultivation of micro-organisms in the laboratory.

Pets Animals in general are known to carry a variety of disease-causing organisms which may be passed on to humans directly, or in food; domestic animals are no exception. There is also a possibility of physical contamination of food with stray hairs and soil. Animals should not be allowed into food rooms. Pet animals may be a problem in domestic premises used as a food business. *See:* Animals, Domestic premises.

pH
- A measure of the acidity or alkalinity of a substance.
- The pH scale runs from 0 to 14 with 7.0 being the neutral point.
- Acids have a pH of less than 7, acidity increasing as the value gets lower.
- Above pH 7 alkalinity increases.
- Pure water has a pH of 7.0 and is said to be neutral.

Many foods, including most meats and vegetables have pH values between 5 and 7, such figures being in the range preferred by most bacteria. Below pH 4.5, pathogens do not normally grow. The term pH is derived from the concentration of hydrogen ions (H^+) in a substance (power of H). The scale is logarithmic, pH 3 being ten times more acid than pH 4 etc. *See:* Acid foods (classification), Canning, Dark-cutting meat.

Phage An abbreviated form of the term 'bacteriophage'.

Phage typing *See:* Bacteriophage typing.

Pharaoh's ant (*Monomorium pharaonis*)
- A small (2-3 mm) pale yellow ant, originally of tropical origin.
- Inhabits warm buildings such as hospitals, bakeries and kitchens.
- Feeds on a variety of foods: sweet (sugar, jam, honey), protein (cheese, meat) and high fat (lard, butter).

- The small worker ants seem able to discover food sources even in closed containers.
- There is no evidence that this ant carries pathogens internally but their bodies and legs may pick up contamination and transmit it to food.
- Infestations may be persistent since nests are constructed in inaccessible places making treatment difficult. *See:* Ants, Juvenile hormone.

Phenol
1. Certain anionic disinfectants, some turning white when added to water, contain phenol as a broad-spectrum bactericide. Due to their strong smell and taste they have no direct food use but are used for toilets, floors and drains. They may be absorbed by the skin producing toxic effects although chlorinated phenols such as hexachlorophene are designed as skin bactericides.
2. During smoking of foods such as fish, phenols and other substances are produced and act as preservatives.

PHLS (Public Health Laboratory Service) Central UK government laboratory which performs analytical work, gives advice and also publishes statistics, for example relating to food poisoning.

Phocanema (**codworm**) A brownish-white round worm, up to 3 cm long, found around the liver and intestines of fish, and sometimes entering the flesh. Freezing and curing kills them but curing alone often does not. There is no evidence that the worm affects humans but badly infested fish are aesthetically unfit.

Phosphatase test Phosphatase is a heat-resistant enzyme found in raw milk. It is an indicator of the effectiveness of heat treatments designed to destroy the bacterium *Mycobacterium tuberculosis*. The test is chemical and results in a yellow colour if phosphatase is present.

Physical contamination The presence of foreign bodies in food. Many physical contaminants are possible including the following examples:

- pieces of machinery (nuts, bolts, saw blades)
- items from people (pens, buttons, cigarette ends)
- cleaning materials
- packaging (paper, cardboard, staples, string)
- flakes of paint
- rust
- wooden splinters

- insects and rodents (hairs, droppings, bodies).

Bacteria and other causes of food poisoning are not considered to be physical contaminants. *See:* Nature, substance or quality.

Phytohaemagglutinin *See:* Red kidney beans.

Phytophthora infestans A fungus which causes the spoilage of vegetable foods, such as potatoes where it forms a scaly material on the surface, making it inedible. It was this organism which was responsible for the Irish potato famine of 1845.

Pickling
1. A method of food preservation using vinegar, a weak solution of acetic (ethanoic) acid. Typical products include onions and red cabbage.
2. During bacon curing, the brine used in some processes is called the 'pickle'.
3. A fermentation process used to preserve vegetables employs a weak salt solution which is converted to lactic acid by bacteria such as *Leuconostoc mesenteroides* and *Lactobacillus plantarum*. Sauerkraut and dill pickles are typical products. *See:* Food preservation, pH.

Pigeons Wild (feral) pigeons are regular inhabitants and entrants of buildings. They are undesirable in food rooms since they are known to carry pathogens and may cause physical contamination. *See:* Birds.

Pilchard Alternative name for sardine. If canned this food should be treated in the same way as canned salmon. *See:* Fish.

"Pipy" liver *See: Fasciola hepatica.*

Plants (poisonous) Food poisoning although most commonly caused by bacteria may be caused by the consumption of many plants. Children in particular sometimes eat poisonous berries. Well known examples of poisonous foods include raw kidney beans, potatoes which have turned green and rhubarb leaves. Non-food poisonous plants include laburnum, holly (berries), deadly nightshade, hemlock and mistletoe. *See:* Alkaloids, Red kidney beans.

Plasmid A small circular piece of DNA in bacterial cells, not located in the nuclear region. It is self-replicating and typically contains a small number of genes. Different plasmids are known, including some which control fertility, some drug resistance, some have metabolic functions and others (known as virulence plasmids) control the production of some toxins, such as endotoxin and enterotoxin by *Escherichia coli*.

Plasmid profile typing A laboratory technique for differentiating between strains of bacteria such as multiresistant *Salmonella typhimurium* DT104.

Plasters *See:* Waterproof dressing.

Plastics Have many food uses since they are non-absorbent, non-toxic and may be effectively cleaned. *See:* Chopping boards, Food contact surfaces.

Plate freezing A method of freezing flat items of food such as burgers and fish fingers using pressure plates containing a circulating refrigerant. The process is slow, taking some hours.

Plesiomonas shigelloides
A Gram-negative rod shaped bacterium which can cause a mild gastroenteritis. It is associated with the consumption of seafood, including oysters and mussels, and contaminated water which has been used for rinsing foods that are consumed without cooking or heating. Most cases occur in the summer months, following contamination of fresh water.

Poliomyelitis ('Polio')
- A disease caused by the polioviruses, which are more stable than most other viruses and can remain infectious for relatively long periods of time in water and food.
- Transmission is mainly by ingestion of water contaminated with faeces containing the virus.
- The virus may cause a sore throat, headache and nausea, but it may affect the central nervous system causing paralysis.
- Control measures include personal cleanliness, adequate heating of food (pasteurisation temperatures are sufficient to inactivate the virus), disinfection of water and prevention of contact with foods by flies.
- Vaccines are available and are highly effective.

Polypropylene A hard plastic material whose major food use is as chopping boards as an alternative to wood. This material is durable and may be easily cleaned although users find that the surface becomes scarred and is somewhat slippery. Sheet polypropylene is also used as a wall covering and in doors (the so-called 'rubber strip' door).

Population (bacterial) growth curve *See:* Bacterial growth curve.

Pork A high-risk food which should be subject to strict temperature control. Pigs are known carriers of salmonellas which will be destroyed only by thorough cooking. The risk of infection by tapeworm and roundworm is also avoided by eating only well-done pork although freezing is known to kill both of these parasites.

Pork tapeworm (*Taenia solium*) The risks and precautions for this are similar to those for the beef tapeworm. This parasite may also form bladder worms in humans which may reinfect the host or infect other people.

Portals of entry and exit The places through which a pathogen enters and leaves the body. For food-borne diseases and food poisoning these are the mouth and anus respectively.

Port Health Authority (UK) At ports of entry such as docks, this is the equivalent of the local authority for the purposes of inspection of imported foods and other matters.

Potable water A term used to indicate that water is fit for human consumption and free from colour, smell, taint and pathogens.

Potassium salts
1. Potassium acetate: a food additive acting as a buffer (stabilises pH), used to preserve the colour of plant foods.
2. Potassium benzoate: a salt of benzoic acid used as a preservative.
3. Potassium hydroxide (Caustic potash): a component of some oven cleaners used to remove hard, carbonised deposits. It attacks human skin and must be used with care. *See:* Sodium hydroxide.
4. Potassium metabisulphite: a component of Campden tablets, used to stop fermentation in the brewing industry and as a disinfecting agent for equipment used in wine and beer-making, particularly home-made. *See:* Sulphur dioxide.
5. Potassium nitrate and nitrite. *See:* Curing, Nitrate, Nitrite.
6. Potassium propionate: a salt of propionic acid used as a mould inhibitor in bakery and dairy products.
7. Potassium sorbate: a preservative, effective in acid conditions, used to control mould growth (and some pathogenic bacteria) in cheese, bread and bakery products, yoghurt, dessert products, seafood dressing and jams. *See:* Sorbic acid.

Potatoes Not normally a high-risk food but, when exposed to the light or cold a toxic chemical (solanin, an alkaloid) is produced in quantities large enough to cause poisoning. Also the green coloured substance chlorophyll occurs and is an indication that the potato should not be eaten. Since most of the solanin is close to the surface, lightly affected potatoes may be deeply peeled and used.

Poultry The main food hygiene problem is that of contamination of both the flesh and eggs with salmonellas. Intensive methods of production and contaminated feed are thought to be the major problems. The percentage of chickens affected in Great Britain has dropped from around 80% in the 1970s to less than 50% in the late 1990s. The figures from Northern Ireland in 1996 were very low but based on a small sample.
Anything with which raw poultry or its juices comes into contact, such as hands, knives, chopping boards, storage containers and other foods is likely to become contaminated. *See:* Cross-contamination, Refrigerators, *Salmonella* (various entries).

Power of Entry An EHO may enter a food premises at any reasonable time, obstruction of which is an offence. Samples, documents, photographs and video recordings amongst other things may be taken and unfit food may be seized.
See: Appendix: Food Law.

Prawns *See:* Shellfish.

Premises (Food) This term includes all places including ships, aircraft, vehicles, stalls etc. used for food production, preparation or sale as part of a food business.
See: Food business.

Preparation surfaces *See:* Food-contact surfaces.

Preservation of food *See:* Food preservation.

Preservatives Substances used to stop the growth of spoilage bacteria, moulds and yeasts in foods. A wide range of substances, all controlled by regulations, is used. Some of them are reported to be toxic to humans. Examples of preservatives with food use include acetic (ethanoic) acid, benzoic acid, biphenyl, carbon dioxide, formic acid, fumaric acid, lactic acid, malic acid, nisin, nitrate, nitrite, propionic acid, sorbic acid and sulphur dioxide. *See:* Food preservation, Individual entries, Sugar.

Preserves Fruit products, similar to jam, with a high sugar content. They are not known to cause food poisoning but are prone to mould growth after exposure to the air, so refrigerated storage after opening is recommended.
See: Food preservation, Sugar.

Presumptive water (coliform) test The initial test used to assess water purity. Samples of water are incubated in a specific liquid broth which contains a sugar (lactose). If fermentation occurs, gas is produced. This is presumed to be from the fermentation of the sugar by coliforms. The test does not completely identify the water contaminant as a coliform, since other waterborne bacteria can produce similar results. Any such positive samples then undergo additional tests, called the Confirmed test and the Completed test. If the presumptive test does not result in growth or gas production, the water is assumed to contain no coliforms, was therefore not contaminated with faecal material and is bacteriologically safe to drink.

Prevention of Damage by Pests Act 1949 Legislation which includes:
- a requirement for pest control by the local authority
- notification of infestations by occupiers of buildings
- occupiers to deal with pest infestations
- the control of methods used in dealing with infestations.

There is power of entry under this Act.

Prohibition notice and prohibition order Following a prosecution, if it is considered that there is a health risk, the court imposes a Prohibition Order that premises, parts of premises, or equipment cannot be used. The order may be lifted after application to the local authority if it can be proved that the risk situation no longer exists.

Prokaryotic A type of cell, possessed by the bacteria, which lack a true nucleus and membrane-bound organelles.

Proofing of buildings In pest control the physical means by which entry into buildings is denied. Examples include close-fitting doors, screens over windows, sealing of all gaps such as those around pipe work and maintenance of drainage systems. *See:* Design of food premises, Pest control.

Propionibacter shermanii A bacterium which produces carbon dioxide in large pockets in Swiss cheeses such as Emmenthal.

Propionic acid An anti-fungal preservative agent used in bakery and dairy products. It is often used as calcium, potassium or sodium propionate.

Propyl parahydroxybenzene (Propyl 4-hydroxybenzene, n-Propyl p-hydroxybenzene) A preservative made from benzoic acid with wide use in drinks, pickles, salad cream and fruit pie fillings. *See:* Benzoic acid.

168 Protective clothing

Protective clothing
- Food handlers should wear clean and washable overclothing to protect food from contamination.
- Safety clothing, such as eye shields when mixing cleaning chemicals, and chain mail gloves if using band saws, may also be needed.
- Waiting and bar staff may wear normal clothing.
- The person running the business should supply all such clothing and also provide somewhere to store ordinary clothing away from food.
- Visitors should be clothed to the same standard

See: Appendix: Food Law, Clothing, Personal hygiene.

Proteins Substances containing carbon, hydrogen, oxygen, nitrogen, sulphur and phosphorus. The basic unit is the amino acid which is joined with other amino acids by the peptide bond (-OC-NH-) into very large and complex molecules. Proteins are structural materials in living organisms and are an essential part of all living cells including bone, muscle, skin, heart and other organs. Foodstuffs rich in protein are favoured by bacteria and fungi, and so need careful temperature storage.
See: High-risk foods.

Protein foods High-risk foods often contain significant amounts of protein upon which harmful and spoilage bacteria feed.

Proteus **species** A group of actively motile Gram-negative coliform bacteria. They are found free-living in water, soil and sewage and are normally present in the human bowel and on the skin. Pathogenic species may cause ear, eye and urinary tract infections, as well as 'summer diarrhoea' in children. Some have been involved in the spoilage of meats, seafood and eggs. *See:* Scombroid food poisoning.

Protozoa A group of single-celled organisms, considered by many to be single-celled animals. They require a moist environment and are found in rivers, stagnant pools and moist soils. They feed on both living and non-living material. Some are capable of producing cysts, which are heat and drought-resistant. The protozoa include the amoebas which live in water and soil, most of which are harmless. Also included is *Entamoeba histolytica*, which causes amoebic dysentery in humans. *See: Giardia lamblia.*

Pseudomonas
- A genus of Gram-negative bacteria, common in the environment; they are found in soil, on plants, in water and as part of the normal skin and gut flora of humans as a commensal.

- In humans it can become a pathogen when the resistance of the host is low, or when it becomes involved with a mixture of other infecting bacteria.
- It can infect burns, the urinary tract and can cause abscesses, septicaemia and meningitis.
- As a result of their growth they produce characteristic brightly coloured pigments (deep blue, yellow-green and brown-black) which may diffuse into their surroundings and change its colour.
- *P. aeruginosa* produces both an endotoxin and an exotoxin and the infection leads to the production of blue-green pus while *P. mallei* causes the disease glanders in horses.
- A number of species are responsible for the spoilage of many foods, particularly high protein foods, producing 'off' tastes and odours.
- Effects include slime on the surface of meats and eviscerated poultry, yellow-green fluorescence on fish and green rots of eggs *(P. fluorescens)*, and 'off' flavours and colourings in milk.
- All species grow well at refrigeration temperatures and in moist conditions (a_w 0.97 to 0.98).
- They are not readily killed by heat, grow poorly if oxygen is not available and are not particularly resistant to drying; they are fairly resistant to many of the commonly-used disinfectants.

Psocids *See:* Booklice.

Psychrophile An organism that grows best at temperatures below 20°C. Many common fungi readily grow at these temperatures, including species of *Cladosporium* and *Penicillium*.

Psychrotroph An organism that grows at temperatures not far above freezing, hence will grow readily at refrigeration temperatures. Such bacteria are found chiefly in the genera *Alcaligenes, Flavobacterium* and *Pseudomonas*.

Ptomaines Substances produced when food decays, thought in the 19th century to be the cause of food poisoning, but later found to be harmless.

Public analyst Laboratory-equipped analyst of food and water appointed by food authorities but also used by others. Many types of analysis including chemical and compositional are possible.

Puffer fish Members of the order *Tetraodontiformes* such as porcupine fish, ocean sunfish and puffers, have poisonous internal organs; the toxin involved (tetradotoxin) may contaminate the flesh. The disease is often fatal (60% mortality) due to respiratory failure. Other symptoms are numbness in the face and a floating sensation. The USFDA have periodically banned imports of this fish because of the risk of contamination of edible parts by tetrodotoxin after processing. *See:* Fugu fish.

Pulegone A naturally occurring biologically active principle (BAP) prohibited as a flavouring in some EU countries but found naturally in peppermint oil.

Pupae (insect) A stage in the life cycle of some insects, between the larva (caterpillar, grub or maggot) and adult. It is the inactive stage, when it is in a cocoon. The adult insect emerges fully-formed from the pupa.

Pus The yellow-white matter produced at the site of an infection, for example in boils and pimples. It consists of dead and living white blood cells, dead and living bacteria, bacterial toxins and fluid. If allowed to contaminate food it may lead to an outbreak of food poisoning. *See: Staphylococcus aureus*.

Pybuthrin A short-lived low-toxicity insecticide.

Pyrethrum Naturally-occurring insecticide found in the pyrethrum flower (*Chrysanthemum cinerieafolium*) exhibiting very quick knockdown with low toxicity to mammals. The substance is effective for a few days and is broken down by sunlight. Piperonyl butoxide is frequently added to prevent recovery of insects.

Pyrethroids Synthetically prepared insecticides similar to pyrethrum, examples being bioallethrin and bioresmethrin.

Pyrrolizidine alkaloids Cereals, honey or milk contaminated with these toxins from various weeds cause varying degrees of liver damage with death in 2 weeks to over 2 years. Recovery is possible if the amount consumed is low. Herbal teas, medicines and folk remedies may also show a degree of risk, the disease being more prevalent in non-developed countries.

Q fever A disease caused by the organism *Coxiella burnettii*, a rickettsia. It produces a pneumonia-type infection, and is rarely fatal. The organism is found in domestic livestock, and animal to animal transmission is by the bites of arthropods. In humans, the disease is most commonly associated with the consumption of unpasteurised milk and through aerosol inhalation in dairy sheds and similar places. Workers in meat and hide processing plants are also at risk. The organism is killed by heat treatment.

Quality assurance (QA)
- A system covering quality aspects of production, distribution and end-use of a product.
- Such a system may commence by detailing exact specifications of raw materials and then go on to closely define each stage of a production process.
- At the end of this, if the system has been adhered to, quality of the product should be both satisfactory and consistent.
- The EC standard ISO 9000 (and similar) and the British Standard BS 5750 are frequently used in industry in this context.
- Safety issues may be incorporated into the system.

See: Due diligence, HACCP.

Quality control (QC) The means of ensuring that product specifications are met. For example, in the food industry bacteriological tests, taste panels (organoleptic testing) and magnetic detectors are frequently used. *See:* Quality assurance.

Quaternary ammonium compounds (QAC or QUATS) Cationic detergent molecules having bactericidal/bacteriostatic qualities. They are both more expensive and limited in their action than hypochlorites but are effective in alkaline solutions and against some moulds.

Quick freezing Produces a better quality product with less drip than slow freezing since water is frozen in place inside cells and is not subsequently lost as drip on thawing. Commercially, quick freezing is most often achieved with small, blast-frozen food items. *See:* Frozen food (production of).

Radiation Particles and electromagnetic waves emitted from various substances and devices, examples being X- and gamma rays used as a means of food preservation. *See:* Irradiation.

Rancidity (hydrolytic and oxidative) The production of substances causing off-flavours and odours in fatty foods such as oils and dairy products.
1. Hydrolytic rancidity involves the release of free fatty acids such as butyric acid which produces the characteristic smell of rancid butter. The reaction is catalysed by lipases (enzymes).
2. Oxidative rancidity is the result of oxygen attaching to double bonds of unsaturated fatty acids forming organic peroxides. Metal such as aluminium foil in contact with foods under refrigeration and freezing speeds up this reaction.

Rats In Britain two main varieties of rat, the black rat and the brown or common rat are pests of food and other premises.

Main problems

- Rodents feeding on human food are known to carry a number of pathogenic organisms including species of *Salmonella*. *Rattus norvegicus* in farms in England and Wales during 1991-1993 were found to be infected with many zoonotic parasites and bacteria including *Cryptosporidia, Toxoplasma, Toxocara, Leptospira, Pasteurella, Listeria, Yersinia, Coxiella* and Hantavirus.
- The bodies are likely to be contaminated due to contact with sewage and refuse.
- Apart from the dangers of disease, rats cause damage and wastage to foodstuffs and damage to buildings.
- The incisor teeth of rats must be continually worn down by constant gnawing, the evidence of which is a common first sign of infestation.
- Rat droppings contaminate food.

Control measures

- Rats avoid open spaces and develop 'runs' in covered areas including undergrowth, false ceilings, behind undisturbed food in storage and in cavity walls.
- Prevention of infestations partly rests on good housekeeping to deny food and water.
- Regular inspections to identify early signs.
- Effective waste disposal and stock rotation.
- Proofing of buildings.
- Rodent control is a specialised task best left to experts.

See: Baits, Black rat, British Pest Control Association, Brown rat, Mice, Pests, Trapping, Sticky boards, Warfarin.

Raw foods Foods which have not been cooked may contain bacteria which can cause problems due to cross-contamination. Examples include *Salmonella enteritidis* from raw chicken and *Clostridium perfringens* from soil on root vegetables. Raw food should be kept apart from cooked food.

Raw milk Milk which has not been heat-treated by pasteurisation, sterilisation or other means to destroy pathogenic organisms. Cases of food poisoning involving *Campylobacter, Staphylococcus* and *Salmonella* species have all been noted, together with other diseases such as listeriosis, tuberculosis and brucellosis. *See:* Milk, *Streptococcus* species.

Red kidney beans (*Phaseolus vulgaris*)   Contain a toxin (phytohaemagglutin or lectin) which affects some people causing severe nausea, vomiting and other symptoms occurring within 6 hours after eating undercooked beans. Recovery is rapid, normally within one day. The toxin is destroyed by rapid boiling for 10 minutes but slow cookers may not reach a high enough temperature to do this since they may only reach 70°C. This has been noted several times in the UK during the 1970s.
Beans should be soaked for some hours, throwing this water away and complete the cooking by rapidly boiling with fresh water for at least 10 minutes. Cooked canned beans do not require this treatment. Similar toxins may be found in other varieties of beans and pulses which should also be well cooked.

Red Whelk (*Neptunea antigua*)   Larger, smooth-shelled relative of the edible whelk. It causes occasional outbreaks of food poisoning similar to paralytic shellfish poisoning due to the release of tetramine (a toxin) from its salivary glands. Symptoms include weakness, muscle cramp, fatigue, dizziness and vertigo between 30-90 minutes after eating affected whelks and tend to last only a few hours.

Refreezing of food Each time food passes through the danger zone of temperatures the numbers of bacteria on it increase. If thawing, reheating and cooling are repeated, the numbers of organisms may build up and become large enough to cause food poisoning.

Refrigerators
- Normal recommended refrigerator temperature is between 1-4°C for the storage of all high-risk foods.
- In refrigerators most harmful bacteria are dormant and spoilage organisms are slow to multiply.
- The shelf-life of products is extended by some days.

Use of refrigerators

1. Locate away from heat sources.
2. Load correctly to allow a good circulation of air around foods.
3. Hot food should be cooled before being placed in a refrigerator.
4. Foods must not be stored in cans except for unopened canned meats; these require only a few hours chilling to facilitate slicing.
5. Containers must be food-grade and covered.

6. It is preferable to have separate refrigerators for raw and cooked foods in commercial premises.
7. If only one refrigerator is available raw meat should be stored underneath cooked foods to avoid any cross-contamination by drips.
8. Cleaning must be regular, not forgetting the door seals.
9. Temperatures of the product and the air in the refrigerator should be taken and recorded regularly throughout the day.
10. Defrosting may be manual or automatic and is essential to avoid build-up of ice which limits the efficiency of the appliance.
See: Cook-chill, Growth requirements (bacterial/fungal), *Listeria monocytogenes*, Temperature control.

Refuse (storage and disposal) Accumulations of waste in food areas must be minimised and confined to closed containers, such as bins with close-fitting lids or heavy duty plastic bags on stands. These containers should be regularly (at least daily) removed to a secure place well away from food areas and collected for disposal. Refuse areas, if managed badly, may be a source of food to rodents and animals and should be maintained and cleaned to a high standard.
See: Compaction.

Registration The proprietor of most existing or proposed food businesses, or the owner of the premises in some cases must notify the local authority so that the extent of the existing and proposed food trade in an area is known to the local authority. There is no charge for registration, it cannot be refused and need not be renewed. The registration however is not a licence. An inspection prior to the business commencing trade may also reduce food safety risks. *See:* Appendix: Food law.

Regulations Many Acts of Parliament (such as the Food Safety Act 1990) contain powers for the appropriate Minister to make regulations. These are more detailed requirements than are contained in such Acts. Examples include labelling, general food safety and temperature control regulations. *See:* Appendix: Food Law, Individual entries.

Reheating As a general rule, food which has been refrigerated or frozen must only be reheated once, to above 63°C (75°C at the centre is preferred) or 'piping hot'. This is to avoid the build-up of bacteria.
See: Refreezing of food, Temperature control.

REHIS (Royal Environmental Health Institution of Scotland) An organisation similar in scope to CIEH.

Reported cases of food poisoning/food-borne disease
- Figures for cases of food-related disease are thought to be unreliable since persons, for various reasons, fail to notify the proper authorities.
- Various estimates from 2 to 10 million cases per year contrast sharply with the official figures of over 60 000 reported in the late 1990s in Britain.
- The reporting system itself may be faulty and people with short-lived symptoms may not go to a doctor; misdiagnosis is also possible.
- Food handlers must report such suspected illnesses.

Reporting of Injuries, Diseases and Dangerous Occurrences Regs 1995 (RIDDOR) These regulations require employers to report all serious accidents including those which result in employees missing more than three days work, acute illnesses and some other matters including explosions and collapse of structures.

Resazurin A colorimetric test carried out on raw milk which determines the bacterial load.

Reservoir of infection The common location where a pathogen may always be found in considerable numbers. Examples include humans as reservoirs of *Staphylococcus aureus* and poultry as reservoirs of *Salmonella* species.

```
        ┌─────────────────────┐        ┌──────────────────────────────────────┐
        │ Nose, mouth, throat │        │ Bowel                                │
        │ Organism: Staphylococci │    │ Organisms: Salmonella, Clostridium, E. coli, │
        └─────────────────────┘        │ dysentery bacilli and others         │
                                       └──────────────────────────────────────┘
```

Sneezing, Coughing,   Hand-Mouth Contact   Poor personal   Sewage
Whistling etc.   hygiene

Food   Hands
(Direct)   Contamination of
                                                         Food e.g. Water,
                                                         flies (Indirect)

              Unbroken skin, skin lesion

                     Food (Indirect)

Human Reservoirs of Infection

Resident organisms Those commonly living permanently in a particular location, for example staphylococci on human skin.

Residual insecticide Substances toxic to insects over a long period, examples being vapour-emitting strips and lacquer-based insecticides. Their use in food rooms is questionable. *See:* DDT, Insecticides.

Resistant strains *See: Salmonella, Staphylococcus.*

Rhizopus A mould causing food spoilage particularly in humid and damp conditions. Typical foods affected include berries, fruits, vegetables and bread.

Rhubarb The leaves of this contain toxic substances (such as oxalic acid) and should not be eaten.

RIDDOR *See:* Reporting of Injuries, Diseases etc Regs 1995.

Rice
- Cooked rice, due to the risk of *Bacillus cereus* food poisoning, should be kept under strict temperature control; this means either refrigeration or keeping it hot.
- It is included in the list of high-risk foods.
- Typical risk situations include takeaways and rice salads in buffets.
- The practice of adding a fresh batch of cooked rice to the remains of the previous one will allow any contamination present to enter the fresh batch.

Rice weevil (*Calandra* **or** *Sitophylus oryzae***)** A pest of stored cereal products including wheat and rice. Adults have a characteristic 'snout' and 'elbowed' antennae and are chestnut coloured insects up to 4 mm long.

Richmond Committee An advisory committee reporting on the micro- biological safety of food to British Government ministries involved with food. The reports are very comprehensive and make detailed reference to a wide variety of issues including food-borne illness, HACCP, legislation, manufacturing processes and poultry meat. The reports make many conclusions and recommendations some of which have been taken up and some, including compulsory licensing, ignored as yet.

Rickettsia A micro-organism which is similar in some respects to both bacteria and viruses, causing diseases such as typhus, Rocky Mountain spotted fever and Q fever. All of these are spread by lice, fleas and ticks but there is evidence to implicate raw milk from sheep, goats and cows in their transmission. *See:* Raw milk.

Rinse (hot, after washing up) Water at 82-88°C is an effective final rinse for utensils and equipment since it will disinfect, remove any traces of chemicals such as detergents and make the clean item hot enough to air dry. This avoids the problem of contamination from cloths. If a high enough temperature cannot be reached then a sanitiser may be added.

Rodenticide A poison capable of killing rodent pests such as rats and mice.

Rodents Animals of the order Rodentia including rats, mice, squirrels and beavers. Rats and mice are significant pests and both are carriers of disease-causing organisms. Their exclusion from food premises is a high priority.

Roe The mass of eggs in a female fish (hard roe) or the milt (reproductive gland) of a male fish (soft roe). They are both high in protein and thus high-risk foods.

Rolled (stuffed) joints These have caused problems since bacteria previously on the outside of the meat, together with those introduced from the food handler or other food items, are transferred to the centre during preparation. They may survive cooking, with *Clostridium perfringens* (a spore-forming bacterium) being a particular problem.

Roller drier A device used for dehydrating 'paste' products including mashed potato or liquids such as milk. It consists of a slowly rotating steam-heated drum upon which the product is spread, being removed when dry by a scraper blade.
See: Dehydration, Food preservation.

'Rope'
1. In bread, a condition caused by the heat-resistant bacterium *Bacillus subtilis* producing a sickly odour and soft, cloying texture.
2. In milk, a slimy condition caused by the bacterium *Enterobacter aerogenes* (*Bacillus aerogenes*).

Rotaviruses
- The most common cause of viral food poisoning in Britain, causing acute gastroenteritis. Six serological groups have been identified, three of which (groups A, B, and C) infect humans; the most common and widespread being group A.
- Over 3 million cases occur annually in the US. In the tropics outbreaks occur

throughout the year, but in temperate regions it occurs mainly in the winter. Rotavirus was reported in 1995 to be the most common enteric pathogen in some parts of Ireland.
- Incubation period is from 1 to 3 days; symptoms include vomiting, watery diarrhoea and fever.
- Transmission is by the faecal-oral route; contaminated hands are probably the most important vehicle, especially in close communities.

See: Viruses.

Roundworms (parasitic) Many of these affect food animals and fish, examples being
1. *Ascaris lumbricoides* causes 'milk spot' in the livers of pigs and also sometimes has severe effects on the growth of these animals.
2. *Oesophagostomum radiatum* causes decomposition of the intestines of cattle and sheep.
3. *Oncocerca gibsoni* rests in beef flesh.
4. *Trichinella spiralis* cysts in the muscle of pigs will develop in humans after consumption of undercooked pork.
5. *Anisakis simplex* affects fish and humans.

Routes of contamination or infection

The path along which bacteria or other organisms travel from one area or food to another. As an example:

Salmonella may be present in contaminated feed,
▼
enter a chicken,
▼
be spread by a wiping cloth to a slicing machine,
▼
contaminate cooked ham,
▼
multiply in warm conditions and
▼
cause food poisoning after consumption.

See: Cross-contamination, Vehicle of food poisoning.

RIPHH (Royal Institute of Public Health and Hygiene) A professional body based in London, England which offers various food hygiene training courses and has an interest in other food and health matters.

RSH (Royal Society of Health) A professional body based in London, England which offers various food hygiene training courses and has an interest in other food and health matters.

Rubber gloves Those used in connection with food should be brightly coloured for high visibility, in case of physical contamination. Manual washing up requires gloves if the final rinse temperature is at 82-88°C. Disposable gloves may be used to prevent hand-contact with foods during production, service or sale. All gloves may become vehicles for bacteria and must be discarded if their condition becomes unacceptable.

Runaway heating A problem in microwave cooking or reheating in which localised 'hot spots' occur. These can be minimised by turning the food during cooking, allowing standing time after cooking and heating only one type of food at a time, since different foods cook in different times. Cold spots are a related problem.

Rust Iron oxide caused by the action of water on iron or steel. A rusty (corroded) surface, of a machine or utensil for example, cannot be cleaned properly and may cause physical contamination of food. A rusted can should be discarded since pin holes may have been made through which the contents may have become contaminated.

Rust-red flour beetle (*Tribolium castaneum*) A common pest of stored cereal products. *See:* Beetles.

Rust-red grain beetle (*Cryptolestes ferrugineus*) A minute insect (3 mm in length) thriving in damp stored foodstuffs. *See:* Beetles.

SAFE (Systematic Assessment of Food Environment) A hazard analysis and control system similar to, but not so detailed as, **HACCP** used in manufacturing.

Safety *See:* Health and Safety at Work etc. (Act) 1974.

Salads Prepared salads are considered to be high-risk foods and should be refrigerated (1-4°C) or eaten within four hours of preparation. Salads containing fruit, rice or coleslaw must be treated in the same way. *See:* Appendix: Food Law.

Salad bars There is a danger of product contamination from initial preparation, public access and from the practice of 'topping up'. The same controls on temperature apply as for salads. Cross-contamination may also occur.

Salmon If fresh, it should be subjected to strict temperature control. If canned (as with other canned fish and meat) it must be treated as a high-risk food once the can is opened, and the contents stored in a refrigerator, in a suitable covered container. *See:* Fish.

Salmonella **species** *Salmonella* is a Gram-negative, non-spore forming, short rod-shaped bacterium. Most forms are motile, all are facultative anaerobes. It grows between 5 to 45°C (optimum 37°C), with a pH range 4 to 9 (optimum 6.5 to 7.5).

There are over 2 000 serotypes, all of which are able to cause illness in humans or animals. Some are specific to birds and certain animals, and some are primarily spread by water (e.g. *S. typhi*) due to poor sanitation. Animals used for food production are common carriers of salmonellas, which can therefore contaminate foods, such as meat, poultry, dairy products and eggs. They are found widely in the environment, including water, soil, insects, raw meats, the gastrointestinal tract of wild and domestic animals of all types (and their faeces), birds (especially in poultry), reptiles, amphibians (e.g. terrapins) and occasionally humans. *S. tosamanga* occasionally infects humans in Europe, its reservoir being reptiles and other cold-blooded animals. Several species including *S. agoueve, S. widemarsh, S. hegenbeck* and *S. havana* were isolated from pet lizards in England in 1996. Up to 80% of lizards are thought to carry salmonellas.

A case of food poisoning caused by a strain of *Salmonella* is called salmonellosis. The *Salmonella* group as a whole have been consistently responsible for the majority of cases of bacterial food poisoning over many years. The incidence of salmonellosis appears to be increasing in most industrialised countries, with around 20 000 cases annually in the UK, and 2 to 4 million in the USA. Common causal agents are *S. typhimurium* and *S. enteritidis.*

Some serotypes have become antibiotic resistant (see entry on *S. typhimurium* DT104) and show 3% fatalities (this is 10 times the figure for normal *Salmonella*). Other salmonellas such as *S. hadar* and *S. virchow* have also shown increased resistance (one drug or multiresistance).

Food poisoning by *Salmonella*

Caused by infection; often large numbers (possibly millions) of bacteria are needed to cause illness, but an infective dose as low as 20 to 30 cells may suffice, depending on

Salmonella species

the age and health of the host and differences between members of the genus. All age groups are susceptible, but the very young, the very old, and the infirm are particularly at risk. Usually the organism has grown in the food. The onset period for the disease is usually 12 to 36 hours, but it may unusually be anything from 6 to 72 hours or longer.

Duration of illness is 1 to 7 days, depending on host factors, numbers of organisms ingested, and the strain responsible. Acute symptoms include vomiting, abdominal cramps, fever, headache, and diarrhoea, with general aching of the limbs following 3 to 4 weeks after the initial onset. The symptoms are usually so severe that medical intervention is necessary. Fatalities are generally uncommon, apart from the high risk groups previously described.

Foods commonly involved

Predominantly raw meats (red and white), poultry and their products, eggs, raw milk and dairy products. In addition, outbreaks have been traced to fish, coconut, sauces of various kinds, salad dressings, cream/custard-filled desserts, dried gelatine and chocolate. Examples include

- *S. gold-coast* in coloured cheddar cheese (NE England 1996),
- *S. indiana* in the UK during early 1996 associated with poultry,
- *S. agona* in 1994-95 outbreak in Jewish children in London eating an imported kosher peanut snack food,
- *S. javiana* infections in Europe mainly from foreign travel although cases have been linked to consumption of spices, particularly pepper and paprika,
- *S. milkawasima*, although widely distributed in animals, the environment and reptiles, is rare in the UK but 60 cases were reported, mainly from doner kebabs in 1992,
- *S. anatum* was held to be the cause of several outbreaks in the UK during 1996 and the dried milk feed manufactured in France was withdrawn.

Note: some *Salmonella* species have been isolated from both the outside of egg shells, and from within the egg. (*See* : entry on Eggs.)

Contamination of food

May be directly or indirectly from human or animal excreta, all farm and wild animals, birds, rodents, all domestic pets (including so-called exotic pets, such as terrapins and iguanas), water and insects.

Control of *Salmonella*

1. Prevention of contamination during food production by ensuring that animal feedstuffs are safe.
2. Prevention of cross-contamination from raw foods such as chickens to other foods during delivery, storage and preparation.
3. Disinfection of all items which have come into contact with any raw food likely to contain *Salmonella*.
4. Thorough cooking of foods such as eggs, poultry and meat.
5. Effective pest control and restriction of contact between animals, food or food handlers.
6. Thorough hand washing after contact with pets of any kind.

S. ealing Responsible for a 1985 outbreak of food poisoning in dried baby food in England. The milk had not been heat-treated prior to drying and although only low numbers were present, over 50 babies were affected with one death. The processing plant was forced to close since the product was withdrawn from sale.

Salmonella enteritidis phage type 4 (PT4)

Generally found in the intestinal tract of animals; common in many waters. Produces both enterotoxin and cytotoxin. The incidence of salmonellosis due to *S. enteritidis* has risen dramatically in both the US and the UK since around the mid 1980s.
Many outbreaks have been reported such as:

- marshmallows made from raw egg white in a recipe which involved no cooking
- strawberry mousse made from raw eggs in a meals-on-wheels outbreak in Kent, England, (1995) from which 3 deaths in 27 elderly people occurred
- bodybuilders consuming a raw egg drink
- lemon meringue and mayonnaise at a Masonic lodge
- a large outbreak affecting 141 people was reported in Colchester, England, during 1991 from sandwiches containing contaminated mayonnaise made from raw eggs prepared at a sandwich bar
- apple pie which was glazed before baking with a raw egg mixture in Leeds England,1992; the bacterium apparently survived baking for 25 minutes at 220°C
- a massive outbreak of 224 000 cases of *S. enteritidis* in Minnesota USA in 1996 was thought to be due to cross-contamination of ice cream in bulk tankers previously used for unpasteurised liquid egg.

The organism has been isolated from the contents of intact shell eggs (the yolk), and it has been demonstrated that reproductive tissue can be infected. It is thought that the organism might be deposited in the yolk by an infected hen before the shell is formed. Other phage types of *S. enteritidis* (6, 21b, 25 and 34) are also pathogenic. *See:* Eggs.

S. napoli Found to be responsible for a large outbreak of food poisoning in Europe in 1982, from eating contaminated chocolate. This was an unusual event in that confectionery products do not normally support growth of bacteria because of their high sugar content.

S. paratyphi* and *S. typhi *See:* Typhoid and paratyphoid infections (enteric fever).

***S. typhimurium* and *S. typhimurium* DT104** Responsible for many outbreaks of salmonellosis. It is commonly found in the intestine of many animals and birds, especially poultry. The excreta of these animals is therefore potentially able to cause food poisoning if allowed to contaminate food.

A recent problem concerns antibiotic resistant strains of DT104. These are classified by A (ampicillin), C (chloramphenicol), S (streptomycin), Su (sulphonamides) and T (tetracycline) resistance. ACSSuT (multi-resistant) resistance is now well known and medical treatment of suffers is difficult.

S typhimurium DT 104 increases have been noted in Europe and in the USA. In England and Wales an increase from 259 cases in 1990 to 4 006 in 1996 was reported.

Salmonellosis A case of food poisoning caused by an organism of the *Salmonella* group of bacteria.

Salting A method of food preservation which causes death of bacteria by osmosis. Meat, fish and vegetables may be so preserved. The technique works since water in bacterial cells is removed due to the high concentration of salt outside the cells. In osmosis, water moves from the higher concentration of water (bacterial cell cytoplasm) to the lower concentration of water (salt). *See:* Curing, Food Preservation.

Sampling of food Environmental health departments and others (such as Trading Standards Officers) regularly check the quality and composition of foodstuffs by a sampling programme involving laboratory analysis. Samples may be purchased informally to detect any problems, and then formally if results indicate the need for this. The way in which formal sampling is carried out involves a set procedure since results from analysis may result in prosecutions and appeals. The procedure is complex and must be performed exactly since evidence for a prosecution may result. *See:* Bacteriological standard.

Sanitary conveniences
- All premises where persons are employed, including food premises, must have suitable and sufficient sanitary accommodation.
- This must be constructed so that it may be kept clean and be well-lit and ventilated.
- WC compartments must not communicate directly with food rooms or other rooms in the workplace and must not be used for any other purpose such as storage.
- As a guide, one WC each for males and females per 15 persons is needed. Exact numbers are contained in the regulations covering this matter.

See: Appendix: Food Law, Personal hygiene.

Sanitiser A specially formulated cleaning chemical capable of both detergent and disinfecting actions. *See:* Cleaning, Disinfectant.

Saprophyte An organism that lives off dead and decaying organic matter. Such organisms secrete enzymes externally into their surroundings, which digest their food, and the digested substances are reabsorbed back into the cell. Many bacteria and fungi are saprophytes, and so are able to spoil food.

Saprotroph An alternative name for saprophyte.

Sarcotases Blood-engorged parasites occasionally affecting fish.

Sardine Also called the pilchard, a member of the herring family. When canned, as with other canned fish and meat it must be treated as a high-risk food once the can is opened.

Sauerkraut A fermented, salted pickled cabbage utilising the ability of the bacteria *Leuconostoc mesenteroides* and *Leuconostoc plantarum* to produce lactic acid, which acts as a preservative. Both of these are good examples of non-pathogenic organisms used in food production.

Sausage A meat product containing cereal binders and spices contained in skins, made from animal intestines or synthetic materials. Some sausages are cured, smoked or cooked. All are generally thought of as high-risk and should be subject to strict temperature control. This means refrigeration (1-4°C) or hot (over 63°C). *See:* Appendix: Food Law, Meat products.

Saveloy A type of sausage subject to the same risks and treatment as other similar items.

Saw-toothed grain beetle (*Oryzaephilus surinamensis*) Similar to the merchant grain beetle, a pest of stored products, principally cereals. *See:* Beetles.

Saxitoxin *See:* PSP.

SBM Specified Bovine Material such as spinal cord. *See:* BSE.

Scampi (*Nephrops norvegicus*) Also called the Dublin bay prawn, Norway lobster or langoustine. *See:* Shellfish.

Scavenger An animal which feeds on dead and decaying animal or vegetable matter. It is likely to be exposed to and therefore carry a large and varied population of microorganisms, including pathogens.

Schistosoma The blood flukes such as *Schistosoma mansoni* and *S. japonicum* are transmitted to humans and other animals by infected water supplies. The resulting disease is called schistosomiasis.

Scombroid food poisoning
- A food-borne illness resulting from the ingestion of spoiled fresh fish belonging to the scombroid group, such as tuna, mackerel and skipjack.
- The onset period for illness is from 5 minutes to 2 hours and lasts for usually less than 6 hours; weakness and fatigue may persist for 24 hours.
- The symptoms resemble those of botulism: headache, dizziness, nausea, sometimes diarrhoea and vomiting, swelling of the face, burning of the throat, difficulty in swallowing and throbbing of the carotid (neck) and temporal (temples) blood vessels.
- Fish contaminated with the toxin (scombrotoxin) have a characteristic bitter or peppery taste. Levels above 100ppm may produce symptoms.
- The symptoms are caused by the release of histamine and similar amines into the fish, possibly as a result of the activity of a species of *Proteus*, a spoilage bacterium.
- Prompt refrigeration of the fresh fish prevents the occurrence of this illness.
- It is likely that this disease is often misdiagnosed as a food allergy.
- *Klebsiella* and *Morganella* species, which are part of the normal flora of many fish, produce histamine from L-histidine at storage temperatures above 4°C.
  Several outbreaks of scombrotoxic food poisoning were reported in 1996-97 in the UK from fresh vacuum-packed tuna steaks which have a maximum shelf life of 11 days, if kept at 4°C, from being caught.

- In the USA in 1973 a very large national outbreak occurred due to canned tuna.

Scombrotoxin A histamine-like substance responsible for the symptoms of scombroid food poisoning, a type of food poisoning associated with the consumption of certain types of fish including non-scombroid types such as sardines, anchovies, herring, pilchard and salmon. Swiss cheese may also be affected. *See:* Previous entry.

Scoops (ice-cream) *See:* Ice-cream.

Scouring powder An abrasive cleaning agent often containing detergent. The use of abrasives may cause minute surface scratches and thus provide harbourage for bacteria.

Screening
1. Medical screening of food handlers involves taking faecal samples and analysing these for the presence of disease-causing organisms.
See: Exclusion of food handlers.
2. Screening of entrances into food premises with mesh or netting is a means of proofing buildings against pests such as birds.

Seafood A general term often used to describe shellfish.

Seasonal variations of food poisoning
- In Britain there has been a general annual increase in food poisoning outbreaks during the Christmas and New Year period and at Easter, due to increased purchases of poultry.
- Similar increases have been noted during the summer months due to warmer temperatures; strict temperature control is vital during these months.
- The use of casual, often untrained staff at these busy times may contribute to these increases.

'Sell-by' date An obsolete method of date-coding showing the last possible date for sale of a foodstuff. It does not indicate the shelf-life of the product to the consumer who may assume that there are some days 'grace' in which to use the food. A more useful marking is the 'use-by' date which states a definite end to the recommended safe life of the product.

Sepsis The growth of pathogenic bacteria in living tissue.

Septic A wound which has become infected with living pathogenic bacteria.

Characteristically it results in swelling, redness, pain and the production of pus.

Septicaemia A condition characterised by actively reproducing pathogenic micro-organisms, together with their toxins, in the blood. It is commonly referred to as 'blood poisoning'.

Serial dilution A laboratory method of determining the actual numbers of bacteria present in or on a substance, such as food. It involves preparing a series of dilutions, each time by a factor of ten. Chosen dilutions are plated out onto nutrient agar dishes, which are then incubated, and the colonies counted.

Serological typing
- A test carried out in order to identify a specific type or strain of an organism, for example a *Salmonella* bacterium.
- Routine staining and physiological tests fail to identify them since they are very closely related.
- Serum is obtained from an animal previously inoculated with a known strain of the bacterium; the serum will contain antibodies specifically against that strain.
- If the serum is mixed with *Salmonella* isolated from a patient suffering from suspected salmonellosis, then the resulting antibody-antigen response makes it possible to identify the strain of *Salmonella* present.
- It may take some time before a positive identification can be made, since there are over 2 000 different serotypes of *Salmonella* known.

Sequestering agents Chemical substances which render ineffective other substances by combining or complexing with them, an example being the chemical removal of the substances responsible for water hardness.

Services Mains water, gas and electricity supplies, sewage and refuse disposal as supplied to premises.

Sewage
- The watery material carrying refuse and wastes in a drainage system or in sewers.
- It consists of rainwater, grit, leaves, industrial effluents (such as metals, solvents, oil, grease and food waste), household wastes (including disinfectants and detergents), food scraps, urine, faeces and toilet paper.
- Over 99% of sewage is water.
- Raw (untreated) sewage often has a high concentration of harmful bacteria (pathogens) of faecal origin.

188 Sewage contamination

- Rats and cockroaches using sewers, or flies and birds from sewage works may easily pick up contaminants and spread them to food.

Sewage contamination The main health risk associated with sewage contamination of foods is:
1. from a range of bacteria, viruses and protozoa that have survived the sewage treatment processes, or from foods prepared using untreated water,
2. food poisoning through eating raw shellfish, such as oysters, harvested from sewage-contaminated water,
3. if untreated domestic sewage is used to fertilise crops there is a chance that the raw plant foods will be contaminated with various harmful bacteria. *See:* Sewage.

Shelf-life The period for which a product lasts in good condition during storage. This may be from a few days (pasteurised milk) to many years (canned meats). Various dating systems are in use. *See:* Best-before date, Sell-by date, Use-by date.

Shellfish A term used to cover a wide range of creatures (molluscs) including:
 - oysters, cockles and mussels, etc. (bivalves)
 - winkles and whelks (univalves)
 - prawns, lobsters, scampi and shrimps, etc. (Crustacea).

In the UK around 2% of all food-borne illnesses involve seafood but this rises to over 70% in Japan.

Problems
- Some shellfish thrive in sewage-contaminated waters, for example in river estuaries and coastal waters, and may take in any bacteria and viruses that this water contains.
- The bivalves, being filter feeders, are most likely to do this, so they must be purified before human consumption by immersion in disinfected or clean water for some time.
- Toxic chemicals from industrial wastes may also be absorbed by shell fish, but these (and toxins and viruses) may not removed by purification processes (see next entry).
- There is an increasing risk of viral food poisoning from these foods.
- Some people are allergic to shellfish.

Use of shellfish
- The smell of shellfish is a guide as to their freshness since they release obnoxious chemicals when decomposing.
- All raw shellfish must be kept away from other foods and cooked shellfish,

to avoid cross-contamination.
- They should be refrigerated whether raw or cooked at 1-4°C.
- Rapid and thorough cooking are essential.
- Shellfish must be purchased through a reputable supplier since there is a real danger of contaminated foods from unreliable sources, including those gathered direct from the sea or river estuaries.

See: Algae, Hepatitis A, Metals, Paralytic shellfish poisoning, *Salmonella, Vibrio parahaemolyticus.*

Shellfish (purification)
1. Depuration: a technique where shellfish are allowed to self-cleanse by immersion in disinfected water for 36-48 hours.
2. Relaying: shellfish are put into non-polluted water for 4-6 weeks before harvesting. Both methods are capable of worthwhile reductions in bacteria but are not effective in lowering levels of viruses, heavy metals, toxins and pesticides.

Shelving In common with all other fittings in food rooms, shelving should be constructed from an impervious material capable of being easily cleaned. Painted or varnished wood, plastics and stainless steel are suitable if kept in good condition. *See:* Design of food premises.

Shigella
- A group of Gram-negative, non-sporing bacteria found in the intestine of humans and other animals, responsible for the disease known as bacillary dysentery or shigellosis.
- It is more common in tropical countries and has many 'local' names including 'Delhi belly' or ' Gyppy tummy'; some cases of traveller's diarrhoea may be cases of bacillary dysentery.
- There are four pathogenic species: *S. sonnei* (which causes a mild dysentery), *S. dysenteriae* (which causes severe dysentery) and *S. flexneri,* and *S. boydii.* All are facultative anaerobic rod-shaped organisms.
- The incubation period is from 12 hours to 2 days; symptoms include diarrhoea, fever, vomiting, abdominal pain and cramps and, in severe cases, blood and pus in the faeces; infections are usually limited to the large intestine.
- There is some toxin production (*Shigella dysenteriae* produces an exotoxin and an enterotoxin), but invasiveness is the more important factor.
- Increases in both Sweden and the UK have been noted during 1994. A large outbreak in Sweden implicated imported iceberg lettuce.

Shigellosis

Control measures
- The organism is frequently found in water polluted with human faeces, so the disease can be waterborne; efficient sewage and water treatments are therefore necessary.
- It is often spread from person to person by the faecal-oral route, particularly amongst children. Good personal hygiene helps prevent this.
- Associated foods include salads (potato, sea food, pasta and meats), raw vegetables, milk and dairy products and poultry.
- Contaminated food, other objects and flies may also spread the disease; control of flies, hygienic preparation of food, and the use of treated water all help to prevent outbreaks of the disease.
- The most likely route is person-to-person contact in crowded populations that have poor personal hygiene and inadequate water and sewage systems.

Although all species of *Shigella* have been implicated in outbreaks of food borne illness, most outbreaks have been due to *S. sonnei*. The other species are more likely to be associated with contaminated water. (There is some evidence to suggest that *S. flexneri* is in part sexually transmitted; incidence is unusually high amongst homosexual men.)

Shigellosis A general name for bacillary dysentery, caused by species of *Shigella* bacteria.

Ships These, when used for the carriage of food, are subject to the same general design, construction and use criteria as other food premises. Similarly, food preparation and service on board ship must follow normal hygienic principles.

Shrimps *See:* Shellfish.

Silverfish (*Lepisma saccharina*) Silvery coloured insects around 10 mm in length having a characteristic pointed appearance with two long antennae and bristly 'tails'. They are of nuisance value and tend to infest badly-maintained crumbling surfaces, such as decaying brickwork, feeding on food scraps and paper. They are nocturnal and thrive in damp conditions. *See:* Firebrats.

Sinks
- In food premises separate sinks should be provided for hand-washing.
- These should not be used for any other purpose such as food preparation or washing up.
- Since hands should be washed after using toilets, the separate sink is a means of limiting the spread of any bacteria which may have contaminated the hands from the intestines.
- The sink should be constructed so that it can be kept clean and maintained

in this condition.
- Sinks for hand washing should have hot water, soap, nail brush and suitable drying facilities.

See: Hand-washing, Personal hygiene.

Skimmed milk Fat-free milk.

Skin
- Unbroken skin presents an impervious barrier to micro-organisms.
- It is thick, dry and scaly, and its secretions are weakly bactericidal.
- Healthy skin however carries large numbers of bacteria, both permanent (resident) and temporary (transient) species.
- Resident organisms, which live on the skin surface, and in cracks, hair follicles and pores, include the bacterium *Staphylococcus aureus*. These are almost impossible to remove by hand washing.
- Transient organisms are picked up through contact with the surroundings and from the intestines through poor personal hygiene after using the lavatory. They are fairly easy to remove from the skin by proper hand washing.

Any infections cause extra hazards since bacteria will grow and multiply extensively in the warm, moist conditions found in lesions such as cuts.

Slaughterhouses Premises licensed for the slaughter of food animals. There are comprehensive regulations covering their design, construction and operation. Slaughterhouse and abattoir hygiene should include an HACCP-type system, ensuring separation of clean and dirty areas, admitting only clean livestock, use of low pressure sprays and removal of offal likely to be contaminated with the agent of BSE.

Slicing machines The main food hygiene problem concerns cleanliness, particularly between uses for different foods, and the risks of cross-contamination. These machines are also dangerous and safety problems should be considered.

Slime layer An alternative name for the bacterial capsule, the outermost layer of some bacterial cells. It helps to confer virulence on pathogenic forms.

Smears Greasy marks left by rats around pipe work, holes or along walls with which their bodies have been in contact. To an expert, the presence of smears is an indication of rodent movement and may for example give useful information regarding trap location or proofing.

Smoke point The temperature at which oils and fats start to chemically break down releasing acrid-smelling smoke. The oil or fat becomes contaminated with unpleasant tasting and smelling substances such as acrolein which can affect the taste and smell of food. Smoke point is in the region of 200°C.

Smoked foods
- Traditionally prepared by hanging foods such as fish, bacon, sausages and cheese over smouldering hardwood wood chips.
- Some smoked meats and fish may be high-risk foods and thus require refrigeration (1-4°C) during storage.
- Foods may be salted or partially cured before smoking; the process produces flavour changes with substances such as phenols in wood smoke having a bactericidal, and thus preservative effect.
- The heat of the process also causes some drying and most non-spore forming bacteria are killed, but *Clostridium botulinum* and others may survive.
- The process is time-consuming (several days) and a modern development has been in the addition of smoke-flavouring to manufactured foods; such additions have little effect on micro-organisms.
- There is some evidence to suggest that smoking produces carcinogenic chemicals.

Smoking (by food handlers) Smoking should be banned in food rooms.
- The main reason is the contact between mouth and fingers and then fingers to food; any bacteria in the mouth may then be transferred to food.
- Smoking also causes coughing which may spread bacteria from the mouth and nose over a wide area.
- There is a possibility of physical contamination of food with ash, cigarette ends and matches.
- Smoking is increasingly thought of as being antisocial and may create interpersonal problems between staff or others; this is not conducive to good hygiene since quality of work is known to be better in a pleasant environment.
- There are other risks, including risks of fire.

See: Personal hygiene, *Staphylococcus aureus*.

Sneeze screens Barriers between open food and people, designed to protect against the aerosols (probably laden with bacteria) created by sneezing. *See:* Personal hygiene.

Snood A covering for long hair/beards designed to prevent stray hairs entering foods.

Soft cheese 193

Snuff (taking of) This is not to be allowed in food rooms for reasons similar to those for the banning of smoking.

Soap Bars of soap have been shown to support the growth of bacteria and may thus pass on contamination from person to person. The preferred soap for food handlers use is an unperfumed liquid soap in a dosing container. Germicidal soaps are also available. Soap is a cleaning agent made by treatment of fats and oils (e.g. palm oil and olive oil) with heat and alkali (e.g. caustic soda) producing chemicals such as sodium stearate and palmitate. *See:* Detergents, Soapless detergents.

Soapless detergents Detergents such as sodium alkyl benzyl sulphonate used in various cleaning chemicals such as washing up liquid. They do not form scum in hard water and are of neutral pH. Their bactericidal effect is limited unless used in hot water.

Sodium benzoate A preservative with wide use in manufactured foods. *See:* Benzoic acid.

Sodium carbonate Washing soda, a mildly alkaline cleaning agent.

Sodium hexametaphosphate (Calgon - TM) A chemical used to complex ions causing water hardness and produce soft water.

Sodium hydroxide (caustic soda) A strongly alkaline substance capable of dissolving many materials, including hair and burnt-on food. It is a common constituent of drain and oven-cleaning chemicals. The substance is corrosive and should be handled with caution.

Sodium hypochlorite *See:* Hypochlorite.

Sodium metasilicate A mildly alkaline cleaning agent commonly used in dish washing formulations.

Sodium nitrate and nitrite *See:* Curing, Nitrite, Nitrate.

SOFHT (Society of Food Hygiene Technology) An organisation based in Lymington, England involved with food hygiene and training in the food manufacturing sector.

Soft cheese Made by a process not involving pressing. Those varieties ripened with moulds or other micro-organisms should, unless ripening, be stored under refrigeration (1-4°C). *See:* Appendix : Food Law, Cheese.

194 Softening of water

Softening of water Water hardness caused by dissolved substances may be removed by several means including boiling or by treatment with chemicals. On a large scale, water may be run through an ion exchange column so that dissolved calcium and magnesium ions which cause hardness are exchanged for sodium ions which do not. *See:* Hardness of water.

Soft ice-cream A product dispensed direct from the freezing equipment which must be thoroughly cleaned at regular intervals. Mobile ice-cream vendors occasionally neglect cleaning (pressure of work being a frequently stated reason for this) and levels of bacteria then build up to a potentially dangerous level. A soft ice-cream machine switched off uncleaned and left overnight may contain large numbers of micro-organisms the following day. *See:* Growth requirements (bacterial).

Soil
- Soil is a complex mixture of solid material, water, air, living organisms and the products of decay.
- It is one of the main reservoirs of micro-organisms, containing vast numbers of bacteria, fungi, algae, protozoa and viruses (usually plant pathogens).
- It has been estimated that just one gram of the top few centimetres of typical garden soil contains about 12 000 000 bacteria and 120 000 fungi, with moulds greatly outnumbering yeasts.
- Even though the vast majority of these micro-organisms are beneficial (helping to improve soil fertility) many of them are potential pathogens or spoilage agents; soil therefore presents important potential hazards in a food preparation environment.

(*Note:* Soil is also a term used in cleaning to mean any undesirable matter.)

Soil micro-organisms
- Many human pathogens can survive in soil for varying periods of time, some for many years.
- Most are spore-forming bacteria such as *Bacillus anthracis* (anthrax), *Clostridium botulinum* (botulism), *Clostridium perfringens* (gas gangrene and food poisoning), and *Clostridium tetani* (tetanus).
- Even non-spore formers, such as *Salmonella* species can survive for considerable periods (weeks or months).
- Also present in soil are members of the following bacteria: *Acetobacter, Alcaligenes, Chromobacter, Enterobacter, Escherichia, Flavobacterium, Micrococcus, Mycobacterium, Proteus, Pseudomonas, Streptococcus,* and *Streptomyces.*

Sous Vide **195**

- Representative fungi include species of *Aspergillus, Mucor, Penicillium, Trichoderma* and many others.

Practical Points

1. Unwashed vegetables are almost certain to have plenty of soil on them, and if they are prepared on the same work surface as for example cooked meat, cross-contamination may easily occur.
2. Surfaces and items coming into contact with soil must be carefully cleaned and disinfected before their use with other food.
3. Separate vegetable storage and preparation areas are preferred to minimise cross-contamination.
4. Soil organisms can be introduced into a food preparation area if personal hygiene is poor, for example if the hands are not washed properly after handling raw vegetables such as potatoes, root vegetables such as carrots, and salad produce.

Solanin A substance, toxic to some people, produced in poisonous quantities in potatoes which have been stored in the light or cold. Since chlorophyll is also produced in these conditions, its green colour is an indication that solanin is present. There is evidence that high levels of this substance causes nausea, headaches and neurological disturbances. *See:* Alkaloids.

Sous Vide

```
┌─────────────────────────────────┐
│          Preparation            │
└─────────────────────────────────┘
                 ↓
┌─────────────────────────────────┐
│ Food placed into plastic laminate pouches │
└─────────────────────────────────┘
                 ↓
┌─────────────────────────────────┐
│         Vacuum applied          │
└─────────────────────────────────┘
                 ↓
┌─────────────────────────────────┐
│          Heat sealed            │
└─────────────────────────────────┘
                 ↓
┌─────────────────────────────────┐
│   Low temperature part-cooking  │
└─────────────────────────────────┘
                 ↓
┌─────────────────────────────────┐
│       Refrigerated storage      │
│ 3°C for 3-5 days or more depends on the system │
└─────────────────────────────────┘
                 ↓
┌─────────────────────────────────┐
│           Reheated              │
│ Microwave, boil in the bag or other method │
└─────────────────────────────────┘
                 ↓
┌─────────────────────────────────┐
│       Eaten immediately         │
└─────────────────────────────────┘
```

Sous vide A French term meaning 'under vacuum' used to describe an interrupted catering process in which lightly cooked food, often of high value (sometimes 'Cordon Bleu' style), is heat-sealed into plastic pouches in vacuum conditions.
- The product has a shelf-life under chill conditions (less than 5°C) of some days and is reheated when required.
- *Clostridium botulinum* favours both the vacuum and temperature found in this product so hygiene standards during production, storage and use are important.
- The process will not destroy spores or toxins.
- Heat treatment by steam cooking at 90°C for 10 minutes achieves a satisfactory reduction in *Clostridium botulinum* numbers, but may affect the quality of the product, as do a pH below 5, an a_w below 0.97 or a salt concentration over 3.5%. However all of these may also usefully reduce anaerobic bacterial levels.

Sorbic acid An anti-mould agent, working best in slightly acid conditions. It is used as a food additive in cheese, bread, jam and other manufactured foods.

Sparrows *See:* Birds.

Species In microbiology, a population of e.g. bacterial cells which are all essentially alike. For example the bacterial genus *Clostridium* has a number of species, including *botulinum, perfringens* and *tetani*. (The species name is always written in the lower case.) Together with the generic name (in this case *Clostridium*) it forms the scientific name of the organism. Different species are thus named, and in this example we have *Clostridium botulinum, Clostridium perfringens* and *Clostridium tetani*.

Species barrier The theory that certain diseases cannot be transmitted between species, for example BSE in cattle and scrapie in sheep to humans.

Spiders More of a nuisance value than a health hazard although there is a risk of physical contamination of food with bodies.

Spirilla A group of rigid, spiral, corkscrew-shaped bacteria. They possess flagella.

Spirillum A curve-shaped bacterium. There are three forms: spirilla, spirochaetes and vibrio.

Spirochaetes A group of Gram-negative, slender, corkscrew-shaped bacteria; they differ from spirilla in that they lack flagella, but move by means of axial filaments. These are similar to flagella, but are contained under an external flexible sheath. Spirochaetes are found in contaminated water, in sewage, soil, decaying organic matter and in the bodies of humans and animals. Included in this group are the pathogenic *Treponema pallidum* (syphilis), *Borrelia* species (e.g. relapsing fever, transmitted by ticks or lice), and *Leptospira* species (leptospirosis, transmitted by contaminated water). Many spirochaetes are harmless saprophytes living in soil and stagnant water.

Spoilage of food
- The development of undesirable changes in food such as 'off' flavours and tastes, or changes in appearance such as colour, consistency or the production of gas.
- It is the result of natural decomposition and/or the effects of microbial growth in or on the food.
- Causes of food spoilage include bacteria, moulds, yeasts, and chemical reactions such as those leading to rancidity.
- Food poisoning bacteria such as *Salmonella* do not cause easily noticed changes in foods and do not make foods go 'off'.
- Food spoilage bacteria include various *Clostridium, Pseudomonas, Achromobacter, Micrococcus, Erwinia, Lactobacilli, Acinetobacter* and others
- Proper, careful storage (e.g. refrigeration or in dry stores) will delay, but not prevent these changes.

Sporadic case An isolated or 'one-off' case of food poisoning not apparently connected with other cases.

Sporangiophore A structure produced by a mature fungal mycelium as part of the reproductive process. It is a stalked structure (an aerial hypha), supporting a spore case (sporangium).

Sporangiospore An asexual spore produced within a sporangium; they are produced as a means of reproduction in some moulds such as the common black bread mould *Rhizopus*.

Sporangium A sac containing fungal spores. Typically each sporangium contains hundreds of sporangiospores.

Spore (bacterial) *See:* Endospore.
Spore (fungal)

Spore (fungal)

- An asexual or sexual reproductive cell, the production of which is how fungi reproduce and spread; this is in stark contrast to the function of bacterial spores which are produced by some forms only, and as a means of survival.
- Millions of spores are released into the atmosphere and they are rapidly distributed by air currents.
- Many, once inhaled, may cause an allergic reaction, producing hay-fever type symptoms.
- Spores are of key importance in the identification and classification of fungi.
- Fungi produce sexual spores less frequently than they do asexual spores; they are produced most often under special circumstances.

See: Ascospore, Basidiospore, Zygospore.

Spray drier A device consisting of a large chamber into the top of which a liquid is sprayed as a fine aerosol. The liquid droplets fall through a rising current of heated air and are dried. A typical product is dried milk. If the feed liquid is high-risk, such as milk, it may require pre-treatment such as pasteurisation.

Springer A stage in the deterioration and spoilage of canned foods in which thumb pressure on one end of the can cause the other to spring out.
See: Blown cans, Canning.

Staining of bacteria Bacteria can be seen under the light microscope but they appear colourless. When stained they are much more clearly visible. A number of stains are commonly employed in the laboratory, including:

1. Gram-staining, which is a counterstaining method, and classifies all bacteria into one or other of two groups,
2. staining of capsules, and
3. the staining of endospores.

A great deal of information can be gained by looking at the stained and magnified organisms, for example when attempting to identify a particular organism. However, the presence of a particular organism can only be confirmed by biochemical tests.

SRSV (Small Round Structured Virus) The numbers of cases of food poisoning reported in England and Wales from these has risen from less than 500 in 1992 to over 2 000 in 1994 possibly because of improved laboratory techniques and increased awareness. SRSV is suspected when stool culture is negative for bacterial pathogens, the illness has a duration of 16-29 hours, vomiting occurs in more than 50% of cases and the incubation period is 15-48 hours (if known). Electron microscope confirmation is also possible. *See:* Gastroenteritis, Virus.

Stainless steel A durable, impervious and readily cleanable but expensive metal alloy with wide use in food rooms. There is a specific food grade containing 18% chromium and 8% nickel and known as 18/8. Care must be taken when cleaning this substance since it may be permanently damaged by the use of steel wool or scouring powers. *See:* Design of equipment in food premises.

Standing time (in microwave cooking) A period of time after initial cooking, during which heat spreads throughout the food (by conduction) and cooking continues. It is an important part of the cooking process. If it is not allowed for the food will be under-cooked.

Staphylococcus Any aggregate of spherically shaped bacterial cells, that exist in random clusters after cell division. They are often described as 'like a bunch of grapes'.

Staphylococcus aureus
- A Gram-positive spherical bacterium (coccus) which is responsible for many outbreaks of food poisoning; it is found in large numbers in cuts, boils etc. and it is also found in and around the nose and throat.
- Found in air, dust, sewage, milk, food and food equipment, surfaces, humans and animals.
- It grows between 7° and 45°C producing an enterotoxin in the food (an exotoxin) which causes food poisoning.
- It is a non-spore former, but the toxin is heat-resistant being destroyed only gradually during boiling for 30 minutes.
- The onset period for the disease is 1 to 6 hours, and the illness typically lasts from 6 to 48 hours.
- Symptoms appear rapidly and are typically nausea, severe vomiting, abdominal pain and cramps, sometimes followed by collapse. Death is rare and diarrhoea is a common secondary symptom.
- Because of these often mild symptoms, it is thought that many cases are not reported, particularly since recovery is often rapid.
- It is a facultative anaerobe, but grows best in the presence of oxygen.
- Resistance to various antibiotics including methicillin, mupirocin and fusidic acid has been noted.
- At least 26 people, including the captain of an aircraft, on flights from Los Angeles to London in 1991 developed acute food poisoning after eating a chocolate dessert contaminated with *S. aureus*.

Control

- Contamination is most often from food handlers, since the organism is found in the nose and throat, and also on the hair and skin of about 50% or more of healthy people; good personal hygiene is vital.
- The toxin may not be destroyed by reheating or light cooking; thorough heating is necessary.
- Foods commonly involved are dishes which have been handled and then kept at room temperature for more than 2 hours, and then eaten cold, such as cold meats, trifles, cream and custard-filled cakes; refrigerated storage before use is important.
- Foods often incriminated include meat and meat products, poultry and egg products, salads of all kinds (e.g. potato, pasta, meat and fish), bakery products (e.g. cream-filled pastries, cakes and pies), milk and dairy products and sandwich fillings. Canned foods contaminated after processing have also been responsible for causing outbreaks.
- It is the most salt and sugar resistant of the food poisoning organisms and so can cause problems with cured products such as ham and bacon; people often assume these are safe because they are salted.
- Similarly, the practice of salting butchers' blocks does not kill all *S. aureus*.
- Custard and cream products favour the growth of *Staphylococcus aureus* since the high sugar content retards the growth of other bacteria (those less osmotically resistant).
- Refrigeration of susceptible foods is the easiest and most reliable method of preventing growth of this bacterium.

See: Exclusion of food handlers, Personal hygiene.

Starlings Sometimes called the 'flying rat' by pest control operators. *See:* Birds.

Star symbols Freezers and the frozen food compartments of some refrigerators carry a star symbol. Each star is 'worth' minus 6°C. This gives an indication of how long a frozen food may be stored and remain in good condition. The symbols are

    *   up to one week   (minus 6°C)

    **   up to one month   (minus 12°C)

    ***   up to three months   (minus 18°C)

    ****   three months or longer (minus 18-24°C)

Note: The 4-star rated freezer is the only type of appliance that is capable of freezing fresh food.

Stationary phase *See:* Bacterial growth curve.

Statutory instruments UK Regulations and orders made under Acts of Parliament and having legal status. *See:* Appendix : Food Law, Codes of Practice.

Steak Tartare A raw minced meat product which should be consumed within six days of slaughter if chilled mince is used. Longer storage periods, up to 18 months for frozen beef and veal, are allowed for in EU recommendations.

Steam disinfection Steam may be used by trained persons during cleaning in the form of jets directed from a lance which is attached to a steam generator. It may also incorporate detergent metering. Accumulations which are difficult to remove and inaccessible areas are often steam-cleaned. Deep cleaning of ducting leading from extraction hoods may also use steam lances. *See:* Cleaning.

Steam fly *See:* German cockroach.

Stenotrophomonas maltophila During 1992 patients in a hospital in England were infected with ice from an ice-making machine.

Sterile Free from any living thing.

Sterilisation
1. Any process that destroys (or removes) all living organisms (including bacterial endospores) in or on an object. It very often involves heat and/or chemicals.
2. In milk processing, a temperature of 110°C for about 30 minutes achieves commercial sterility. Other products such as ice-cream and cream may also be sterilised.
3. Canning achieves commercial sterility.

The term is often misused and confused with disinfection. Sterilisation means 100% destruction or removal of all living organisms including their spores and is very difficult to achieve. Disinfection (reduction of micro-organisms to a safe level) is more likely in processes such as cleaning. *See:* Fo, Pasteurisation, Turbidity test.

Sterilising sinks In washing up, a method of disinfecting crockery and cutlery etc. by standing them in hot water (82-88°C) for at least 30 seconds. The term 'sterilising' is incorrect but is in common use. *See:* Washing up.
Sticky boards Adhesive-coated traps used in pest control for insects and rodents

in small infestations, or for survey purposes.

Stock rotation A system in which older stock is used first thus minimising risks of pest infestation and stock deterioration. *See:* Best-before date, Shelf-life, Use-by date.

Storage of foods Correct storage conditions for foodstuffs are essential to ensure

freshness
maximum shelf-life
prevention of food poisoning and spoilage
prevention of pest infestations.

Elements of good storage
- Thoroughly check all goods inward by trained and authorised persons to ensure that only good quality items are accepted.
- Damaged goods or those delivered at unacceptable temperatures (for example partly thawed frozen foods) should be rejected.
- Each type of food has optimum storage conditions, for example
  - raw meat and poultry at around 0°C
  - meat products at less than 8°C
  - canned foods and many vegetables in dry conditions at 10-15°C
  - dried foods such as flour in tightly closed containers at 10-15°C.
- In storage areas, construction and design should be so that proper cleaning is possible with foods stored off the ground.

See: Appendix: Food Law, Dry goods stores, Refrigerators.

Streptococcus Any group of spherically-shaped bacterial cells that remain attached in chains after cell division.

Streptococcus **species** These are microaerophilic non-sporing Gram-positive bacteria, four groups of which are important in foods.

1. **Enterococcus.**
Five species are known, including *Streptococcus faecalis*, which can be transmitted to humans by food. It is unusual in that
a. it is thermoduric and likely to survive pasteurisation
b. it is tolerant of high salt concentrations and can grow on bacon and cause spoilage of canned ham
c. it can grow in alkaline conditions
d. it has a wide temperature range for growth (5 to 50°C).

It is found in the intestinal tract of humans and animals, and is sometimes used as an indicator of faecal contamination of foods. *Streptococcus faecium* (more commonly from plant sources) is a very similar organism with similar properties. Outbreaks of food poisoning (associated with meat, milk, cheese and poultry) are not common; symptoms are similar to those of staphylococcal food poisoning. They are usually the result of under-processing or unsanitary preparation, storing, or handling of food.

2. Lactic acid forming.
Examples are *Streptococcus cremoris* and *Streptococcus lactis*, which are used as starters for hard cheeses. The latter has been shown to cause spoilage of raw milk, causing souring and ropiness. These organisms are not very salt tolerant.

3. Pyogenic (pus forming).
Examples are *Streptococcus agalactiae* (mastitis in cows) and *Streptococcus pyogenes* (septic sore throat and scarlet fever), both of which have been found in raw milk. *S. pyogenes* has also been found in foods containing eggs or milk. Entrance into food is the result of poor hygiene, food handlers working whilst ill, and the use of unpasteurised milk.

4. Viridans.
Examples are *Streptococcus thermophilus* (used as a starter for 'continental' cheeses and yoghurt) which may cause spoilage of canned foods and *Streptococcus bovis*, found in cow manure and saliva. Both forms are thermoduric.

Streptomyces A group of Gram-positive aerobic bacteria, commonly isolated from soil, which can cause undesirable flavours and appearance when growing on foods. They produce a musty or earthy taste, which may be absorbed by nearby foods. (Many species of *Streptomyces* have been used extensively for the production of antibiotics and more recently for the industrial production of enzymes.)

***Strongylus* species (Nematodes)** Small worms affecting internal organs of food animals, which if badly affected, should be condemned.

Stuffing Should be cooked separately from poultry since filling the body cavity makes cooking times longer and increases the risk of organisms such as salmonellas surviving. It is possible that the stuffing will become contaminated and thus more dangerous than the poultry itself. *See:* Centre temperature.

Sublimation The direct change from solid (ice) to water vapour without liquid forming. *See:* Accelerated Freeze Drying.

Sucrose Table sugar.

Sugar A preservative which causes the removal of water from cells, including bacterial cells, by osmosis. Moulds are less affected. Foods with a high sugar content such as jam, confectionery and some bakery items are unlikely to cause food poisoning, but if mould growth is apparent, such contaminated foods should be treated with caution due to possible aflatoxin presence. *See:* Aflatoxin, Available water, Osmosis.

Sulphiding A chemical reaction between sulphur-containing amino acids in meats and some vegetables (e.g. peas) and iron in cans produces iron II (ferrous) sulphide. This is a blackish-coloured substance which may stain food in cans, or the inside of cans especially along side seams. It may be safely trimmed off corned beef and similar foods.

Sulphur Dioxide An acidic gas which is the active component of a number of preservative compounds. It is very widely used in beers, wines, meat products and many other foods. It is toxic to most animals and levels in food are controlled.

Sun-drying An ancient method of preservation, used in Mediterranean and other regions for thousands of years to produce raisins, sultanas and other dried fruits, meats and fish. The technique is still in use today, problems being attack by birds and pests. Food poisoning bacteria will not normally live on dried foods.
See: Dehydration.

Surfactants (Surface-active agents) *See:* Detergents.

Swine erysipelas An infectious bacterial disease of pigs causing skin discoloration and septicaemia which may affect humans and other animals.

Sycosis barbae A staphylococcal-caused rash, occurring in the beard region of the face. It results in the formation of many pus-containing spots, which, if allowed to contaminate food (e.g. by the fingers), could cause staphylococcal food poisoning.

Symbiosis A close physical relationship between organisms of two different species that may or may not be beneficial to the organisms involved.
See: Commensalism, Mutualism, Parasitism.

Symptomless excreter Some people who harbour disease-causing organisms inside their bodies sometimes excrete them, which may then contaminate foods, surfaces etc.

They themselves never show any symptoms of any disease. They are of great importance in the food industry since such people can easily be responsible for causing outbreaks of bacterial food poisoning, without being aware of it. As they show no symptoms, they would not be excluded from work, as for example would someone suffering from diarrhoea. *See:* Carrier, Typhoid Mary.

Symptoms of food poisoning Generally these are
- nausea
- vomiting
- diarrhoea
- abdominal pain and cramps.

These may vary widely from symptoms so mild that they are ignored, to those which are so severe that affected individuals suffer collapse and/or severe discomfort and even death. There may also be additional symptoms, such as fever or chill, headache, aching of limbs, and in some cases (such as in botulism) paralysis and death are not uncommon. Similarly onset/incubation times may range from hours to days (commonly), but unusually to weeks and even (rarely) months.

Synergism When two kinds of micro-organisms or chemicals act together, they may be able to bring about changes (such as fermentations) that neither could produce alone.

Taeniasis The disease caused by parasitic tapeworms, particularly the Cestoda.

Taenia hydatigena A tapeworm whose intermediate host is cattle and other food animals, the final host being dogs.

Taint in meat Undesirable odours and tastes, resulting from the growth of bacteria on the surface of meat, often evident before other signs of spoilage.

Tasting of food If food is to be tasted during cooking, such as to check seasoning, it is important that a clean implement is used, which should then not be re-used without prior washing. It is certain to be contaminated with saliva from the mouth, which may contain bacteria, including *Staphylococcus aureus*. The re-use of spoons without washing in between has been found to be responsible for outbreaks of food poisoning. Similar dangers of probable contamination of food are likely if a finger is used in order to taste the food. *See:* Hands, Mucous membrane, Personal hygiene.

Tap proportioner A metering device connected to a water tap which controls the amount of liquid substances such as detergents which require mixing with the water.
Tapeworms

Tapeworms

- Parasitic worms having a small head and a long body consisting of many segments (proglottids). The head possesses suckers (some also have hooks) which enable the worm to attach itself to the lining of the intestines.
- Segments are continually produced at the neck region of the worm as long as the worm is alive and attached. Some adult worms grow up to 15-20 metres in length and may live for up to 25 years.
- The worms are hermaphroditic (each segment containing a set of male and female reproductive organs) and segments furthest from the body contain fertilised eggs which pass out with the faeces of the host.
- Several species exist which affect food animals, domestic animals and others. Examples include *Diphyllobothrium* (fish), *Taenia* (beef and pork), *Echinococcus* (dog, sheep. cattle and horses) and *Toxocara* (many animals including dogs, cats and foxes).

Eaten in infected and undercooked meat

Bladderworm or CYSTICERCUS
Head
Hollow bag

Secondary host-pig or cow

SINGLE EGG

Primary host-man

RIPE SEGMENT, full of eggs passed out with faeces

Head with HOOKS and SUCKERS

ADULT WORM develops in primary host and attaches to wall of intestine

End segment break off

Note: Stages not to scale

Life cycle of the tapeworm

The beef tapeworm is typical of the risks and necessary precautions to be taken for most of these parasites. Generally, symptoms are not severe but vomiting, anaemia, diarrhoea and loss of appetite may occur. Freezing for several days kill the cysts in meat.

Temperature Several temperatures are important in food hygiene from freezer temperature at minus 18°C to the process temperature of 132°C for UHT milk.
See: Danger zone, Temperature Control.

Temperature control
- The practice of keeping high-risk food outside the range of temperatures in which food poisoning and food spoilage bacteria grow.
- This is 8-63°C and is often called the 'Danger Zone'
- Refrigeration and cooking are the two most common methods of controlling temperature.
- A commonly quoted motto in food hygiene is:

    KEEP IT HOT, KEEP IT COLD OR DON'T KEEP IT AT ALL.

- Many reported outbreaks of food poisoning have poor temperature control as a root cause.
- In England and Wales foods which support the growth of harmful bacteria or the formation of toxins which would result in a risk to health must be kept above 63°C or below 8°C.
- These foods (often called 'high-risk' or 'perishable') include dairy products with a pH over 4.5, cooked foods, meat and fish products and pastry and dough products.
- A number of foodstuffs such as those which have been preserved, raw foods which are to be cooked and those needing to be ripened at ambient temperature are excluded.
- There are some exceptions for high risk foods including display of previously chilled food for a once only maximum time of four hours above 8°C or of previously hot food for up to two hours. This allows for food service in catering. There are provisions for limited fluctuations of temperature during loading or breakdowns of equipment and for scientifically proven arguments to allow foods to be kept outside these temperatures.
- Regular monitoring, either manually or by various recording devices including computers, is needed. Product and air temperature may be taken. Any probes used need to be disinfected.
- In Scotland, there is no set chill temperature. A centre temperature of 82°C is required unless quality is affected.

208 *Temperature Zones*

- Generally food should not be stored at a temperature likely to result in a risk to health and there are separate EU recommendations for other foodstuffs including minced meats, in many cases well below 8°C.
- Cooked or reheated food should reach 75°C at the centre (core temperature) as good practice.

See: Appendix: Food Law, Bacterial growth requirements, Mesophiles.

Temperature Zones

°C	
180	Hot cooking oil
132	UHT milk (one second)
121	Fo-*Cl.botulinum* killed in 3 minutes
100	Water boils. Bacteria killed more quickly
88	Final rinse in washing up
82	Hot cupboard
72	Pasteurisation (milk)
70	Minimum centre temperature for cooked foods
63	Top of danger zone. Bacteria killed slowly
55	Main wash water in washing up
37	Human body temperature
20	Comfortable room temperature
15	Dry goods store
10	Bacteria start to become dormant
8	Lower danger zone for high-risk foods
5	
4	Refrigerator
1	
0	Water freezes
-6	One star freezer
-12	Two star freezer. Some ice-cream freezers.
-18	Deep freeze storage
-25	
-35 and below	Blast freezer. Very low temperature storage

Tenebrio species Large oval dark coloured beetles which include *T. obscuris* the dark mealworm and *T. molitor* the yellow mealworm. Adults (which may grow to 3 cm) and larvae affect mainly cereals and thrive in damp dark conditions. Their presence is an indication of long-standing cleaning problems since infestations take many months to develop.

Terrapin Many pets, including such 'exotic' types, are known carriers of *Salmonella*.

Tetra-Pak (TM) A laminated paper container developed for packaging UHT milk and other liquids such as fruit juices. The container is made by machine from a roll of laminate while the liquid is being filled under aseptic (sterile) conditions.

Thawing
- The raising of the temperature of frozen food from as low as minus 18°C so that all ice is melted.
- If food is to be cooked, adequate thawing is vital to ensure that the heat of cooking can kill any pathogens and is not wasted in melting ice.
- Thawing in a refrigerator at less than 8°C may take many hours but will limit growth of bacteria. It is probably the safest method.
- Thawing at room temperature or in cold water results in an increase in numbers of bacteria on the surface while the inside may remain frozen. If cooking is thorough, this may not be a problem although some bacteria may produce toxins which are not destroyed by cooking.
- Controlled thawing at 10-15°C, keeping food separate and taking care that all equipment used is disinfected and that juices do not cause cross-contamination, are important factors.
- Microwave thawing has the disadvantage of producing localised hot or cold spots. It must be done on the correct setting following the manufacturers' recommendations and can be very effective.
- Certain small sized foods such as vegetables and beef burgers do not require thawing and may be cooked from frozen. This is not true for large items such as frozen poultry.

Thermal death rate curve A graph of the log (logarithm) of the number of surviving cells against time of heating at a constant temperature. From this graph the thermal death time curve is derived.

Thermal death time The length of time required to kill all bacterial cells of a given species at a given temperature.

Thermal death time curve A graph of time against temperature showing equivalent time/temperature combinations lethal to an organism. For example *Clostridium botulinum* may be destroyed by heating at 100°C for 6 hours or at 121°C for 3 minutes. *See:* Fo value.

Thermoduric Heat resistant. Such micro-organisms endure high temperatures, waiting for more favourable conditions to develop. Examples include the *Bacillus* and *Clostridium* groups of bacteria. *See:* Endospore.

Thermometers Probe thermometers are now commonly used in many food premises. They should be

1. calibrated before use (iced water at 0°C and boiling water at 100°C are useful tests) to check accuracy; manufacturers may periodically re-calibrate probes
2. disinfected in between uses to avoid cross-contamination, a disinfectant wipe is often used both before and after taking a reading
3. inserted at the correct depth to ensure that it is the temperature at the centre of the food which is being measured.

In refrigerators and freezers, a fixed thermometer may be fitted by the manufacturer or a small strip thermometer used.

Infra red 'gun' thermometers are a non-invasive method of taking surface temperatures.

Temperatures of refrigerators (1-4°C) and freezers (minus 18°C) should be checked and recorded several times per day. Some larger installations use chart recorders or computer controlled systems fitted with alarms. *See:* Due diligence, Refrigerators.

Thermophile An organism whose optimum temperature for growth is above 45°C. *Bacillus stearothermophilus* is such an organism which sometimes causes spoilage in canned foods.

Tiling Ceramic or other impervious tiles with a suitable waterproof grout are excellent surface materials for food room use including walls, floors and partitions. They are durable if the correct cleaning agents are used but initially expensive. The main disadvantage is that they are brittle and may crack on impact becoming unsatisfactory since the crack may harbour bacteria and food scraps. Cracked tiles are impossible to clean properly.

Toxoplasmosis

Tin
1. A corrosion-resistant metal used to coat the mild steel plate from which cans are made. The common name for cans is tins.
2. Food poisoning has been reported from opened cans which have become contaminated with tin dissolved from the can by the action of acids. It is advisable to decant the contents of part-used cans into suitable covered containers, if they are to be refrigerated.

TMA Some types of fish produce the chemical substance trimethylamine during decomposition. The amount may be used as an indication of freshness. *See:* ATP.

Toadstools A popular, non-scientific term used to describe large fungi other than the common edible mushroom. Toadstools are generally thought of as being poisonous.

Toilets *See:* Sanitary conveniences.

Torry kiln A mechanical trolley-loaded kiln used in the smoking of fish.

Total Viable Count (TVC) *See*: Bacteriological Standard.

Total volatile basic nitrogen A laboratory method for assessing freshness of certain species of fish.

Towels (hand, paper, roller) *See*: Drying of hands.

Toxic Poisonous.

Toxin A poison of bacterial or other origin. Ingestion of toxins in foods is a common cause of food poisoning. *See:* Endotoxin, Enterotoxin, Exotoxin, Haemagglutin, Lectin, Neurotoxin Paralytic shellfish poisoning.

Toxocara Tapeworms which are common parasites of dogs (*T. canis*) and cats (*T. felis*) producing larvae which may cause serious damage to various organs in humans. Infection is thought to be by ingestion of eggs following contact with animal faeces, the urban fox being one reservoir of this organism.

Toxoplasmosis The protozoan parasite, *Toxoplasma gondii* and *T. cati* whose definitive host is the cat, causes a variety of symptoms, including neurological disorders, in humans who may consume cysts or tachyzoites (an early stage in the parasite's life cycle) from infected raw or under cooked meat or milk, or through contact with cats that shed cysts in their faeces. *T. gondii* has been found in virtually all food animals. Many human cases are not food-borne. Symptoms in humans vary from mild to life-threatening. Around 1 500 000 cases of toxoplasmosis occur annually in the US, with over 300 deaths. Toxoplasmosis is common throughout the world but rare in the UK.

Trans fatty acids (TFAs) Formed during the hydrogenation of oils in margarine manufacture and have been associated with coronary heart disease by increasing blood plasma cholesterol. A safe daily intake has not yet been suggested.

Training of food handlers
- Persons handling food should possess sufficient knowledge of food hygiene to enable them to act in a safe and hygienic manner.
- A trained work force is likely to be more confident and efficient, less likely to cause food poisoning or other problems concerning the product and be better motivated.
- It is unlikely that due diligence could be proved if a food business was operating with untrained staff and problems concerning food safety occurred.
- Various types of training are appropriate, depending on levels of responsibility and work done.

Induction courses (1-2 hours)
- for all previously untrained workers giving the most important principles before any food-related work starts, this may be combined with supervision after work starts.

Basic courses (about 6 hours)
- for all food handlers such as cooks, chefs, production workers, bar staff etc.

Intermediate courses (about 18 hours)
- for supervisors and some management.

Advanced courses (about 36 hours)
- for managers and trainers.

An appropriate level of training and/or supervision related to the risk to the food from the food handler is legally required in the UK. *See:* CIEH, Due diligence, HACCP, Pennington Report, RSH, RIPHH, SOFHT.

Transient organisms Micro-organisms that are present on an animal, including humans, for a short time without causing disease. *See:* Skin.

Transmissible disease *See:* Communicable disease.

Traps Insects, birds and rodents may be physically controlled by catching them, normally in a baited trap. Such devices need expert location and there should be no alternative foods available if the bait is to be successful. There is a problem in disposing of live or dead bodies. Traps may also be used in surveys to estimate the extent of an infestation. *See:* Fly papers, Sticky boards, Ultra violet.

Traveller's diarrhoea Common name for food poisoning acquired in foreign countries caused by a number of organisms, such as *E. coli.*

Trematodes Flatworm parasites of animals and humans, the most common being the liver fluke (*Fasciola hepatica*).

Tribolium The flour beetles including *T. castaneum* (rust red flour beetle), *T. confusum* (confused flour beetle) and *T. destructor* (dark flour beetle). They are common pests of stored cereals, especially flour. Adults vary from 3-6 mm in length and are brown in colour with *T. destructor* sometimes being black. *See:* Beetles.

Trichinella spiralis

- The parasitic trichina worm which produces cysts in humans, rats, pigs, seals and bears.
- Eating pork containing viable cysts results in small worms (up to 4 cm) maturing in the intestines.
- Fertilised female worms burrow into the intestinal lining and deposit large numbers (thousands) of larvae which enter the bloodstream and are carried throughout the body.
- The larvae form cysts in muscles including the diaphragm and tongue and may cause severe problems; after some time the cysts in humans calcify and die.
- The reservoir of infection is the pig which contracts the disease from eating undercooked food containing infected pork or from rats.
- Pork may be made safe by freezing (10 days at minus 18°C) or cooking to 75°C.

Trichinosis was reported in France from eating horse meat imported from the USA (23 cases in 1991), Canada (538 cases in 1993), Mexico (7 cases in 1994) and Poland (125 cases in 1976). The first such incident was as long ago as 1881.

Trichiniasis or trichinosis The disease in humans or animals caused by the parasitic worm *Trichinella spiralis*.

Trisodium phosphate (TSP) A sanitising rinse capable of reducing the level of *E. coli* on carcass meat and adipose tissue.

Tuberculosis In humans, a chronic communicable disease of the respiratory system caused by the Gram-positive bacterium *Mycobacterium tuberculosis*. It may be contracted from food such as milk or by droplet infection. There are two forms human and bovine, with bovine having been eradicated by a control programme in some countries including Great Britain but is rife in many others. Heat treatment of milk destroys the bacterium. *See:* Milk, Pasteurisation.

Turbidity test A post-processing test for sterilised milk depending on soluble proteins being denatured by heating above 100°C. A positive test indicates insufficient heating or the presence of raw milk.

Turkeys Share common food hygiene problems with chickens but the large size of some birds makes thawing, cooking, cooling and temperature control in general more difficult. *See:* Poultry.

Two-sink system (Double sink system) A manual method of washing up using

1. a sink containing hot water at 55°C with a detergent, and
2. a second sink with water at 82-88°C or with cooler water containing a chemical disinfectant.

Less soiled items such as glasses are washed first. The sequence of washing up is:

a. pre-clean or scrape items to remove large deposits
b. wash in the first sink to remove grease and soil
c. rinse in the second sink to remove residues and to heat up and disinfect cleaned items; this may take around 2 minutes.
d. air-dry the hot items
e. final storage away from possible contamination.
See: Cleaning, Dishwashing, Soil.

Typhoid fever (enteric fever) Caused by *Salmonella typhi B*. Reservoir of infection is usually the gastrointestinal tract of humans, both cases and carriers. Transmission is mainly food-borne from consumption of food contaminated with faeces by a human case (sufferer) or occasionally from a symptomless excreter. Water contaminated with sewage has also been found to be responsible, both through drinking and through washing fruit and vegetables. Person to person spread has occurred in poor hygiene conditions, especially where overcrowding occurs. Outbreaks often occur following natural disasters such as floods and earthquakes. Efficient sanitary control by sewage removal and treatment and water purification are the best control measures.

Typhoid fever is much more serious than paratyphoid fever and is often fatal. Bacteria colonise the small intestine, the walls of which are penetrated, and may become ulcerated. The organisms become distributed all over the body, including the blood and lymphoid tissue. Symptoms typically include headache, fever, malaise, enlargement of the spleen and constipation resulting from damage (necrosis) to the lymphoid tissue and the liver. If bacteria localise in the gall bladder (sometimes necessitating its surgical removal) or kidney, they may be excreted in the faeces or urine by carriers over many months or years. Most individuals stop excreting the organisms in their faeces in around three months. There are around 400 to 500 cases annually in the US, and very few in the UK of which eighty per cent of cases are acquired abroad, mainly in Asia. Antibiotic therapy is effective, despite rapid development of drug resistance. Care is needed with such treatment (particularly with the elderly) as it may lead to a loss of intestinal flora which ordinarily keeps such pathogens in check. Recovery confers permanent immunity against further infections; a vaccine is available for high-risk groups.
See: Aberdeen typhoid outbreak, Food-borne disease, Milk, Paratyphoid fever, Typhoid Mary.

Typhoid Mary Mary Mallon, who worked as a cook in New York State in the early part of the 20th century. She was a carrier of typhoid fever and was responsible for several outbreaks of the disease, which resulted in three deaths. Her case became well known through the attempts of the State to restrain her from working in the food trade, which included periods of imprisonment.

Tyrosine An amino acid causing aesthetically unacceptable white spots in the livers of sheep.

UHT (Ultra Heat Treated) A preservation process developed for milk in which commercial sterility is achieved by heating to 132°C for one second followed by aseptic filling into sterile containers, normally made from plastic laminated board. The product has a shelf-life of six months without refrigeration.

Ultra sonic sound Attempts have been made to control various pests with emissions of high frequency sound above the range of human hearing. The technique has worked for a time but acclimatisation then occurs.

Ultra violet radiation (UV) A type of radiation used in electric flying insect killers to attract these pests. It also has limited use for sterilisation purposes such as the surfaces of fruits and for small quantities of water. *See:* Electromagnetic radiation.

Undulant fever *See: Brucella abortus.*

Unfit food Food which is not suitable for human consumption. The possession of such food in a food business (unless in refuse containers) may be illegal since all food is deemed to be on food premises for the purpose of human consumption. Unfitness may be judged by bacteriological standards or by organoleptic assessment including the presence of physical contaminants. Food found to be unfit, including other batches, may be seized and destroyed by authorised officers such as an EHO.

Untreated milk *See:* Raw Milk.

Urinals One per 25 persons and then 1 per 40 persons after 100 persons is sufficient.

'Use-by' date A date reserved for labelling perishable high-risk foods which may cause a health risk due to growth of micro-organisms after a certain date. Typical foods include
- meat products
- cook-chill foods
- dairy products such as soft and semi-hard cheeses, mousse and fromage frais (unless sufficiently acid to halt bacterial growth)
- any cooked food
- smoked or cured meat and fish (except when ambient stable)
- pre-prepared ready-to-eat foods including sandwiches
- uncooked or partly cooked pastry or dough products such as pizza, pasta and sausage rolls.

Labelling of these foods with a 'use-by' date is a legal requirement in Britain. Food so labelled should not be consumed after the date marked has elapsed.
See: Best-before date, Food Labelling Regs, Stock rotation.

USFDA (United States Food and Drug Administration) The body in the USA roughly equivalent to MAFF and DoH in the UK in respect of some food matters.

Vacuum-packed foods Mainly meats and fish which are heat-sealed into laminated plastic or nylon pouches. The oxygen-free conditions may favour the growth of

Clostridium botulinum and the process must be hygienically operated to prevent any product contamination. As soon as the pack is opened, the food should be treated as if it were fresh and may require refrigeration before use. *See:* Sous vide.

Vector A transmitter and reservoir of disease. They may be :
1. inanimate (non-living), including food, water, saliva, pus and contaminated eating utensils
2. animate (living), generally insects or animals, including humans.
See: Animals, Droplet infection, Personal hygiene, Rodents.

Vegetables
- Should be stored separately to keep soil bacteria away from other foods.
- Most store best in cool conditions (10-15°C).
- They should be prepared in a separate area since there is a risk of cross-contamination from the soil on the surface onto other foods.
- Freshly cooked vegetables should be safe as long as they are eaten straight after cooking.
- Cooked vegetables, if not to be eaten immediately, should be refrigerated or kept hot.
- All salad vegetables should be washed thoroughly before consumption.
- Some salad vegetables are treated with a dilute hypochlorite solution which should be washed off before use.

See: Appendix : Food Law, *Clostridium perfringens*.

Vegetative cell Cells which are actively growing as opposed to those which are reproducing or 'resting' (in the endospore state). It is during the vegetative phase or state that exotoxins are produced and released.

Vehicle of food poisoning
- The means by which micro-organisms may travel from place to place.
- This includes food itself, hands, wiping cloths, cutting boards, knives etc.
- The same categories of food, commonly meat, meat products and poultry, regularly appear in statistics for reported cases of bacterial food poisoning.

Vehicles (delivery) Such vehicles used for food must be constructed and maintained so that they are clean. Temperature control in refrigerated delivery vehicles is important and should be regularly checked. *See:* Cross-contamination, Delivery vehicles.

Ventilation
- Depending on the use of a room, a certain number of air changes per hour are required so that heat, water vapour and fumes generated by people and

equipment do not build up to unacceptable levels.
- Kitchens may require up to 20 air changes per hour.
- Systems range from simple hoods and ducting to complex air conditioning systems; all of these must be included in the routine cleaning and maintenance programme.
- Filters and ducting should be regularly inspected otherwise they will lose efficiency and may become a fire hazard.
- In air conditioning systems, there is a risk of creating conditions favourable to the growth of the bacterium causing Legionnaire's disease
- The design of ventilation systems is a specialist task.

Vermin An undesirable pest such as rodents, cockroaches, starlings etc.

Vibrio
1. A term used in the lower case ('vibrio') to describe the shape of certain bacteria, which are curved or comma-shaped.
2. When written as *'Vibrio'*, the name of a group (genus) of bacteria.
3. At least three vibrios are found in British waters (*V. parahaemolyticus, V. fluvialis* and *V. alginolyticus*).

Vibrio cholerae **(Serogroup 01)**

- A slightly curved rod-shaped Gram-negative bacterium, *V. cholerae 0139* is responsible for Asiatic or epidemic cholera. The organism survives well outside the body, for example in cool, moist places it will survive for days. It is easily killed at high temperatures (10 minutes at 55°C.) and is sensitive to chemical disinfectants.
- The organism may be found in estuarine and brackish waters (fresh and salt water mixed).
- Transmission is by consumption of polluted untreated water, contaminated water, shellfish, and foods eaten raw or washed in contaminated water. Person to person spread by the faecal-oral route is a contributory factor in epidemic spread in underdeveloped countries, where sanitation and personal hygiene are poor.
- Incubation period varies from 6 hours to 5 days.
- Symptoms vary from a mild, watery diarrhoea to an acute diarrhoea (due to the release of a potent enterotoxin), with abdominal cramps, nausea and vomiting.
- No major outbreaks have occurred in the USA since 1911. Sporadic cases have occurred, for example in the 1980s due to consumption of raw shellfish

- or of improperly cooked shellfish, or recontamination after cooking.
- The disease rarely occurs in the UK and then only as imported cases.
- Over 340 000 cases have been reported in the Western Hemisphere between 1991 to 1996, with over 3 600 deaths.

Vibrio parahaemolyticus
- A slightly curved rod-shaped Gram-negative halophilic bacterium, which causes food poisoning by infection.
- It usually inhabits coastal salt waters, particularly in warm climates, and is transmitted to humans mostly by consumption of untreated water, contaminated shellfish, and foods eaten raw or washed in such waters.
- Improper handling of cold seafood salads is often responsible.
- Symptoms are caused by the release of a toxin in the gut, and include a burning sensation in the stomach and abdominal pain, together with vomiting, headache, fever, chills, and watery diarrhoea. The illness is usually mild to moderate, but can be fatal.
- The incubation period is less than 24 hours and the illness lasts from 1 to 7 days.
- The organism is easily killed by proper cooking of the seafood, hence prevention of recontamination of cooked shellfish by raw shellfish or by sea water is essential.
- It is a very common causal agent of food poisoning in Japan (45-70% of total reported cases).

Vibrio vulnificus A serious contaminant of seafood in the Atlantic and Pacific oceans and the Gulf of Mexico. Consumption of raw or re-contaminated oysters, clams and crabs may result in illness. The organism can give rise to various illnesses, infection of wounds, a condition known as 'primary septicaemia', as well as gastroenteritis. It has the nickname 'terror of the deep', since it can produce septicaemia (blood poisoning) in its victims, who have eaten contaminated seafood; it can result in around 50% fatalities. Sporadic cases occur, more common in the warmer months of the year. It is not found in British waters.

Vinegar Contains acetic (ethanoic) acid and has a sufficiently low pH (less than 4.5) to prevent the growth of pathogens. Pickled foods however are subject to mould growth and preservatives such as benzoic acid are also incorporated in commercially produced pickles.

Vinegar fly (*Drosophila* species) Various fruit flies which may breed in fermenting materials such as overripe fruit, decaying vegetables, vinegar and brewing liquid.

Refuse control and covering of food are the best control measures.
See: Flies.

Virion A fully complete unit of a virus particle, usually composed of a nucleic acid core surrounded by a protein coat. Some forms also possess an outer envelope.

Virucide Literally means an agent used to 'kill' viruses. However since there is some debate as to whether viruses are living organisms, it is more accurate to describe a virucide as an agent used to inactivate viruses. The application of heat is a simple but effective agent and some viruses are sensitive to chemical disinfectants.

Virulence The degree to which a pathogen can cause harm in a specific host, i.e. relative pathogenicity. It may be due to toxicity and/or aggressiveness (invasiveness). There is a range of virulence, extending from avirulent (harmless) to highly virulent (extremely virulent/deadly).

Viruses
- Cases of food poisoning caused by viruses (viral gastroenteritis) were recorded as being over 15 000 in Britain in 1990.
- The major cause of these viral outbreaks is probably by the faecal-oral route although contaminated foods, water and shellfish have also been noted. There is a risk of infection from aerosols of projectile vomit.
- In the UK the most common appear to be the small round unstructured viruses (SRSV) of the Norwalk type although Astrovirus and Calcivirus have been noted in seafood.
- Viral food poisoning normally develops within 48 hours and causes nausea, vomiting, cramps and diarrhoea; symptoms usually subside after 2 days.

Characteristics of viruses

- Very small and simple parasitic agents which must be inside living host cells in order to reproduce (obligate intracellular parasites).
- Due to their non-cellular nature they are not considered to be living organisms.
- They mostly consist only of a core of nucleic acid (DNA or RNA) surrounded by a protein coat, but some possess an outer envelope as well; the single unit is called a virion.
- Their size is measured in nanometres (billionths of a metre) and they are only visible under the electron microscope.

- The number and variety of viruses is unknown as is the range of diseases they may cause.

Viruses are generally subdivided into three main groups based on the kind of host they infect:

1. bacterial viruses (bacteriophages)
2. animal viruses
3. plant viruses.

Viruses are unable to multiply unless they are inside a living host cell, hence they cannot increase in numbers in foods. However they can remain viable in food or water for variable periods of time. Following ingestion of the virus-contaminated food or water, the virion, after entering the host cell 'takes over' the cell totally to produce many copies of the virus particle. This often results in damage to or death of the host cell. Very small numbers of virions are required to cause disease. *See:* Enterovirus, Hepatitis A/B, Norwalk virus, Poliomyelitis.

VTEC (Verocytotoxin producing *E. coli*)
- First identified as a specific pathogen in 1982 in beefburgers in the USA.
- A third to a half of cases are admitted to hospital, up to 7% develop haemolytic uraemic syndrome. Around 3% fatality is noted.
- Less than 10 cases were notified in England and Wales in 1985, rapidly increasing since then to 173 cases in 1992-94.
- The incidence in Scotland, for reasons which are unclear, is the highest in the British Isles with a an outbreak in Lanarkshire during 1996 resulting in 20 fatalities.
- The reservoir is farm animals, particularly cattle with the majority of outbreaks associated with undercooked meat products.
- Cases reported in Scotland and Devon during 1994 were from milk.
- An outbreak in Bavaria (March 1996) was suspected from consumption of Teewurst and Mortadella (fresh sausages).
- A very large outbreak in Osaka, Japan 1996 (almost 10 000 cases) involved mainly schoolchildren eating school lunches. Cold noodles, raw cow's liver and undercooked hamburgers were implicated and it has been noted by ACMSF that children under 4 years old appear to be at a greater risk.
- A small outbreak in the East Midlands, England in 1994 appeared to have been the result of contact with animals at a farm visitor centre allied to poor hand washing facilities.
- Person to person transmission is also possible with faecal-oral transmission

- noted amongst children.
- High standards of hygiene are needed at schools and nurseries to limit the spread of *E. coli*.
- The infective dose is believed to be very low with a level of 2 organisms in 25 grams reported to have caused illness in South Wales during 1995.
- HUS (haemolytic uraemic syndrome) caused by VTEC 0111 was reported in France during 1992-1993. Some victims had eaten fromage frais made from raw cows' and goats' milk.
- Outbreaks among children in Scotland and London have been linked to paddling pools.
- Laboratory workers are at high risk.
- Most cases occur between July-September, possibly due to higher ambient temperatures and more frequent barbecues, but large winter outbreaks have occurred both in the UK and USA.

See: Escherichia coli.

Walls As part of the structure of food rooms, these should be constructed with a durable, impervious surface capable of being easily cleaned. A light colour is preferable so that cleanliness may be seen and also to assist in lighting. Several costly but effective wall finishes are ideal for food rooms, particularly if there is likely to be contact with food. Examples include:

1. ceramic tiling with a waterproof grout
2. plastic coated boarding
3. stainless steel
4. fibre glass
5. purpose-formed polypropylene or other plastic sheeting.

Painted surfaces, using a special food grade finish are satisfactory as long as flaking does not occur. Washable wallpaper may be of limited use and normal domestic wall finishes should not be used in production areas. Where there is likely to be contact with trolleys or fork lift trucks the finish should be capable of withstanding this. *See:* Design of food premises.

Warehouse moth (*Ephestia elutella*) A very common pest of stored products including cereals, chocolate, dried fruit and nuts. *See:* Moths.

Warfarin An anticoagulant rodenticide developed in the 1960s. It causes rats and mice to die slowly so that others do not associate eating the poison with their death. Resistance to it is now widespread. *See:* Rats.

Wasps These can be a nuisance and also theoretically carry food poisoning organisms on their feet and bodies. From midsummer they are attracted by sweet substances, such as fruit juice, sugar, syrups and preserves. A 3 mm mesh screen will prevent entry into premises.

Washing up
Several systems ranging from manual to machine are in use, many being based on the following sequence of operations.
1. Pre-cleaning (scraping of plates, pans etc.).
2. Main wash using detergent at around 55°C. This removes greasy soil and is not so hot that food (such as egg) is baked onto surfaces.
3. A rinse in water at 82-88°C for 2 minutes. This removes traces of detergent, heats up items so that they may air dry and also disinfects them. The rinse may contain sanitising chemicals, particularly if the water temperature is too low.
4. Air-drying.
5. Correct storage away from contamination.

In manual washing up one sink may suffice, working on a fill and empty system, but two sinks are preferable. The first contains detergent and the second is the rinse sink, often called the sterilising sink. Automatic systems normally use similar cycles and it is important to use chemicals correctly and to monitor temperatures.
See: Cleaning, Disinfectant, Sterilisation, Two sink system.

```
         Pre-clean/scrape -
         Cold rinse if needed
                  |
                  v
                      Main wash (1st sink)
                      - Scrub in water at
                        55°C with detergent
                                |
      Storage -                  v
   Clean dry conditions
         ^                Rinse (2nd sink)
         |     Air dry -  - Water at 82-88°C (cooler
         |  Avoids contamination   if sanitiser is used)
              from cloths
```

Washing Up

224 Washing facilities

Washing facilities Suitable washing facilities for food handlers must be provided in food premises so that the required standard of personal hygiene may be achieved. As a rough guide, one wash hand basin per 15 persons is required; the exact numbers being determined by the risk to food safety, but one per 10 persons is more desirable, particularly in high-use areas. *See:* Hand washing, Personal hygiene.

Wash hand basins Separate wash hand basins, not used for any other purpose, should be provided in food premises. They must have soap, hot water, suitable drying facilities and a nail brush if needed. *See:* Basins, Hand washing, Personal hygiene, Washing facilities.

Waste (control and disposal of) In food premises, a suitable number of containers with close-fitting lids must be provided for wet and dry waste. Plastic sack holders or waste bins are often used and must be periodically emptied to separate refuse areas for the wet and dry waste. These must be kept clean to discourage for example dogs, flies and rats. Collection from these areas must be regularly carried out. It is important that waste is covered and contained at all stages and that all containers, as well as the general refuse collection area, are kept in good condition. *See:* Compactors.

Waste disposal units Electrically operated devices which finely chop food waste and deliver it to the drainage system. These require frequent maintenance and cleaning.

Water
1. A food business cannot operate without an adequate supply of wholesome water. It is the responsibility of the supplier to ensure suitable quality in mains water delivered to a building. Contaminated water may affect food.
2. Water may be classed as being food, for example a glass of water given to a customer in a restaurant, or ice-cubes given in a drink.

Almost a third of private drinking water supplies tested in 1994-95 in England and Wales were below standard while in Scotland a list of SMRVs (Significant Medical Risk Values) is used to assess water quality. Many substances such as aluminium, fluoride and zinc are listed as are coliform bacteria. The SMRVs are often higher than PCVs (prescribed concentration or value) and are for short term use while a potential problem is under investigation. Pesticide levels should be a maximum of 0.1 mg/litre.
See: Aberdeen typhoid outbreak, Food-borne disease, Infections (waterborne), Personal hygiene, Washing facilities.

Water activity *See:* Available water (a_w).

Waterproof dressing
- It is recommended in the food industry to cover skin lesions such as cuts

with such dressings.
- They not only prevent the lesions from becoming infected, but they also prevent the escape of blood and/or pus from the wound, both of which may contain bacteria such as *Staphylococcus aureus,* which may then contaminate food.
- Special bright blue (and other non-food coloured) versions are available which are easily seen should they get into food.
- In food manufacturing, metal strips may be incorporated into the dressing for magnetic detection.

Waterborne infections *See:* Infections (waterborne).

Wax Used as a coating on various fruits. It is not edible.

Weedy fish Foul smelling iodine-like smell caused by fish eating various marine organisms.

Weevils Small beetles (up to 5 mm in length) having a characteristic snout.

Weil's disease
- A disease caused by a parasite of rats (*Leptospira icterohaemorrhagiae,* a spirochaete). It is commonly present in their kidneys and urine, and is apparently not harmful to them.
- It also occurs in dogs (in which it is pathogenic), in pigs and other rodents such as field mice.
- The parasite may enter the human body through the skin, mucous membranes or skin abrasions, following contact with water contaminated by the urine of infected rodents.
- It is possible that infection may follow ingestion of food or water contaminated by infected rodent urine and cases of infection have followed rat bites.
- The use of stagnant water for drinking, preparing food and for bathing or recreation (e.g. wind surfing) should be avoided.
- The disease has been frequently reported among workers at slaughterhouses and refuse tips after contact with items contaminated with rat urine.

WHO (World Health Organisation) Based in Geneva, Switzerland and having interests in communicable diseases of all kinds, including food poisoning and many other health matters.

Windows As part of the structure of food rooms these must be constructed from durable and impervious materials capable of being effectively cleaned. Screens and

Wood

nets may be attached as part of proofing against the entry of flying insects and birds. Windows may also be a source of heat (solar gain) and their position may be of importance when considering location of equipment such as refrigerators.

Wood
- Potentially a problem material in food premises due to its absorbent properties, splintering and difficulty in cleaning.
- Bare wood should be restricted in food rooms with the possible exception of cutting boards for the sole use in raw meat preparation. These must be constructed of high density wood and be capable of being cleaned.
- To date, a completely acceptable substitute for wood has yet to be found.
- The practice of salting wooden butchers' blocks is of some use, but it does not destroy toxins, spores or staphylococci.

See: Chopping boards.

Work-flow *See:* Linear flow.

Work tops *See:* Food contact surfaces.

Wrapping materials Materials which come into contact with food should be inert and not cause any contamination.
See: Aluminium, Cling film, Packaging.

Worms Many parasitic worms which are harmful to humans and animals may be found in food. These include *Ascaris lumbricoides*, Nematodes, Roundworms, *Taenia* species, and Trematodes.

Xenopsylla cheopsis **(rat flea)** It is responsible for the transmission of 'plague', known in the Middle Ages as the Black Death.

Yeasts
- Single celled fungi, widely distributed in nature, frequently seen as a white powdery coating on fruits and leaves.
- Some are capable of the fermentation of carbohydrates to produce alcohols and carbon dioxide.
- Carbon dioxide is used in baking for raising bread, while alcohol production is the basis of the brewing and wine-making industries; in both industries species of *Saccharomyces* are widely used.
- Wild types of yeasts are responsible for the spoilage of many types of food such as meats, wine, beer, and fruit juices.
- Most common yeasts grow best with a plentiful supply of water but need

- less moisture to grow compared with bacteria.
- The temperature range for growth is similar to moulds, which is an optimum of 25 to 30°C, and a maximum of 35 to 47°C; some can grow at 0°C or less.
- They prefer an acid environment, around pH 4 to 4.5.

Yellow swarming fly (*Thaumatomia notata*) A small insect, 3 mm in length, occasionally invading dwellings and food premises at the start of cold weather. *See:* Flies.

Yersinia enterocolitica
- A small rod-shaped Gram negative bacterium which causes the infrequent food-borne illness known as yersiniosis.
- Gastroenteritis-type symptoms are produced (diarrhoea and/or vomiting), but classical symptoms include fever and abdominal pain. (Many cases in children mimic those of appendicitis.)
- Foods involved are commonly pork and other meats, raw milk or any contaminated raw or leftover food.
- The organism can multiply at 4°C. Thorough cooking, protection from contamination and rodent control are effective control measures.

Yoghurt A milk product formed by the action of bacteria such as *Lactobacillus bulgaricus* and *Streptococcus thermophilus*. These consume lactose (milk sugar) and produce lactic acid which causes milk protein to clot (denature). If the pH is below 4.5, yoghurt is not a high-risk food. If above this figure it must be stored in a refrigerator before use. *See:* Appendix : Food Law.

Zinc One of number of metals which can cause food poisoning. It may enter food by being dissolved by fruit acids. *See:* Galvanised steel.

Zone of maximum ice crystal formation The speed of freezing determines the quality of the final product since the less time food spends in the temperature range of 0 to minus 4°C the smaller the ice crystals which are formed. Modern quick freezing rates are around 3-10 cm/hour (movement of ice front) in blast or fluidised bed freezers, whereas slow freezing would occur at about 0.2 cm/hour. *See:* Frozen food.

Zoonoses Diseases that occur primarily in wild and domesticated animals, but they can be transmitted to humans. Transmission can occur by many routes:

1. direct contact with infected animals

2. contact with hides, fur or feathers
3. by insects
4. contamination of food and water
5. consumption of infected animal products.

Many such diseases occur including anthrax, foot and mouth, glanders, salmonellosis, swine erysipelas, taeniasis, trichinosis, tuberculosis, undulant fever and vaccinia.

Zygospore A large sexual fungal spore, produced as a means of reproduction; it is enclosed in a thick resistant wall. Such spores are formed by *Mucor*, a common spoilage mould.

APPENDIX 1: Food Law, UK and the USA

Generally, Food Law is similar in UK countries. This section is not intended to be a comprehensive guide to the wide-ranging and complex subject of food legislation, but is meant as an overview to the more important issues affecting food hygiene. Other entries may be found in the main text. Readers should be aware that there are some differences between law in England and Wales, Scotland and Northern Ireland. The term 'UK law' is used generally, not specifically throughout this volume.

UK Food Hygiene Law

A. Food Safety Act 1990
A major piece of consumer protection legislation which modified and repealed existing law. The main provisions include:

1. Definitions (Sec 1)
a. Food
- Anything consumed for food including drinks, chewing gum, water and all ingredients used including additives such as flavourings and colourings.
- Live animals, except when eaten live, such as oysters, are excluded.

b. Food businesses - do not have to make profit, so non- commercial premises such as hospitals and charities are included.
c. Food sources - are defined as growing crops or live animals. There is a power to make regulations governing these at a later date.
d. Contact materials - packaging materials and all food equipment may be subject to later regulations.

2. Sale (Secs 2, 8, 9, 14, 15)
Food given away or offered as a prize, food advertised for sale, possessing food for sale, as well as actually selling food may be included.

3. Human consumption (Sec 3)
- All food kept or sold which is normally for human consumption is deemed to be for that purpose unless proved otherwise.
- Food in a proper waste bin, for example, would not be for human consumption even though it was on food premises.

4. Injury to health (Sec 7)
- This includes temporary and permanent injury as well as cumulative effects caused to a person by eating food.
- Making food injurious may be caused by adding substances to food, removing them from food or by a process which affects the food.

5. Selling food not complying with food safety requirements (Sec 8)
- Food which is sold, intended for sale, put on sale or advertised for sale and which does not comply with any food safety requirement causes an offence to be committed.
- For example, food which is injurious to health, unfit for human consumption or contaminated would not comply, neither would animals killed in a knacker's yard.

6. Parts of batches (Sec 8)
The whole of a batch, lot or consignment may be judged on the condition of one part.

7. Power to inspect and seize food (Sec 9)
- The local authority has a legal right to perform routine inspections or to act on complaints from the public. These may occur at any reasonable time and at any place including vehicles.
- The food, if judged not to comply with food safety requirements, may be seized or detained by serving a legal notice. The food may then not be moved or used and may be taken to be destroyed.
- There is a right of appeal with compensation payable if the actions are found to be unjust.

8. Improvement notice (Sec 10) 'Minded to' notice
- If conditions are found which do not comply with food safety requirements and place food at risk, then an improvement notice may be issued by the local authority to the person running a food business.
- It states what is wrong, why it is wrong and what must be done to put matters right.
- Times must be specified for work to be done (minimum 14 days) and for appeals to be lodged.
- It is an offence not to comply with an improvement notice.
- Under an order made in 1996 an authorised officer must inform a proprietor that an improvement notice is being considered and invite the proprietor to discuss the matter verbally or in writing. This 'minded to' notice must allow 14 days for consultation. The requirement is restricted to improvement notices, and is under review.

9. Prohibition order (Sec 11)
- After the proprietor of a food business has been convicted of a food safety offence, an order prohibiting the premises, parts of the premises, individual processes or persons from involvement in a food business may be issued by

APPENDIX 1: *Food Law, UK and the USA* 231

the court.

10. Emergency prohibition notices and orders (Secs 12, 13)
- Without going to court, an authorised officer such as an EHO may issue a notice having immediate effect, and have this confirmed within three days by a court order.
- Such a notice could be used to close a premises if there is serious and imminent risk to health, such as filthy premises or pest infestations.
- In other respects this is similar to a prohibition order.
- The notice is conspicuously fixed to the premises and remains in force until the local authority issues a certificate, lifting the order.

11. Emergency control order (Sec 13)
In national or widespread food safety emergencies, the Minister may make such an order for example to stop a process or to have food seized or destroyed on a large scale.

12. Food not of the nature, substance or quality (Sec 14)
- An offence is committed when food which is not what the ordinary person would normally expect or demand, is sold.
- The legal term 'prejudice' is often used, meaning that the purchaser has received inferior goods .

See: Entries in main dictionary for examples of nature, substance and quality.

13. False descriptions (Sec 15)
- Food labels, descriptions, menus and advertisements must accurately describe foods. *See:* Section D, Labelling Regulations

14. Power to make regulations (Secs 16-19, 48, 53 and 59)
Regulations covering the following are all possible under the Act:

- composition of food.
- microbiological standards.
- processes.
- practises.
- premises.
- labelling.
- food contact materials.
- 'novel' foods.
- special milk designations.
- registration and licensing of food premises.

15. Defences (Secs 20-22)
- Possible defences include proving that the offence was due to the act or default of another person or that all due diligence was exercised.
- Due diligence implies that all reasonable precautions were taken.

16. Other provisions (Sec 23 onwards)
a. Local Authorities may provide training courses in food hygiene.
b. Public analysts must be appointed.
c. Authorised officers may 'perform inspections', take samples, photographs and may seize food.
d. Food sampling methods are specified.
e. Entry to food premises must be permitted at all reasonable times, obstruction of authorised officers is an offence,
f. Appeals against notices and prosecutions are detailed as are the ways in which legal action is to proceed.
g. Crown Immunity is partially removed.
h. Penalties include fines, (depending on the type of court this may be unlimited) and/or up to 2 years imprisonment.

B. Food Safety (General Food Hygiene) Regulations 1995
These regulations made to implement EC Directive 93/43 deal with hygiene in all food premises, except primary production (such as farming) and those high-risk food businesses with their own more detailed regulations (such as meat product manufacturers and dairies).

The main purpose of these regulations is to protect the health of the consumer and the regulations differ from the previous ones in requiring hazard identification and control as well as training and/or supervision for food handlers. The regulations are more general than previous versions and allow flexibility of solutions to food safety problems.

There is provision for proprietors to negotiate with the local authority on many matters such as the suitability of surfaces and waste disposal systems. A risk-related solution is thus possible without the law being prescriptive for all situations.

1. Reg 4
An analysis of potential food hazards must be carried out and those critical to food safety must be identified, controlled and the controls monitored. These measures must be periodically reviewed and reviewed after any changes.
See: ASC, HACCP.

APPENDIX 1: Food Law, UK and the USA

2. Reg 5
Food handlers with food-borne diseases or infections such as skin infections, infected wounds etc. must notify the proprietor of the food business who should notify the local authority.

3. Reg 6
Penalties under these regulations range from fines and/or two years in prison.

Schedule 1 - Rules of hygiene

Premises (general requirements)
- Kept clean and well maintained.
- Designed to allow proper cleaning and prevent accumulation of dirt, condensation and mould.
- Prevent cross-contamination by any means.
- Allow for suitable temperature control.
- Provided sufficient facilities for personal hygiene (such as washbasins, WCs, changing facilities).
- Adequate lighting and ventilation.
- Adequate drainage.

Premises (specific food room requirements)
- Floors, walls, ceilings, doors, fixtures and fittings to be suitable (e.g. floors in a sound condition and easy to clean, ceilings not to accumulate and shed particles).
- Windows of suitable construction and screened against insects if necessary.
- Facilities for washing food as needed.

Temporary and moveable premises, domestic premises used as a business, vending machines and occasional premises requirements
- Constructed to avoid pest infestation.
- Risk of food contamination to be avoided as far as in reasonably practicable.
- Personal hygiene facilities to be provided.
- Cleaning facilities where necessary.

Transport
- Clean vehicles and containers. Food to be protected from cross-contamination.

Equipment
- Kept clean, well maintained and installed so that the surrounding area may be cleaned.

Food waste
- Not to accumulate in food rooms.
- Separate closed containers.
- Adequate collection frequencies.

Water supply
- Adequate supply of potable water.

Personal Hygiene
- High standard must be maintained by food handlers.
- Exclusion of persons suffering from certain diseases or conditions.

Foodstuffs
- Must be fit for human consumption.
- Protected from contamination.
- Pest control measures in place.
- Dangerous substances labelled.
- Food waste clearly identified.

Training
- Food handlers to be trained and/or supervised commensurate with their work activities.

C. Food Safety (Temperature Control) Regs 1995

There is a general requirement not to keep food (which includes raw materials, intermediate and finished products) so that the growth of pathogens occurs.

Chilled food
- Food likely to support the growth of pathogens should not be kept above 8°C.
Note that a refrigerator temperature is not specified in Scottish law.
The regulations exclude foods which are -

for sale or service for one occasion only of up to four hours
kept hot
preserved in some way
ripening
intended for further processing
safe above this temperature (a scientific assessment for this is needed)
in transit between a vehicle and the food business

APPENDIX 1: Food Law, UK and the USA

unavoidably kept above 8°C (for example by the practicalities of handling, temporary breakdown, defrosting etc) for as short a time as possible.

Hot holding
- Food to be kept above 63°C.
- This includes food for service or display but excludes food which has been at less then 63°C for a one-off period of up to two hours.
- A proven scientific assessment may show that other times and temperatures are safe.
- Food which is to be cooled should be cooled as quickly as possible.

Scotland
- Reheated food must reach at least 82°C.
- Gelatine (used for meat and fish products for example) must be kept at 71°C for 30 minutes or boiled immediately before use.

D. Food Labelling Regulations 1996
These regulations are extremely complex with many exceptions and readers who need detailed information should refer to them direct. Most food for human consumption must be labelled with:

- name of the food
- ingredients list in weight descending order
- a 'best-before date' or in the case of high-risk or perishable food a 'use-by' date
- any special storage information
- name and address of the manufacturer supplier or packer.
- if the food has been irradiated.

The **'best before'** category is a statement of quality (for example in many confectionery products) and is often long term.
The **'use by'** category is for food which will become micro-biologically unsafe after the short-term date has elapsed (for example cook-chill high protein foods). Food so marked must not be used after this date.

Exempted foods include:

- uncut fresh fruit and vegetables
- bread
- chewing gum
- flour confectionery
- sugar, vinegar, cooking and table salt

There are specific requirements for vending machines, pre-packed food, alcoholic drinks, raw milk, nutritional claims, medicinal properties, baby food, misleading labels and the use of certain words such as cream, cheese and wine.

E. Milk and dairies legislation.
- A large number of regulations are in existence dealing with registration, licensing and hygiene standards in milk, milk products, ice-cream and egg producers.
- The heat treatment, packaging and labelling of milk is closely specified.
- The sale of raw cows' (but not sheep and goats') milk is restricted to farm visitors or to the ultimate consumer by way of a licensed distributor. It cannot be sold for resale to a restaurant for example.
- It is an offence to sell ungraded eggs with cracks in their shells.
- Egg products manufacture is licensed, for example pasteurisation plants.

F. Slaughterhouse, meat, poultry and fish trades law.
- General hygiene standards are similar to other food premises with EC standards being very strict.
- All meat and poultry for human consumption must have been killed in a licensed slaughterhouse and inspected in the prescribed way by authorised officers supervised by veterinarians. Satisfactory meat is marked.
- Animal by-products (such as meat for the pet food market) must be stained or sterilised before leaving a slaughterhouse.
- Waste food including meats used for feeding animals must be heat processed by a licensed operator.
- Premises used for the manufacture of meat products have separate detailed regulations.
- There are specific regulations dealing with bivalve molluscs and fish.
- 'Home Killed' meat must be inspected and marked.

G. Public Health (Control of Diseases) Act 1984 and Public Health (Infectious Diseases) Regs 1988
- Food poisoning must be notified to the local authority by medical practitioners or by persons in control of food businesses.
- A food handler or any other person may be excluded from work by the local authority consultant in communicable disease control (CCDC), known as the 'proper officer', if they have certain infectious diseases such as typhoid fever, scarlet fever or food poisoning.

H. Health and Safety at Work etc Act 1974.

- Legislation requiring employers to ensure safe conditions in workplaces for employees and others and to prevent danger to the public caused by workplace activities.
- There are a huge number of regulations made under this and other safety law, including reporting of accidents and injuries, manual handling, use of personal protective equipment, COSHH, electricity, radiation, lead and noise.

I. Food Premises (Registration) Regs 1991
See entry in the text.

J. Statutory Codes of Practice
Documents which detail standards of enforcement by local authorities on matters such as sampling (COP7), food hygiene inspections (COP9), temperature control (COP10) and qualifications and experience of authorised officers and experts (COP19).

Law in Scotland.
There are many historical differences between the Scottish and English legal systems at all levels. Most alleged food hygiene offences are heard in the Sheriff Court, the Sheriff being a full-time legally qualified official. Each Sheriff Court has cases referred by an administrative department headed by a Procurator Fiscal. More serious matters may be referred to the High Court which has a presiding Law Lord and jury. Fines are similar to those in England in the Sheriff Court but an unlimited maximum fine and/or one year in jail for other courts.

Scottish Food Hygiene Law
1. The Food Safety Act 1990 replaces the Food and Drugs (Scotland) Act 1956.
2. The main Scottish food hygiene regulations were made in 1959 and have been amended several times and generally revoked, apart from temperature control requirements listed above. The Food Safety (General Food Hygiene) Regs 1995 apply.
3. Licensed premises must have a hygiene certificate issued by the Environmental Health Department.
4. Market stalls, late night caterers, places of public entertainment and street traders must also have a hygiene certificate similar to the above.
5. There are specific regulations covering milk and dairies, ice-cream and some aspects of egg production.
6. Slaughterhouse hygiene regulations and meat and poultry inspection regulations are similar to those in the rest of Europe but there are additional regulations governing meat distribution and export.

APPENDIX 1: Food Law, UK and the USA

Food Law in the USA

1. The Federal Food, Drug and Cosmetics Act 1938

Based on the adulteration principle, this is the current main statute in the USA. It has been significantly amended and many regulations subsequently made (for example, Good Manufacturing Practices, Pesticides, Additives, Meat and Poultry, Packaging, Labelling etc.). Product liability is an important concern in US law in which manufacturers and others must supply safe products.

2. Good Practice in the USA

FDA also offers its Electronic Inspection System (FDAEIS) for adoption by local, state and federal agencies in tandem with the Food Code. The Field System component, which may be installed on a portable computer, contains comprehensive regulatory technical references, accepts the input of inspection data, generates inspection reports, and communicates with the Office System, the database. The system may be used by industry or others, such as health-care or day-care providers, consulting organisations, or trade associations, for conducting mock inspections as part of quality assurance activities. The system includes EPI-TRACKER, a computerised epidemiological tool for use in investigating suspected food-borne illnesses.

3. Food and Drug Administration (FDA) Food Code

A reference that guides retail outlets such as restaurants and grocery stores and institutions such as nursing homes on how to prepare food to prevent food-borne illness. It is based upon the Hazard Analysis Critical Control Point (HACCP) concept.

Local, state and federal regulators use the FDA Food Code as a model to help develop or update their own food safety rules and to be consistent with national food regulatory policy. Also, many of the over 1 million retail food establishments apply Food Code provisions to their own operations. Although the Food Code is neither federal law nor federal regulation and does not pre-empt state or local laws, authority to provide such guidance is granted by federal law.

Prevention of food-borne illness, the primary focus of the food code, is emphasised in several provisions. These include:
- detailed charts that give specific guidance for time, temperature and humidity for cooking meat and other raw foods derived from animals. For example, ground meat must be cooked to an internal temperature of 155°F (68°C) for 15 seconds to be safe. The cold holding temperature is 41°F (5°C) or lower

APPENDIX 1: Food Law, UK and the USA

- recommendations to retail managers on how to ensure food service workers health and hygiene practices (including restricting infected employees), how to clean and sanitise food utensils, and how to maintain equipment and facilities.

In order to comply with the Food Code, retail management must be able to demonstrate knowledge of food-borne illness prevention as it relates to their own food operation.

The Food Code includes provisions for:

- setting time limits for holding cooked foods safely outside of controlled temperatures.
- allowing the temperature of frozen foods to be raised, short of thawing, before cooking, which is sometimes desirable for improving the texture of cooked foods.
- using food additives safely.
- marking the date of preparation on all potentially hazardous refrigerated ready-to-eat foods that are prepared and held for more than 24 hours in a food establishment.
- preparing game animals, exotic animal species, and wild mushrooms.
- ensuring honest presentation of foods to consumers.
- advising consumers that certain foods should be ordered and eaten fully cooked in order to ensure their safety.

The Food Code also has provisions for the safety of molluscs shellfish, such as oysters, clams and mussels.

Seven reference sections help users apply the codes provisions uniformly and effectively to their jurisdictions. The sections are:

- compliance and enforcement - shows model provisions
- references - cites relevant scientific studies, laws, and regulations
- public health reasons - explains the purposes of each code provision
- establishment inspections - guides in planning, conducting and reporting inspections under the code
- HACCP - explains in detail the principles, terminology and applications of the concept
- food processing criteria - gives factors to be considered when preparing, evaluating and approving HACCP plans pertaining to certain food processing operations at the retail level.
- sample forms

The Food Code is updated every two years, to coincide with the biennial meeting of the Conference for Food Protection. The conference is a group of representatives from regulatory agencies at all levels of government, the food industry, academia, and consumer organisations that works to improve food safety at the retail level.

APPENDIX 2: Scientific Names

Note: Many of these and others including most micro-organisms appear in the main body of the text.

Acarus siro	flour mite
Agaricus bisporus/brunescens	common white cultivated mushroom
Alexandrium tamarense	alga (poisonous)
Alphitobius laevigatus	black fungus beetle
Amanita phalloides	death cap mushroom
Amanita verna/virosa	destroying angel mushroom
Anagasta kuhniella	Mediterranean flour moth
Anthrenus species	carpet, furniture and museum beetles
Blatta orientalis	oriental cockroach (also known as black bat black beetle or black clock)
Blattella germanica	German cockroach or steam fly
Bruchus ervi	lentil beetle
Bruchus pisorum	dried pea beetle
Buccinium undatum	whelk or buckie
Calandra granaria	grain weevil
Calandra oryzae	rice weevil
Calliphora erythrocephala	blowfly/bluebottle
Cancer pagurus	crab
Candida albicans	mould
Cerastoderma edule	cockle
Cheyletus eruditus	mite (parasite of flour mite)
Chlamys opercularis	queen escallop
Chloromyscium thyrsites	protozoan (milky hake)
Chloromyscium pisiformis	protozoan (rabbits)
Chloromyscium serialis	protozoan (rabbits)
Contracaecum	roundworm
Coxiella burnetii	rickettsia (Q fever)
Crangon crangen	common/brown shrimp
Crassostrea angulata	Portuguese oyster
Crassostrea gigas	pacific oyster
Cryptolestes ferrugineus	rust-red grain beetle
Ctenocephalides canis	dog flea
Ctenocephalides felis	cat flea
Dermestes lardarius	bacon/larder beetle
Dibothriocephalus latus	tapeworm (fish)
Dinophysis	marine alga (poisonous)
Diphyllobothrium latum	tapeworm (fresh water fish)
Distoma hepaticum	liver fluke
Distoma lanceolatum	liver fluke

Drosophila melanogaster	fruit fly
Echinococcus granulosus	dog worm (hydatid diseases in humans)
Ephestia elutella	warehouse moth
Ephestia kuhniella	Mediterranean flour moth
Fannia cannicularis	lesser housefly
Fasciola hepatica	liver fluke
Filaria bicol	codworm
Gambierdiscus toxicus	marine alga
Giardia lamblia	protozoan (diarrhoea)
Gnathocerus cornutus	broad-horned flour beetle
Gnathocerus maxillosus	slender-horned flour beetle
Gonyaulax catanella	alga (poisonous)
Gonyaulax tamarensis	alga (poisonous)
Hofmannophila pseudospretella	brown house moth
Homarus gammarus	lobster
Hysterothylacium	roundworm
Iridomyrmex humilis	argentine ant
Lasioderma serricorne	cigarette beetle
Lasius niger	black or garden ant
Lepisma sacharina	silverfish
Liposcelis granicola/ Bostrychophilis	booklouse
Littorina littorea	periwinkle
Lucilia sericata	greenbottle
Maestomys ratalensis	multimate rat
Monomorium pharaonis	pharaoh's ant
Monosodium glutamate	flavour enhancer
Mus domesticus	house mouse
Musca autumnalis	autumn fly
Musca domestica	housefly
Mytilus edulis	mussel
Nephrops norvegicus	dublin bay prawn/langoustine/norway lobster/scampi
Neptunea antigua	red whelk
Niptus hololeucus	golden spider beetle
Nitzschia pungens	marine diatom (poisonous)
Oesophagostum radiatum	roundworm (cow, sheep)
Oncocerca gibsoni	roundworm (cow)
Oryzaephilus surinamensis	saw-toothed grain beetle
Ostrea edulis	oyster
Palinurus elephas	crawfish/langoustine/pink shrimp/ spiny lobster

APPENDIX 2: Scientific Names

Pandalus borealis	prawn
Pandalus montagui	pink shrimp
Pecten maximus	escallop
Periplaneta americana	american cockroach
Periplaneta australasiae	australian cockroach
Phaseolus vulgaris	red kidney bean
Phocanema species	roundworm (cod)
Phormia	bluebottle fly
Plodia interpunctella	indian-meal moth
Prorocentrum concavum	alga
Prorocentrum mexicana	alga
Ptinus tectus	australian spider beetle
Ptychodiscus brevis	alga
Pulex irritans	human flea
Pyrodinium bahamense	alga
Rattus norvegicus	brown rat
Rattus rattus	black rat
Saccharomyces species	yeast
Sarcophoga carnaria	flesh fly
Schistosoma japonicum	blood fluke
Schistosoma mansoni	blood fluke
Sitophilus granarius	grain beetle or weevil
Sitophilus oryzae	rice weevil
Sitophilus zea-mais	maize weevil
Stegobium paniceum	biscuit or drug-store beetle
Sporotrichum	mould
Taenia hydatigena	tapeworm (dog)
Taenia saginata	tapeworm (cow)
Taenia solium	tapeworm (pig)
Tenebroides mauritanicus	cadelle beetle
Thamnidium elegans	mould
Thaumatomiyia notata	yellow swarming fly
Thermobia domestica	firebrat
Tineola bisselliella	clothes moth
Trichinella spiralis	worm (pig)
Trichurus tricuria	roundworm
Tyrophagus casei	cheese mite
Tyroglyphus farinae	flour mite
Venus mercenaria	clam
Vespula vulgaris	wasp

ACMSF	Advisory Committee on the Microbiological Safety of Food
AFD	Accelerated Freeze Drying
APC	Aerobic plate count
ASC	Assured Safe Catering
ASP	Amnesic Shellfish Poisoning
ATA	Alimentary Toxic Aleukia (Aleukia)
ATP	Adenosine Triphosphate
ASC	Assured Safe Catering
a_w	Available Water
BAP	Biologically Active Principle
BFMIRA	British Food Manufacturing Industries Research Association
BHA	Butylated Hydroxy Anisole
BHC	Benzene Hexachloride
BHT	Butylated Hydroxy Toluene
BPCA	British Pest Control Association
BS	British Standard
BSI	British Standards Institution
BSE	Bovine Spongiform Encephalopathy
CAMPDEN	Campden Food Preservation Research Association
CCDC	Consultant in Communicable Disease Control
CCP	Critical Control Point
CDR	Communicable Disease Report
CDSC	Communicable Disease Surveillance Centre
CEN	Committee for European Standardisation
CIEH	Chartered Institute of Environmental Health
CIP	Cleaning-In-Place
CJD	Creutzfeldt-Jakob Disease
COMA	Committee on Medical Aspects (of food)
COP	Code of Practice
COSHH	Control Of Substances Hazardous to Health Regs 1994 (amended)
CPU	Central Processing Unit
CPHL	Central Public Health Laboratory
DAFS	Department of Agriculture & Fisheries for Scotland
DDT	Dichlorodiphenyl Trichloroethane
DH	See: DoH
DHSS	Department of Health and Social Security
DNA	Deoxyribonucleic Acid
DoH	Department of Health
DSP	Diarrhetic Shellfish Poisoning
EC	European Community
ELISA	Enzyme Linked Immunosorbant Assay
EHEC	Enterohaemorrhagic *E. coli.*
EHO	Environmental Health Officer
EIEC	Enteroinvasive *E. coli.*
EPEC	Enteropathogenic *E. coli.*

APPENDIX 3: Abbreviations

ETEC	Enterotoxigenic *E. coli*
FAC	Food Advisory Committee
FAST	Food Authentication by Spectroscopic Techniques
FDA	See: USFDA
FDF	Food and Drink Federation
FEPA	Food and Environmental Protection Act 1985
FMBRA	Flour Milling and Baking Research Association
FOOD RA	Leatherhead Food Research Association
FSA	Food Standards Agency
FWA	Fluorescent Whitening Agent
GNVQ	General National Vocational Qualifications
HACCP	Hazard Analysis Critical Control Points
HASAWA	Health and Safety at Work etc Act 1974
HAZOP	Hazard Operability Studies
HAV	Hepatitis type A virus
HBV	Hepatitis type B virus
HCH	Hexachlorcyclohexane
HEV	Hepatitis type E virus
HMSO	Her Majesty's Stationery Office
HSC	Health and Safety Commission
HSE	Health and Safety Executive
HTST	High Temperature Short Time
HUS	Haemolytic Uraemic Syndrome
IEHO	Institution of Environmental Health Officers (now CIEH)
IFST	Institute of Food Science and Technology
IOSH	Institute of Occupational Safety and Health
ITSA	Institute of Trading Standards Administration
ISO	International Standards Office
IVS	Intervening Ventilated Space
LACOTS	Local Authorities Co-ordinating Body on Trading Standards
LC_{50}	Lethal Concentration (50%)
LD_{50}	Lethal Dose (50%)
MAFF	Ministry of Agriculture, Fisheries and Food
MRL	Maximum Residue Level
NACCB	National Accreditation Council for Certification Bodies
NAMAS	National Measurement Accreditation Service
NCC	National Consumer Council
NFU	National Farmers' Union
NHS	National Health Service
NSP	Neurotoxic Shellfish Poisoning
NVQ	National Vocational Qualification
OA	Ochratoxin A
OHP	Overhead Projector
PACE	Police and Criminal Evidence Act 1984
PDA	Potato Dextrose Agar

APPENDIX 3: Abbreviations

pH	Hydrogen ion index (measure of acidity/alkalinity)
PHLS	Public Health Laboratory Service
PT	Phage Type
PUFA	Polyunsaturated Fatty Acid
QA	Quality Assurance
QAC/QUAT	Quaternary Ammonium Compound
QC	Quality Control
PSP	Paralytic Shellfish Poisoning
REHIS	Royal Environmental Health Institution of Scotland
RH	Relative Humidity
RIDDOR	Reporting of Injuries, Diseases and Dangerous Occurrences Regs 1995
RIPHH	Royal Institute of Public Health and Hygiene
RSH	Royal Society of Health
SAFE	Systematic Assessment of Food Environment
SOFHT	Society of Food Hygiene Technology
SMRV	Significant Medical Risk Value
SRSV	Small Round Structured Virus
TB	Tuberculosis
TFA	Trans fatty acid
TMA	Trimethylamine
TSP	Trisodium phosphate
UHT	Ultra Heat Treated
USFDA	United States Food and Drug Administration
UV	Ultra Violet (light)
V-CJD	New variant CJD
VTEC	Verocytotoxin producing *E. coli*
WC	Water Closet (lavatory)
WHO	World Health Organisation
WO	Welsh Office

Organism	Onset Period	Duration	Symptoms	Foods Commonly Involved	Comments
Bacillus cereus Gram-positive, normally aerobic, spore forming.	Diarrhoeal: 6 to 16 hours; Vomiting (emetic): 30 min to 6 hours commonly; exotoxin in food.	Generally less than 24 hours.	Diarrhoeal similar to those of *Clostridium perfringens*; Vomiting similar to those of *Staphylococcus aureus*.	Diarrhoeal type- a variety including meats, milk, vegetables and fish; Vomiting type- cereals, such as cooked rice, particularly boiled, but eaten cold (as in salads), fried rice (especially reheated) and corn flour.	Widely distributed, found in soil, cereals, vegetables and dairy products; refrigeration of cooked rice essential.
Campylobacter jejuni/coli; Gram negative spirally-curved bacilli, non sporing, microaerophillic to anaerobic.	Two to seven days; enterotoxin in gut.	7-10 days to several weeks.	Start by resembling influenza, and includes diarrhoea, which usually contains blood.	Raw or uncooked meat (especially poultry), and offal; contaminated water, raw and inadequately heat-treated milk.	Contamination is usually from the excreta of humans and animals, birds (particularly poultry), cattle and domestic pets. Wild birds pecking milk bottle tops are reported to have infected this foodstuff.
Clostridium botulinum, Gram-positive anaerobic bacillus, spore-former	18 to 36 hours (exceptionally 12 to 96 hours); neurotoxin (an exotoxin).	Death in 24 hours to eight days, or slow convalescence over six to eight months.	Slurring of speech, double vision and loss of balance: death may result to various paralysis of the brain centres such as that involved in the control of breathing.	Any food which is not acid (above pH 4.5) particularly in any improperly proceeded or contaminated canned or bottled foods, which provides anaerobic conditions.	Contamination of soil, meat and fish is likely since spores of the bacterium are widely distributed in nature.

APPENDIX 4: Major causes of food poisoning and food-borne disease

Organism	Onset Period	Duration	Symptoms	Foods Commonly Involved	Comments
Cryptosporidium parvum, a coccidial protozoan.	About seven days. Infection occurs when cysts (known as oocysts) are swallowed.	One to three weeks	Watery diarrhoea, abdominal pain, vomiting and fever.	Water, raw milk and offal. Infection in cattle and sheep is common and may be passed to water supplies via contaminated slurry and manure.	Source of infection may be animal or human, person to person spread is not uncommon.
Escherichia coli, Gram-negative, non sporing aerobic bacillus. Four recognised groups: EIEC, EPEC, ETEC and VTEC. (Last group contains *E. coli* O157:H7.)	8 to 72 hours (depending on the strain); infection and enterotoxin.	One to seven days.	Abdominal pain, watery or bloody diarrhoea, vomiting and sometimes fever.	Raw foods of animal origin; meat, poultry and fish, and their products.	Its presence is an indicator of poor hygiene or improper processing. Common cause of 'traveller's diarrhoea'.
Listeria monocytogenes, Gram-positive, non-sporing bacillus; facultative anaerobe.	8 days to 3 months. Infection.	Varies, often long lasting.	Influenza-type illness, followed by nausea, vomiting and diarrhoea. More serious symptoms may follow of septicaemia, meningitis, and in pregnant women, the possibility of miscarriage and stillbirth. (the mother usually survives)	Commercial chilled foods, such as prepared salads, sandwiches, pates, cooked meats and ready-to-eat meals which just require heating.	Widely distributed in nature; found in sewage, decaying vegetable matter, soil, insects, birds, ruminants (e.g. cows), humans, all types of farm animals and domestic pets. Grows at all temperatures down to 2.5°C.

Organism	Onset Period	Duration	Symptoms	Foods Commonly Involved	Comments
Salmonella species, Gram-negative, non-spore forming short bacillus. All are facultative anaerobes.	12 to 36 hours, but it may unusually be anything from 6 to 72 hours or longer. Infection.	1 to 7 days.	Vomiting, abdominal cramps, diarrhoea, fever, headache, and, with general aching of the limbs.	Raw meats (red and white), poultry and their products, eggs, raw milk and dairy products.	Widespread; found in water, soil, insects, raw meats, the gastrointestinal tract of wild and domestic animals of all types (and their faeces), birds (especially in poultry), reptiles, amphibians and occasionally humans.
Shigella species, Gram-negative, non sporing bacillus, facultative anaerobe.	12 hours to 2 days. Infection and toxin production.	Several days.	Diarrhoea, fever, vomiting, abdominal pain and cramps and, in several cases, blood and pus in the faeces; infections are usually limited to the large intestine.	Salads (potato, sea food, pasta and meats), raw vegetables, milk and dairy products and poultry.	Contaminated food, and other objects and flies may also spread the disease; control of flies, hygienic preparation of food, and the use of treated water all help to prevent outbreaks of the disease.
Staphylococcus aureus, Gram-positive spherical bacterium (coccus), non-spore former.	1 to 6 hours. Extoxin in food.	Typically 6 to 48 hours.	Nausea, severe vomiting, abdominal pain and cramps, sometimes followed by collapse, diarrhoea is a common secondary symptom.	Dishes which have been handled and then kept at room temperature for more than 2 hours, and then eaten cold such as cold meats, trifles, cream and custard-filled cakes.	Contamination is most often from food handlers; good personal hygiene is vital. Most salt and sugar resistant organism.

APPENDIX 4: Major causes of food poisoning and food-borne disease

Organism	Onset Period	Duration	Symptoms	Foods Commonly Involved	Comments
Vibrio parahaemolyticus, Gram-negative non-sporing curved bacillus, faculative anaerobe.	Less than 24 hours to several days. Infection, with toxin release in the gut.	Several days. (1-7)	Burning sensation in the stomach and abdominal pain, together with vomiting, headache, fever, chills, and watery diarrhoea.	Consumption of untreated water, contaminated shellfish, and foods eaten raw or washed in such waters.	Usually inhabits coastal salt waters, particularly in warm climates. A very common causal agent of food poisoning in Japan.
Hepatitis A virus. (All viruses are unable to grow in food; they can only grow and multiply inside a living cell.)	10 to 50 days	1 to 2 weeks	Usually a mild illness with a sudden onset of fever, malaise, abdominal discomfort followed by several days of jaundice.	Cold meats, sandwiches, salads, raw and steamed shellfish, bakery products and iced drinks, all contaminated by infected persons.	Usually spread by the faecal-oral route; outbreaks occur through the transmission of the virus in water, food and milk. Recovery from illness usually confers lifelong immunity.
Norwalk virus	1 to 2 days	1 to 3 days	Nausea, vomiting, abdominal cramps, and diarrhoea.	Raw or insufficiently cooked shellfish (clams and oysters); foods other than shellfish are usually contaminated by food handlers.	Transmission is by the faecal-oral route, and water is the most common source of outbreaks.

The above organisms and others have a full entry in the main text.